THE JOY OF SCHOLARSHIP:

TEACHING LAW AND WRITING HISTORY

David J. Langum, Sr.

Cover: photograph by Mike McAndrew, Port Townsend, Washington of portrait of David J. Langum, Sr., © 2018 by Michael Hale, Port Townsend, Washington.

Library of Congress Cataloging-in-Publication Data
Langum, David J., Sr., 1940-author.

 The Joy of Scholarship: Teaching Law and Writing History
 Includes index.

DISAC # BIO019000
ISBN 978-1-0878-8310-6 (hardback) 1. Memoir, David J. Langum, Sr., 1965-2020. 2. Legal education, 1968-2005. 3. Research and Scholarship, 1975-2020. 4. Scholarly publication, 1974-2020. 5. Social conditions in San Francisco, 1962-1968.

David J. Langum, Sr.
2809 Berkeley Drive
Birmingham, Alabama 35242
360.809.0465/djlangum@samford.edu

This book is dedicated to my grandfather, Henry Langum; my fourth grade teacher, Carol Redecker; and my friend Barbara Jeskalian, for reasons described in the Preface.

TABLE OF CONTENTS

Preface

Since this memoir is centered on my academic career, composed of teaching and scholarly writing, it is not in the form of most memoirs. The major themes begin with law school, and I rarely look backward from then, except for a slight discussion of college at the very beginning. Childhood is largely omitted. I do not discuss my wives in detail, except as needed to explain crucial events in my life. I have only briefly discussed my children, and if Virginia seems to be discussed more than my other children it is only because she is much older than my other children, and has had opportunity for her own academic and scholarly accomplishments that my younger children have not yet really had the opportunity to attain. I hope they will in due time.

Other elements of my personal life are not discussed. For example there is next to nothing here about my relationships with women, before and in between my marriages. It is not that there is nothing to say. When I was in my 20s and 30s I was pretty amoral and followed too much the devices and desires of my own heart. I had adulterous relationships with three married women, three live-in girlfriends, and four wives. Discussion of this aspect of my life is better addressed to my confessor than the reader of memoirs centered on teaching and writing.

While there is nothing in the text about my religion, I am an Anglo-Catholic, and attend an Orthodox church while I am in Port Townsend. That might be inferred from my occasional allusions to the Elizabethan Book of Common Prayer.

There are no footnotes or endnotes for two reasons. First, they are not in common use with memoirs. Second, all of the written sources may be found in my papers at the Abraham Lincoln Presidential Library in Springfield, especially in the boxes of papers concerning my published books (fulsome) and articles (slight) and in the daily diary I have kept since 1988. Beyond this are only my personal recollections.

I do have some thanks. My wife Grace read the manuscript and found a few typos. More important, she gave me considerable emotional support and encouragement while I was writing this book. My son, David Jr., also read the text and found still more typos and some grammatical infelicities. My friend and colleague William G. Ross read the entire manuscript and made useful suggestions, especially where I was writing about faculty relationships in Cumberland School of Law. I also must thank Natalia Holtzman, my editor and copyeditor. I am grateful for her close reading, many suggestions, and especially for working up the manuscript to the point where it was ready for the press.

I also want to thank my deceased parents, John K. Langum and Virginia de Mattos Langum, who gave me invaluable early training for a scholarly life. My mother promoted personal stability and, although I have not always followed her precepts, this has been a help at difficult times. My father continuously expanded my intellectual horizons and gave me the example of his fantastic work ethic.

I also want to explain my dedication to three persons who were absolutely essential to my pursuit of scholarship. All three were *sine qua non*, and I would never have written my eight books without them.

Henry Langum, my grandfather, was the first Langum ever to leave the farm and seek a larger life through a college education. When he presented himself at St. Olaf College, a traditional Norwegian-American school, the admissions office determined that his preliminary training was insufficient, and it was necessary for him to take four years of St. Olaf's academy before he could even enroll in the college. He had already graduated from public high school, and even himself taught in a country school, but the quality of education in South Dakota then was apparently so poor that he had to spend another four years of preparation. Henry wanted a college education so badly that he worked in the dining hall as a waiter and repeated high school, his classmates in the academy and in the college being four years younger than he.

Henry Langum went on to become a high school biology teacher, a state-licensed chiropractor (requiring an additional academic degree), and an ordained Lutheran minister (also requiring additional academic training). Biology teacher, chiropractor, and minister make quite a combination of professions, yet he practiced them all in different phases of his life.

Three of his direct descendants, his son John, his grandson David (me), and his great-granddaughter Virginia have acquired academic doctorates. All three of us have written and published much scholarly writing, and taught in universities, although my father later left the academic world to become a nationally prominent economic consultant. The chances of our doing this without the examples of our fathers are remote. Henry Langum began this, giving an example to his son, John, who passed that example along to me. Henry was never in a financial position to help much with my father's education, but John Langum, his son, provided me with a splendid education as I believe I also gave my daughter.

Carol Redecker, my fourth grade teacher, taught me how to read. In 1946 I was in three different schools for my first grade, the place where reading was then introduced. I missed the introduction at all three schools, and was out-of-step whichever school I attended. By my second grade I could read only very elementary sentences. By third grade I was regarded as mentally challenged, and my third grade teacher told my parents most solemnly that they would be lucky if I were able to graduate from high school.

In fourth grade things turned around. My teacher, Carol Redecker, recognized some capabilities in me. She organized a special phonics class, gave me individual attention, and ultimately made me read one of Carl Sandburg's Rootabaga Stories before all the parents (including mine!) at a Parent-Teacher Conference meeting. I was so nervous that while waiting in my classroom to be summoned to read, I accidentally stuck my finger in the ink pot on my desk. We still wrote with steel tipped pens and needed ink pots. However, the reading went perfectly, or close enough to that, I guess. I was never again anxious about reading, although I think that whole experience in early school left a mark. I read more slowly, but just as keenly, than do most people who read as much as I must in my work. Of course, the key skill to do scholarly research is the ability to read well, and for that ability I thank my wonderful fourth grade teacher, Carol Redecker. As Henry Adams reminds us, one can never tell where a teacher's influence stops.

After I began to practice law in 1966 I told various people that *someday* I was going back to school and earn a master's degree in history. *Someday, someday*, and I told that story quite often. I was still saying that after I moved to San Jose to practice law. After a few years I purchased a home on Chapman Avenue, my first wife, Bernadette, and I became friends with a couple who lived across the street. They both worked at San Jose State University, the husband, Franklin Dalkey, in the university photo lab and the wife, Barbara Jeskalian, in the university library as music reference librarian. The four of us got together every so often to have dinner, take a walk, go to a restaurant, and so forth. I was still singing my *someday* song about a master's in history. Barbara must have heard it a few times before she called my bluff and put in my hands, without my asking, all the forms I needed to complete to apply for admission to San Jose State's graduate program in history.   Obviously it was time for me to put up or shut up.

I did apply and after several years of night classes, thesis research and writing, and practicing law I did obtain my master's in history. It was a transformative experience.   I not only enjoyed the climate of academe, but in this master's program I came to enjoy the process of scholarship, the necessary research and writing. I began to write and published a few scholarly articles even before I had the master's degree in hand.

If Barbara Jeskalian had not called my bluff, I might have gone on forever saying *someday, someday* to the idea of returning to the university. If I had gone down that path I would never have come to know the joys of scholarship and would never have become a scholar myself.

So thank you to Henry Langum, Carol Redecker, and Barbara Jeskalian. Without your example, help, and prompting I would never have become an academic and scholar.

David J. Langum, Sr.   June 2020

Birmingham, Alabama
Port Townsend, Washington

Chapter 1

From Beginning Stanford Law School:
1962 through Summer 1968

When I began studies at Stanford Law School I was hardly a scholar.

My deficiencies with scholarship had little to do with the excellent education I had received at Dartmouth College; it had more to do with me. I wasted my opportunities at Dartmouth, spending vast amounts of time in trivial activities such as running a student laundry. I also managed the finances of the college humor magazine, the *Jack-o-Lantern*. In the 1920s the *Jacko* served as an outlet for the considerable talents of Ted Geisel, soon to be known as Dr. Seuss. But I avoided challenging courses. I did not attend nearly enough the lectures of the outstanding speakers brought to the campus. I took insufficient advantage of the magnificent natural beauty of the region with its abundant opportunities for hiking. I drank too much; I studied too little, conditions then common with many Dartmouth students. Yet I remember being busy most of the time, but I now understand that the time was wasted in trivial pursuits, partying, and inefficient cramming sessions.

I did reasonably well in grades, garnering a B- overall average with a B average in my major subject, History, in the days before grade inflation when a B truly meant "good." I graduated in the upper quarter of my class. Yet I could have done so much better had I applied myself. Dartmouth made no demands for true scholarship, beyond four or five term papers based on research entirely within secondary sources, even in my major field. This was hardly scholarship and not much beyond the searching for apt quotations in numerous books and journals, work that I already had done as a debater in high school forensics. This was no deficiency of Dartmouth, but an adherence to the then-current model of teaching history. Under that model, the faculty crammed undergraduate students with historical facts and interpretations. The use of primary sources, that

1

is to say real scholarship, was reserved for graduate studies. Thankfully, this is no longer the reigning paradigm, and undergraduate history majors today can enjoy the pleasures and challenges of working with original materials, the raw sources of history.

After graduation from Dartmouth, I spent the summer of 1962 in San Francisco before beginning law school at Stanford that fall. Dan Miller, a college friend, had promised me a place to stay that summer. He had been living with a doctor, an engineer, and a couple of other young men in a large apartment on top of Nob Hill. One was away for the summer, and they had a spare room to rent. I enthusiastically agreed, but when I actually showed up found that one of his flat mates had also offered the room to another fellow who had appeared just the day before I arrived and had already occupied the spare bedroom. The best they had for me was a large couch in the living room, which I took. Staying in the living room meant that I could not go to sleep until everyone else had gone to their own beds.

Actually, it was a pretty nice "pad," as we called sleeping arrangements then. The apartment complex, called the Babylonian Gardens, was on the very top of exotic looking garden units built on top of each other and off into side terraces. To reach our apartment, one had to climb precisely 128 steps. Once there, the living room had a commanding view of San Francisco, the Bay Bridge, and Treasure Island. I became acquainted with the fellow who had beaten me out on the spare bedroom. Stanley Siddle, an Englishman, was working in San Francisco during the summer between his first and second years at the Harvard Business School. He returned to the Bay Area after his graduation, and eventually became one of my best friends, and that has remained true to this day.

Stanley is fourteen years my senior and a very knowledgeable and intelligent man. He served in the Royal Air Force in India during the closing months of W.W. II, and then returned to England to finish his education, graduating from the University of Durham. Stanley then worked many years for the British Foreign Service, stationed in Ghana, and found time to travel by primitive back roads throughout Africa. He came to the United States in 1961 to attend the Harvard

2

Business School. After graduation in 1963, Stanley returned to the San Francisco Bay area to live and build a career, primarily in the equipment leasing business. He remained a bachelor until later in life, marrying Joan V. Lavin in 1988. Stanley is a good conversationalist, and, with his wide experiences in many parts of the world, an excellent raconteur.

The apartment, or rather the beginning of the steps to the apartment, was at 1230D Washington Street, and was very well located: just a few blocks to Chinatown, same distance to North Beach, and an easy cable car ride to downtown. San Francisco then had almost a plethora of jazz joints and also beer and banjo Dixieland bars. I had fun that summer discovering them all, with my favorites in the jazz category being Jumbo's Bop City, Pier 23, and Mr. Otis, and in the Dixieland group, the Red Garter, Honey Bucket, and Earthquake McGoon's. These are only a sampling of what was available in both jazz and Dixieland. There were also opera bars where one could have a drink and listen to quite well-sung opera arias. Numerous second-hand bookstores formed another category of interest.

My father was a good friend of Ray Lapin, the President of a large mortgage-generating company, later the first President of Fannie Mae, the federal insurer of mortgages, and he arranged for a summer job for me. The job at Bankers Mortgage was not terribly demanding but at the same time it was creative. For its salesmen to work most efficiently, the firm needed to develop a system whereby it received notice of new subdivisions at the earliest possible moment. That is easy to state, but with hundreds of independent planning commissions and other pertinent agencies in the Bay Area, and well before the Internet, it was a challenge to gather the information. My task was to develop a systematic approach to garnering this data, something that in the hectic growth of the company had not yet been done.

I thought I might prepare myself for law school by reading books offering an introduction to legal studies. I recall going to the Chinatown branch of the San Francisco Public Library on Saturday mornings and afternoons to find a quiet place for reading these. The books I read were hopelessly out-of-date and filled with long discussions of old English writs, Latin legal maxims, and long historical digressions. They had little to do with contemporary law or studies at modern law schools, and the discussions were so complicated and foreboding that I seriously questioned whether this law business was for me at all. I also wondered that summer in the midst of the first large Vietnam buildup whether I ought to volunteer for the draft, to serve two years and get that over with before law school. I called Dean William Keogh at Stanford, and he dissuaded me from this.

Later in the summer I went down the San Francisco peninsula to Palo Alto to find an apartment to live in while at the law school. I found a house in East Palo Alto that had been broken up into three units, the house itself upstairs, and two lower semi-basement units below, the two separated by an actual basement. The available basement apartment was very basic: living room, bedroom, kitchen area with refrigerator, hot plate, sink, and no stove. It came furnished, albeit poorly, at only $75 per month, including all utilities except telephone. A 15-20 minute drive through downtown Palo Alto and then down beautiful Palm Drive on the campus would take me to the law school. East Palo Alto is quite distinct from Palo Alto, which adjoins Stanford. East Palo Alto is in a different county, San Mateo rather than Santa Clara, and had much looser zoning and law enforcement. Whereas Palo Alto was and is a quite affluent town, East Palo Alto is poor, filled with minority groups, and has significant drug and crime problems. I did not know all this when I rented my apartment.

I was certainly not the ideal student that first year of law school. Indeed, I missed so many classes that many classmates thought I had dropped out. I was absent from class for a number of reasons. First, we had 8:00AM classes, and I was just too lazy, up too late at night, or distracted by waking up every morning with a live-in girlfriend at my side, to get up that early. Second, I was busy buying and selling land in the Santa Cruz Mountains, and my dad and I had just completed our first purchase of land in Big Sur. These transactions took time for document preparation and, especially in the case of the Santa Cruz properties, travel to show land to potential buyers. Third, and most

4

important, I really did not care for the Socratic method, then still practiced in the major law schools.

The Socratic method of teaching requires that students read actual judicial opinions, contained in a casebook, and then be subjected to a series of very nit-picky questions about the case. Usually the professor would call on a student, ask him (we were still almost entirely males; I believe there were only four females in our class of around 120) to read his brief, a tightly circumscribed analysis of an appellate case. Then the professor would slightly alter the facts of the case and ask whether the reasoning of the court in deciding the case would still apply. Or whether the statute the court relied upon in deciding the case would still be applicable. Very little time was spent in discussing what the law actually was. We were supposed to learn this incrementally through the cases themselves. We still use questions in today's law schools, but there is far more time spent in actual description and discussion of the law itself; students are no longer left to flounder about trying to intuit larger concepts from the cases alone. Curiously, when I turned to teaching myself, I felt compelled by the recollection of my excellent Stanford professors to be more Socratic than I otherwise might have been.

In my student thinking, this Socratic method was a big waste of time. I had looked at some old examination questions and saw that what the school tested had little to do with what we were doing in class. Law school examination questions, then and now, generally consist of a statement of incredibly convoluted facts followed by a broad question such as: "define the rights and duties of the parties." To answer these questions one must have a thorough knowledge of the substantive law, that is, specific principles of actual law, together with a good ability to apply the law to actual facts, just as a practicing lawyer does after a client comes into the office with a tangled story of woe. In addition to its irrelevancy to our examinations, the Socratic method itself could be intimidating. I remember one day in Torts class, Robert Girard, a young whipper-snapper professor whom Stanford had recently lured away from Harvard, called on me to brief a medieval case involving an assault. I was fully prepared that day, but made the fatal mistake of beginning casually rather than in strict legal form. I started out: "Well, this is an old case that … " At that point Girard interrupted me and asked, "Mr. Langum, what does it matter that the case is old? Are cases like wine that improve with age?" I just did not want to put up with that sort of nonsense.

I did attend enough classes to note the distinctive mannerisms of some of our leading faculty. John Bingham Hurlbut, a courtly elder gentleman who taught us Contracts, was noted for his long questions that he would pose to students. They were always incisive and went to the nub of the legal reasoning and principles behind each case. Yet he usefully phrased them rhetorically, so all the student in the spotlight, so to speak, had to do was agree. The questions were so keen that it was a pleasure to listen to them. We called him the Silver Fox, in part for his shock of silver hair.

Moffatt Hancock, a crusty older man who taught us Property, had a serious visual problem. He held the seating chart close to his face, and moved it around like a bombing chart, deciding on which student he would drop a question. As we had fixed seats in the large classroom we could tell whether he was getting close. One day in the late fall I walked in nonchalantly, even though I had not been there at all the preceding week, carrying my casebook, notebook, and a cup of coffee, and took my seat. Before he began the class Hancock boomed out, "Mr. Langum, would you please see me after class?" I thought, oh boy, now I am really going to get it for skipping class so much. After class I approached the podium with real trepidation, and reminded Hancock that he had wanted to see me. He only said, "Mr. Langum, please do not bring coffee into the classroom." What a relief! I did wonder how he could see the cup of coffee, as I was fairly far back in the room. Perhaps his distance vision was just fine.

For Thanksgiving 1962 my parents decided to cruise to Hawaii and have me fly over to join them for a few days at the Royal Hawaiian Hotel. The best flight for me would have cut through my last class before the brief break, and I would have to miss it. Although I thought nothing of that, having skipped so many classes before, my parents did not know that and insisted I inquire whether missing that single class would get me into trouble. I inquired about this with a secretary in the administration office. She told me that professors generally did not take notes on attendance; there was certainly no rule regarding cuts just before a break and law students generally did leave a day or so early; and, moreover, I was the first student who had ever raised this question in the three years she had worked at the law school. Not only were my parents relieved about this single class cut, but I was relieved about my multiple skips. There would be no retribution for the absences alone. A comment on this. Lesser law schools, forced by economic necessity to admit students with poorer law-aptitude exam scores, often have attendance policies. For example, at Cumberland School of Law, where I taught for 20 years and am still a research professor, absence for over 20% of class time will result in a lowering of the student's grade, regardless of how good or bad his examination grade. The reasoning is that poorer students need to be forced to attend class. I did go to Hawaii for a brief Thanksgiving break, and my mother remarked for years on the anomaly of my sitting on the beach in a lounge chair, a Mai Tai in one hand and an open treatise on Contracts in the other.

In late December we had preliminary examinations in Contracts and Torts. They would not count unless the grades were good. By late January we had the results. I had a C in Torts and in the two questions in Contracts I received an A in one and a D in the other. That should have relieved me somewhat, but it did not. By late March I was sure that I would flunk out of school. I was far behind, partly because of a three-week illness in late January and February and partly because of my general sloth. I felt myself in serious academic trouble, far more than I had ever experienced before. Fortunately, I did not panic but devised a solid plan to deal with it. I did begin to attend class more regularly, hoping to hear hints on what might be on the exams. However, the main thing I did was to build upon my earlier discovery of the nature of the final exams.

I began a rigorous reading program to learn the basic legal principles and trusted my own intelligence to gauge their applicability to facts. For each academic legal course, such as Contracts, Torts, Property, and so forth, there are corresponding treatises that have solid explanations of the law and all its details. Generically these are called hornbooks, although technically Hornbooks are only treatises in a series of that name published by West Publishing. Shorter outline booklets also covered each subject, as well as "canned" briefs, prepared and printed briefs designed to dovetail with the cases in specific casebooks. I looked over the outlines and canned briefs and found them worthless, but not so the treatises, especially the Hornbooks, which I thought were excellent in clearly describing the law and its components but in enough detail and with just the amount of explanation so that the concepts would stick in the brain. I had to travel to the legal bookstores in San Francisco, but I bought treatises on every course I was taking. The law school would not then allow the Stanford Bookstore to carry them, as it was insistent that students should learn legal concepts only through reading cases.

In April 1963 I began a serious study regime, working at my apartment reading five or six treatises of some 350-400 pages apiece, and from cover to cover. I concentrated, and if any passage seemed unclear, I re-read and re-read it until it was clear in my mind. At the same time I read all the cases we were assigned for class discussion. I did not write the formal briefs that we were supposed to write, but I wrote what law students call a "book brief." I have always had a good skill in analytical and analogical thinking. I had taken the Law School Aptitude Test while a junior at Dartmouth and scored in the 99% national percentile. If I concentrated, and at this point I had to, I could read a case of 10-15 pages and distill its precise legal meaning, what lawyers call its "holding," and express that in one, two, no more than three sentences. I did that for each and every case I was supposed to have studied over the past year, and wrote those few sentences at the beginning of the case within the casebook, hence the term "book brief." It is easy to describe my method in a few sentences, but the effort was enormous. I worked 12-14 hour days with great concentration, working harder intellectually than I ever had before in my entire life. I had never before been so behind in my studies to need this effort.

I had taken my final exam in Torts at the end of the winter term. Although I am certain they had been graded, the school would not release the grades until June, together with the other grades. I surmise the reason for this withholding of the Torts grades was that if students could not stand a significant delay waiting for an outcome, they had no business being lawyers. After all, lawyers have to prepare their cases for trial over a year's time, perhaps more, and then try their cases and wait additional hours or days more for the "outcome" represented by a jury's verdict. Patience and delay of outcome is inherent in any trial practice.

For my final exams in May and June, I developed a little ritual that I followed throughout my law school career. I worked very hard on the material for the course being tested, up until around 6:00PM of the evening before the exam. Then I would go out and have a nice dinner, preceded by two (and only two) scotch and sodas to help me sleep that evening. If I stopped working a bit earlier, I might also take in a movie. I went to bed early and got up very early. Then I drove to Stanford and had breakfast in Tresidder, the student union. After eating I went to the drug store at Tresidder and bought two new Bic ballpoint pens to write in my exam booklet, the so-called "bluebook." Then I walked to the steps at the front of the university quad and watched the cars pour in along Palm Drive. After a few minutes of this I would walk a few paces to the law school, then located at the front of the quad, and take my exam at 9:00AM.

I did not study at all the morning of an exam. I thought that study immediately before an exam would clog up my brain and make it less efficient in recalling material. I think I was right about that and have always recommended similar pre-exam procedures to my own students. As mentioned before, the exams themselves were monstrous statements of convoluted facts, coupled with broad general questions, such as "Please state the rights and obligations of all of the parties." I felt comfortable with the amount of law I had mastered. The business of applying the law to the actual facts is a matter of talent and skill more than knowledge. I knew students were graded on spotting legal theories as much as anything, and I was careful to note what legal theories were definitely applicable to the given facts. I also discussed what legal theories *might* be available if a small additional fact, not inconsistent with the given facts, were also present. If I had time I brought up the "red herrings," legal principles that might superficially seem to apply to the facts but were not, with my own explanation of why not. I always prepared an outline on blank paper before writing anything in the examination bluebooks. That way I had a checklist of what I had to cover in my essay. All this said, they were frightfully difficult examinations.

9

When the exams were over I felt exhausted. I had just broken up with my live-in girlfriend, so depression was added to exhaustion. My general feeling was that I had passed. I would not flunk out. I also thought I had not done particularly well. The school did not formally announce grades until later in the summer. However, a benevolent tradition allowed students to place self-addressed post cards inside the last bluebook, with just a simple statement, "Contracts," "Civil Procedure," etc. After grading his exams, the professor wrote your grade on the postcard and posted it. This cut off at least a month of anxiety. There is, by the way, a long-standing tradition in American law schools that professors personally grade their own exams, without assistants, and that the examination booklets are identified only by an anonymous number.

I was amazed as the postcards came in. In the major subjects of Property, Civil Procedure, Contracts, and Torts, I received grades of A, C, B+, and A-. In the shorter courses of Unjust Enrichment (restitution and remedies) and Agency, I had a B+ and C+. This was in the era before grade inflation, and would be graded higher today. I think it is important that my lowest grades, Civil Procedure, C, and Agency, C+, came when my troubles with my girlfriend were at their height. I took the Agency exam on the morning after she had spent the evening running around with some other fellow and had come in drunk at 4:00AM. I later learned that about 5% of my classmates had flunked out and were academically disqualified from continuing on to the second year. About the same percentage left voluntarily, concluding that law studies were not for them.

These grades put me in the upper 15% of my class. That made me eligible to participate on the *Stanford Law Review*, a pivotal matter that has affected my entire career and served also as my initial entry into the world of scholarship. I was between the 10% line and the 15%. I calculated that if I had been about five individual places higher, I would have been in the upper 10%. That would have made me eligible for the Order of the Coif, a very prestigious legal fraternity.

However, being on the Board of Editors of the Review was prestigious itself, as I soon learned.

My second and even third year at Stanford Law School was dominated by my participation on the *Stanford Law Review*. With the sole exception of my scholarly writing, the work on the *Review* was the most intellectually stimulating of my life. Its real significance was that it gave me the intellectual focus and discipline that made the later books and journal articles possible. The training involved a grueling three-week program with intense work on legal citation and research, far deeper than what non-review students received in the general curriculum. Other general work of the reviewers included work on (1) preliminary analyses of specific areas of the law to determine whether the *Review* ought to assign a member to write on that area and to ensure that it had not been "pre-empted" already by other reviews; (2) citechecks that checked the accuracy of each and every citation in professional or student articles by tracking down the sometimes obscure sources and checking the original against the manuscript; (3) ascertaining whether the author had used the proper signals, such as *see, but see, compare,* and numerous others, as the proper introduction to a footnote, depending on the exact relationship of what the case or other material cited in a footnote bore to the text to which the footnote was attached; and (4) extensive and painstaking proofreading of other persons' articles.

However, the most important work of the law review at Stanford was the preparation of two significant writings. In their first year on the *Review,* their second year in the law school, most reviewers write a case comment, in which the student makes a thorough analysis of a significant recent opinion of an appellate court. The comment could be favorable or unfavorable toward the outcome of the case, but it had to include a detailed analysis of the procedural and more broadly historical background of the case, comparisons with other states' or nations' handling of similar matters, a detailed and thoughtful consideration of the policy and further legal implications of the court's opinion, and a reasoned recommendation as to whether a higher appellate court ought to reverse the lower court's opinion or, if the opinion commented upon came from a state supreme court, whether the state legislature ought to adopt legislation to the contrary of the opinion. All law reviews try to publish these case comments as quickly as possible, with the hope that a higher court in reviewing the case will cite the particular law review in their opinion. The second important writing comes in the final year of law school when the reviewer writes a note on a much broader legal topic and of significantly greater length than the comment.

An article in *Time* magazine of April 24, 1964 commented on the educational function of the law reviews:

> The country's 100-odd law reviews are wholly run by the aristocrats of U.S. law schools – fearsomely bright students who toil around the clock polishing deep-think articles that influence U.S. law right up to the Supreme Court. ... Law reviews – most notably those published by Chicago, Columbia, Harvard, Michigan, Pennsylvania, Stanford and Yale – are more influential than ever. A law-review job shapes a man's entire later life. ... New staffers often slave 14 hours a day [to write] a debut article of three to five pages, knowing well that top editors will do their best to rip it apart. In his two years on the law review, a staffer can expect to write only about three pieces [the norm at Stanford was two], though he will spend several hundred hours checking other writers' sources. On graduation, however, he has the most impeccable credentials: the case-hardened polish of a law-review man.

Yale's Dean Eugene V. Rostow, summed it up by once saying that "law reviews are by far the best training that any American law school can offer. Their educational value is unmatched by anything in the law schools themselves."

My own training on the *Review* began in September 1963 with the formal research and citation work. Next was a huge amount of citechecking and proofreading. In October I selected a case for my comment, and my research was well underway in November. A Nebraska Supreme Court decision had invalidated more than $400 million worth of installment contracts as usurious, even though they were written in good-faith compliance with a state statute, also struck down, that purported to regulate them. I had numerous conferences with Gene Robinson, the Comment Editor, who proved to be a nice person but a tough editor. I submitted the first draft at the end of November, followed within days by critique and demands for revision. I submitted a second draft of the comment in early January, and I was now up to 52 long footnotes as well as text, again followed within the week by critique and demands for revision. During this writing I was also citechecking and proofreading other work, and the hours spent on the *Review* sometimes were as many as 30 per week. A third draft came in late January, and I believe there was even a fourth draft.

At our final conference in late March, I noticed that Robinson had almost completely rewritten the text, substantially toning down my criticisms of the Nebraska Court. He told me not to be upset, because he had left the important part, my footnotes, completely alone. After I recovered from my shock, I saw that in a sense he was correct. The footnotes were the most important part because it was there, in long discursive footnotes, that the law reviewer demonstrated his well-honed analysis and budding erudition. It was published in the July 1964 issue as "Nebraska Vitiates Time Sale Doctrine Retroactively." Apparently my editor had not been completely successful in toning down my criticism of the Nebraska Supreme Court. I understand from several reports that a representative of the Nebraska Bar called the Stanford Dean to complain about my criticism of their Court. Apparently the Dean commiserated with him that, indeed, students could be troublesome, but regretfully noted that they had to consider the First Amendment as well.

In 1963-1964 I attended more classes than I had in my first year, although I was often unprepared because of the nearly overwhelming work on the *Review*. Faculty understood about those pressures and cut the reviewers a bit of slack. My final grades for the year were slightly but not dramatically better: Corporations, B; Legal Process, A; Taxation, B; Trusts and Estates, B+; Constitutional Law, B-; Municipal Corporations, B-; and Criminal Law, B.

I also worked for a few hours a week at the Legal Aid Clinic, helping indigent clients with their legal problems. The Palo Alto Legal Aid Clinic, like the *Stanford Law Review*, was entirely student run. Every student volunteer had the opportunity to work individually with clients through the entire stage of their problems, from initial interviews through the courts. No attorneys hovered about checking anything. If we actually had to go into court, we called in an attorney of our own selection. But anything we could possibly do without an attorney – settlements, releases, drafting complaints or answers, and so forth – we did ourselves. It was very gratifying work. I had a couple of divorces and one truly different and interesting case where a woman had her security clearance revoked. That was essential for her job, and we had to process her ultimately successful claim for its reinstatement all the way from petition to actual administrative trial in San Francisco.

I began to work part time, in January 1964 and thereafter, for a tax preparation firm, San Mateo Tax Service, twenty miles up the San Francisco Peninsula in San Mateo, and became good friends with its owners, Robert and Sue Miller. For the next two years they invited me to dinner and pool parties. When I was in practice in San Jose, I represented them. Even after I had moved out of California we kept in touch, by letters and otherwise. Sometime in the 1980s, Sue and a relative of hers were passing through Alabama on their way to Florida. We arranged a visit, and they stopped by my house in Birmingham for wine and then dinner at a local Chinese restaurant. Later, in 1998, when I gave the History Department commencement speech at San Jose State University, Sue flew in from Los Angeles to hear me and afterwards to visit. Although I almost never worked more than ten hours per week at San Mateo Tax Service during my law school days, I was happy to earn the extra income, with the partial independence that represented. My father was very upset, and once confronted Bob Miller, demanding to know how he could take my valuable time away from my law studies, they were much more important, etc. Bob and I just ignored that.

Of course, I also had classes in 1964-1965. Most of the courses in my last year of law school were electives. My grades were decent but not stellar: Oil and Gas, A; Evidence, C+; Administrative Law, B; Land Use Control, B; Real Estate Transactions, B-; Conflicts, C; Commercial Law, C+; Creditor Rights, C; and Legal Profession, B-. My overall average, weighted by units and for my entire law school career, was 3.04, not high by today's standards yet good then, before grade inflation had set in. My grades in property courses demonstrate this. Although I had an A in first year property and another A in Oil and Gas, I also had a B- in Real Estate Transactions and a B in Land Use Control. Yet those grades cumulatively were the highest grades in real property courses for my entire class. Just before graduation I received the Lawyers Title Award, a certificate and $100, given by the title company of that name, for being the "graduating student whose achievement in the law of real estate has been most notable." Translated, that meant that I had the highest grade point average of the class for real property courses.

Just as was true of my second year, in my final year, work on the law review was intense. The citechecks and proofreading diminished sharply; after all, another fresh crew of second-years had arrived. However, this was the year of the note, intended to be a long piece with deeper analysis than the case comment of the second year. I chose as my topic an issue arising out of oil and gas production, with significant antitrust implications. A special problem presents itself when two or more oil producers have wells tapping a shared underground oil pool. A moment's thought suggests that some limitations must be put on each firm's drilling. Otherwise, the effect would be similar to two "unregulated" boys, each with a straw, sipping from a single soda glass. Their incentives are to sip as rapidly as possible to maximize share. If two or more oil producers followed this "Rule of Capture," their shared field would not only be depleted rapidly, but actual oil would be lost compared with the ultimate total recovery from a slower withdrawal.

Every oil field has a geologically determined maximum efficient rate of production (MER) that will provide for the highest ultimate recovery over time. Most oil states have a state agency that regulates the withdrawal of oil producers in accordance with the MER, and allocates that among the various producers. However, these state agencies also regulate this withdrawal to assure price stability as well, a questionable activity done under the banner of conservation. California was unique in that her regulation of oil production was made by a private body controlled by the oil industry itself, the Conservation Committee of California Oil Producers. Private limitations on oil production by a group controlled by those same producers raise the serious threat of price control and an antitrust violation. This was the concern that I decided to address in my note for the *Stanford Law Review*.

I did a great deal of research on this question during the fall of 1964, and held initial meetings with Bill Bryant, the note editor, at the end of October. For some of the research I had to use the facilities of the Stanford Geology Library. That was a lot of fun since I sensed for the first time the power and extent of knowledge involved in a true *university*. On December 7, 1964 I flew to Los Angeles and spent an entire day with William R. Wardner, the General Manager of the Conservation Committee. He advised that the Conservation Committee restricted its recommended production limitations only to those established by the MER concept and it did not consider price stability or price control in its work at all. It is difficult to prove a negative, yet he had some documentation he showed me, in the case of a few specific wells, as to how the Conservation Committee went about its business.

I returned to my note editor convinced that the Conservation Committee was not violating antitrust laws after all. Bill Bryant thought I was gullible and had been hoodwinked. I said I would reflect a bit, but I was sure that I was not going to have an article over my signature stating that an organization was violating a law when I did not believe it really was.

I thought there was a middle position, and I presented it to Bill. I would be happy to take the view that there was too much of a possibility of price control; the operations as then conducted by the Conservation Committee presented so great a danger of future antitrust violation, that it ought to be regulated by government. We agreed to this compromise, and I proceeded to write the article.

I did not have much time as the note was due on December 21, 1964. This would allow enough time for citechecking and my response to the citechecks in order to make the spring issue. I worked furiously and the manuscript was submitted as due. The citechecks came back in early January, and whatever revisions or corrections were needed had to be in by January 25, which was extended to an absolutely final deadline of February 8, 1965. These seem like tight deadlines on their face, but they are even tighter when one factors in the size of the note. In its final printed form it ran 23 pages including 91 footnotes. These notes were long, many of them running over 12 lines and one alone running 31 lines. The article was published in early May 1965 as "Private Limitations of Petroleum Production – California's Approach to Conservation." For the piece, the Rocky Mountain Mineral Law Foundation conferred on me its Award for "demonstrating superior ability and diligence in the study of Mineral Law," a certificate, and $200. It also republished the article in its house organ, *Rocky Mountain Mineral Law Foundation Review*, that it distributed to lawyers in that field of work.

Yet another thing I had to worry about in my last year of law school, besides women, the draft, my courses, and my law review note, was employment following graduation. Although I did interview with several law firms, I really wanted to clerk for an appellate court. These appellate clerkships are very prestigious, and there is a lot of competition for them. I interviewed with Justice Murray Draper, presiding justice of a division of the California Court of Appeal, and also Justices Raymond Peters and Mathew Tobriner of the California Supreme Court. Although Tobriner ultimately offered me a job with the California Supreme Court, he did so on the very last day of the hiring process. Obviously there was someone else he preferred who had turned him down. In any event, I had already accepted Draper's offer, and by spring 1965 my job for the following year was assured, subject of course to my local draft board giving me an additional deferment.

One other event was important to my intellectual growth that final year at Stanford. I had a chance to hear the noted author Arthur Koestler speak in Memorial Auditorium on January 21, 1965. I thought him a most interesting speaker. I have forgotten much of what he said, but I distinctly recall Koestler's discussion of how he disciplined his mind when he needed to work out writing difficulties or to recall forgotten material. Koestler said he took a cold bath, dried

17

himself off, sat still, and usually the solution to the problem or the forgotten material would float into his head. I have skipped the step of the cold bath, but have learned that intense concentration followed by a mental release of the issue very often results in a solution to a problem or in forgotten material coming to mind. The insight has been helpful to me, and the ability to hear such a talk reinforced the desirability of *university* as a concept, an institution making available to its colleagues a wide variety of learning.

Graduation arrived on June 13, 1965. My maternal grandfather had died in 1961, but my three living grandparents, all attended my Dartmouth graduation, and came with my parents to the Stanford graduation. They were to meet me at the law school a few hours before the graduation, so we could have lunch together. I was by a window on the second floor of the school and saw my grandparents and parents walking toward the entrance. I remember thinking that was really the end of a long journey for both my parents and myself. I was done with my formal education, subsidized by my parents, and henceforth would work and earn my own living. I had no inkling that three more advanced academic degrees awaited me, although my parents would not be called upon to pay for them.

Following graduation from law school I moved to San Francisco to take up residence in a turn of the 20th century mansion at 1654 Taylor Street. The House of the Flag, as it was called, sat on top of Russian Hill, and its grand spacious living room held a commanding view of the entire downtown, the Bay Bridge, Oakland, and parts of Berkeley. Skyscrapers had not yet come to dominate San Francisco's skyline – the Wells Fargo Building at 44 stories being the tallest and far to the right from the viewpoint of the House of the Flag – and the entire city seemed to unfold from the prospect of the living room. That room also held a magnificent fireplace, Georgian style moldings, and a 16 foot ceiling. Toward the street was a very large anteroom with piano, and further toward the street was a small library. In another direction from the living room was a large dining room, with another fireplace, and further on, the kitchen. A large circular staircase ran up a hallway running parallel with the dining room, and led to three large bedrooms, two lavatories and a sleeping porch, with another full bath on the first floor. The House had a long history, including its storied saving from the 1906 earthquake and fire by virtue of a flag from a tenant's flag collection waving defiantly from its top, thus leading to its name, House of the Flag.

Stan Siddle and his friend David Palmer had rented the mansion and in the spring of 1965 were looking for fellow bachelors to fill up its remaining bedroom and sleeping porch. I took the bedroom, really two large rooms, with a private bathroom, and Dan Miller, the friend from Dartmouth who had promised me a room for the summer of 1962, took the sleeping porch. I recall that my share of the rent for this prime piece of real estate was just $125 per month. One unexpected amenity arose from the culinary abilities of Martha Ficzere, our Hungarian maid. For a slight increase in compensation we induced her to cook dinner for us on Thursday evenings. San Francisco then had hundreds of small grocery stories scattered throughout its neighborhoods, and we established an account with one that Martha favored. Every Thursday afternoon she walked down a block to the grocery and ordered whatever inspired her. The grocery delivered the food to the house, and she prepared a delicious meal that she personally served at 6:00PM. If we wanted to bring guests to these feasts, and our dining room table had a service for 10, or if we needed to cancel ourselves, we had to call Martha by 1:00PM Thursday. We had some fabulous dinner parties through this arrangement.

I had one highly unusual encounter in the summer of 1965. I left the Russian Hill apartment of a woman I was dating around 1:00 in the morning and walked to my car. I had just gotten in when suddenly a young lady came rushing up to the right side of the car, pounded on my window, and yelled "Help me! He's trying to kill me!" I opened the door to let her in, and drove off as quickly as I could. I asked her to explain. She said she was a prostitute and worked in the Tenderloin, a well-known vice district. She explained she had committed the stupidest stunt known to hookers – going to an unknown customer's own place without telling anyone where she was headed. Once they were at his apartment he had tried to choke her, but she had run off, and could I please take her back to the Tenderloin.

When we were stopped at a stoplight she yelled, "There he is!" A pickup truck stood to the right, and I saw the driver pull out a gun and point it towards us. Immediately I stepped down on the gas, and fortunately no one was in the way. The pickup followed us, not on our tail, yet close enough. We were now on Nob Hill, adjoining Russian Hill, and just past California Street, where a series of one-way streets, such as Pine and Bush, run parallel with one another, down the side of Nob Hill toward the Tenderloin, a flatter area near Market Street. There was little traffic, and I deliberately decided to go down those streets the wrong way. If he continued to follow us my hope was that a cop would stop us. But there was no cop as I worked my wrong way down these streets toward the Tenderloin. When we reached the edges of the Tenderloin, and more traffic was in play, to our relief the Pickup veered off onto another street. I took the hooker to a corner where she asked to be let off. She thanked me profusely.

I was busy preparing for the bar exam, when one day in mid-August 1965, in the early afternoon, I experienced some stomach pains that seemed to become worse as the day went on. I ignored them for some time, and went about my business, thinking that something I had eaten just did not sit well. As they became stronger and more urgent, to the point where I could no longer concentrate on my work, I went out to buy some antacid, hoping that this might help. I persuaded myself that I was getting better and continued to work, but by the evening I could no longer convince myself that things were okay. After consultation with a doctor I went to Mt. Zion Hospital for an emergency appendectomy. During my three week stay in hospital I also developed severe blood clots that passed into my lungs, and then staph pneumonia. At least twice during my experience at Mt. Zion I was close to death, and the experience gave me an awareness of my own personal mortality. I had never even been seriously ill before. I was impressed with the patience I developed when I was most seriously sick and along with that patience an incredible ability to withstand sustained pain. I thought at the time that my experience would be life-transforming, leading me to greater serenity, patience, and appreciation for the gift of good health. However, I was too immature to allow my hospitalization to significantly affect me, to my great loss. However, there was one other significant result. The final reports of my doctors were that I was permanently precluded from heavy physical labor, and that there probably was an element of heart trouble along with the embolus. These reports, with the guidance of my local draft board's medical examiner, who was my friend Ann Glashagel's father, led my local board to change my classification to 1-Y, medically disqualified, and ruled that I was "not acceptable for induction under present standards." I had escaped Vietnam.

In the second week of October I was cleared to go to work, and I began to work at the Court of Appeals on October 15, 1965, exactly one and one half months late. The California District Courts of Appeal handle appeals from the superior courts which are the trial courts of unlimited general jurisdiction. Although litigants may attempt to appeal further to the California Supreme Court, in fact the decisions of the Courts of Appeal are final in more than 96% of their cases. Situated in San Francisco, the court for which I worked served a population of more than four million. Each justice had his own clerk who prepared a memorandum for each of the four, sometimes five, cases assigned each month by the clerk's office. They could be criminal or civil, although the majority were civil. With each case came a clerk's transcript, with reports of procedural matters associated with the case; a reporter's transcript that included a transcript of all the testimony taken during the trial and often arguments over motions made in the course of the proceeding; and the parties' briefs. The briefs consisted of a large opening brief submitted by the party, defendant or plaintiff, who brought the appeal; a substantial reply brief submitted by the prevailing party at trial, either defendant (in a civil trial) or the plaintiff/prosecutor; and a smaller closing brief submitted by the appealing party in rebuttal of the reply brief.

Each brief contained a concise statement of facts, the legal issues presented, the legal cases relied upon as precedent outlining the law, and the argument of counsel relating the law to the facts of the specific case at issue. They varied in complexity and also in length, but the typical opening brief and reply brief each would be 50-60 printed pages of dense legal reasoning. Likewise, the reporter's transcripts were extremely variable, some short trials resulting in transcripts of only 200-300 pages. Longer trials yielded transcripts of well over 1,000 pages.

My job was to read over these materials carefully, do any additional legal research I thought necessary, and then prepare a detailed memorandum, discussing the facts, critiquing the legal arguments of the briefs, reaching my own conclusions, and making a recommendation as to whether the court ought to affirm or reverse. The memoranda were due two weeks before the oral arguments before the three-judge panel. I also was to sit in on the oral arguments of counsel and, if warranted, make any additional observations based on these oral presentations.

I enjoyed the work, but soon came to resist the regularity of the work-day rhythm, the coming in at predictable times, working, then leaving at set times. I had a key, not just to my personal office but also to the entry of the suite of offices and library that constituted the Court, and I had twenty-four hour access to the State Building that housed our Court, the California Supreme Court, and several other state offices. I began to work in the evenings and even very early mornings, and to absent myself at times from the regular workdays. I continued my land speculation, buying and selling lots in the Santa Cruz Mountains. I was in my office most of the workdays, but also was absent a fair amount of time, compensated of course by work during the early mornings and evenings.

I still faced the bar examination, and the next testing came up in the first few days of March 1965. Justice Draper suggested I take a week off work to study. I did not have the time to repeat the series of lectures I had begun during the summer, but I had very detailed commercial outlines, more than one thousand pages of densely-worded expositions of the law. I read those outlines with concentration, and then walked into the toughest testing of my life. It was exhausting, and far more difficult than any testing I had endured at Stanford, although that was tough enough. I celebrated finishing the end of the second day a bit too much, and I began the third day with a slight headache. I really did not know whether I had passed or failed, but felt cautiously optimistic. Simply because I had recognized the incredible complexity of the issues presented by the facts of the questions, I thought I had done reasonably well.

The San Francisco *Chronicle* published the names of those who passed on the release day of the results, and that created a minor rush for that issue of the newspaper. I knew of a *Chronicle* vending machine in North Beach that usually had the morning papers by 6:00AM, so I got up very early on the release date, drove down from Nob Hill to North Beach, put a quarter into the vending machine, opened my newspaper, and discovered that I had passed. Hah! No more exams, ever, I thought, not having any inkling of my future academic pursuits.

The only burden between bar passage and swearing in was a review by the Character Committee, concerning our ethics. The Committee placed no hold on me, and so I proceeded to the swearing in ceremonies, held June 28, 1966. My parents came out for the event, and I also invited Martha, a young woman then high in my feelings, to join us. Everyone gathered in the auditorium of the Veterans Memorial Building, adjacent to the opera house on Van Ness Street. The fledgling attorneys sat in front, the California Supreme Court sat on the stage, and the friends and relatives were in the rear. A few short speeches were made, and then the President of the California State Bar made a motion that those before the Court and listed on an accompanying paper be admitted to the California Bar.   Roger Traynor, the Chief Justice, said simply, "The motion is granted," and there I was, a lawyer.

Martha had to leave after the state ceremonies. However, the day was not over. Now that we were attorneys recognized by the State of California, we were entitled to practice law in the federal courts within the state. After lunch, at 2:15PM we all trooped into the ceremonial courtroom of the United States District Court for the Northern District of California, a beautiful spacious room generally used to give the oath of allegiance to newly naturalized citizens. That day, however, a federal judge made the many hundreds of us officers of this court and members of its Bar. We then walked to the nearby courthouse of the United States Circuit Court of Appeal for the Ninth Circuit. The Ninth Circuit has a beautiful, pre-earthquake structure, filled with interior mosaics. After we were all admitted there, my mother, father, and I re-united for a real celebration. I am sure my parents felt gratification for the culmination of many years of anxiety and financial struggle on their part. Their only child had made his way and was truly now out of the nest and into the world.

I think Justice Draper began to believe I was shirking my work, although I never missed a single deadline and my memoranda were just as complete as always. Yet I failed to make a positive projection of effort, and I did not realize until late in my tenure at the Court that it bothered anyone so long as I actually accomplished the tasks. Draper had no way of knowing that I often worked in the evenings and on weekends. I should have told him. One of the things appellate judges do for their clerks is to scout out employment possibilities for after their clerkship. I took it as a sign of distain for my work habits that Draper came up with only one suggestion, a discipline-enforcing job at the State Bar. I did not even consider it because I wanted to practice law, not ride herd over allegedly unscrupulous lawyers.

I wrote letters to several law firms, asking for an interview. About 15 responded affirmatively to the request for an interview, but most had no immediate need for an additional associate and advised only that they would keep my resume on file. I received a warmer response from only two: Dunne, Phelps & Mills and Littler Mendelson. I went to the Dunne, Phelps & Mills firm because one of its partners, Edward Mills, had advertised for a lawyer to take over a class in Trusts he taught at San Francisco Law School. I interviewed with him about that job, part time work that paid only $15 per week. Apparently he was impressed at our meeting as he indicated that he and his partners had talked about adding an associate and that he wanted to talk with his partners about me for that position.

He called me back with an offer for employment as an associate at the going rate, left unspecified. Dunne, Phelps & Mills was a small firm of a traditional nature. It had a general civil practice, although a solid part of that practice was defending railroads in Federal Employers

Liability Act cases involving injuries to their employees. It had about ten lawyers, of which about half were partners. Littler Mendelson was a smaller firm specializing in the representation of management in employment and labor disputes. It was founded as early as 1942, but was still small, with six young lawyers. Although it did practice some general civil law, the firm intended to specialize in labor law, and related fields. It also extended an offer, so now I had two prospective employers.

I spoke with Justice Draper about the two firms. He was enthusiastic about Littler Mendelson, calling it a top firm that had a good reputation with the National Labor Relations Board. It definitely was not a union-baiting firm, and sometimes when there was no conflict of interest it represented unions. Its six attorneys, Draper said, were young and dynamic. He was sure the firm would grow, double to twelve lawyers he foresaw, and become the best labor firm in the area. He was less enthusiastic about Dunne, Phelps & Mills. Draper affirmed that it had a more general practice than Littler Mendelson, but had doubts about its growth.

Draper also asked me to consider if I would feel comfortable in a Jewish firm, as Littler Mendelson was. That did not bother me in the slightest. My employers at the San Mateo Tax Service, Bob and Sue Miller, were Jewish, and they had treated me wonderfully as an employee and had become friends personally. More compelling to me was my doubt that I wanted to specialize in labor law. I had not taken labor law at Stanford, and I was not sure I would like that field. I did hear things about Dunne, Phelps & Mills from other lawyers that were more affirmative than Draper's impression.

In the end I made my decision to go with Dunne, Phelps & Mills because I really wanted exposure to a wide variety of civil practice, and I just was not sure I wanted to specialize in labor law. From one perspective it was a huge mistake, a disastrous decision. Dunne, Phelps & Mills never had any significant growth. Littler Mendelson, on the other hand, began on an exponential growth curve after I had the opportunity to join its six lawyers. It expanded significantly in the Bay Area into the 1990s, and then went nationwide and even global. It is now an acclaimed labor law firm with over 1,000 lawyers on its staff and 70 offices nationwide and globally. I could have been on the ground floor of that growth.

I began at Dunne, Phelps & Mills on November 8, 1966. At first I really enjoyed my work there and was certain I had made the right choice. Remembering the need to project my effort, I often went into the office early. I got up early in the morning and walked to work, going down Russian Hill, then crossing Chinatown where I would buy a pork-filled hot bun for my breakfast, and then continue down to the firm's Montgomery Street offices. After a year or so I became more and more dissatisfied with my employer. The firm's idea of the market rate for my compensation turned out to be only $700 per month, only a pittance more than I had been paid at the Court of Appeals. I brought in several clients, not a huge number, but enough to make me think I should see something of their fees. The firm's policy was to keep it all, and not share fees with associates even when they had brought in the clients themselves. Then the generous variety of cases assigned to me morphed into almost exclusively railroad defense work. The final straw was that after about 18 months I received a raise in the token amount of only $50 per month, making my salary $750 per month.

Four of us, in different firms and circumstances, began talking together about beginning our own firm. I knew one, Joseph Moless, fairly well, since he had been a fellow clerk with me at the Court of Appeal. We were all young, had done well at law school and had served on our respective law reviews, and more to the point, we all chaffed at the restrictions on us in the stuffy environment of our San Francisco law firms. We wanted to be our own men and to practice law in booming San Jose. Although the term "boutique" was not yet in use regarding law firms, in a rapidly expanding city that did not have such a practice, we wanted to become one. On April 30, 1968, I gave a month's notice to Ed Mills, the partner who had hired me.

The men who had talked so bravely about leaving their secure employment came to have cold feet. Of the four of us, I was the only one ready to embark on the new venture as of the end of May, although Joe Moless and Dick Turrone ultimately did come down to San Jose, only later; the fourth, Harold Collins, showed no interest in our San Jose project beyond our initial meetings. Dick Turrone and Joe Moless both spent time in San Jose with me, talking with several small firms about arrangements for sharing space. But eventually the decision was mine alone, and I was impressed by a small firm headed by Bruce Christenson and Earl Hedemark. We reached agreement as to my rent and costs for sharing our single secretary. Using money I borrowed from my grandmother, Phyllis de Mattos, I bought some office furniture, ordered stationary and insurance coverage, rented an apartment, and was ready to move down to San Jose at the end of May 1968.

In 1966 I had taken the teaching post offered by Edward Mills, as well as the associateship in his firm. I do not remember much of my first law teaching, at San Francisco Law School one evening per week for the academic year 1966-1967. I taught Trusts, a subject never of much interest to me. I do recall being always short of time for adequate preparation, and therefore not as fully prepared for classes as I should have been. I thought the students were not working hard enough, so I graded my midterm examinations half to a full point below what I would have graded them had they been final examinations. Several students received Ds and a few received flunks. That had the desired effect of inducing more effort out of the students. A few weeks later I announced that the midterm grades would not lower final grades and would only be used to improve on the final exam.

One other thing I recall from that teaching year that, while really nothing in itself, caused me considerable embarrassment at the time. In my initial night of teaching, the first case in our casebook involved an early nineteenth century trust where the assets of the trust consisted of slaves. A standard technique of teaching law is to call on students to discuss the facts of the case and the legal rules involved. This was before I had any acquaintance with my students and by sheer fortuity and a portion of bad luck I happened to call upon the only black student in our class of about 45. That unfortunate happenstance had no significance or repercussions, but it was the sort of thing that bothered anyone of good will in 1966.

My 1966 reading of Bernard De Voto's *The Year of Decision: 1846* whetted my interest in Mexican California, and I began reading more widely in California history, especially in the Hispanic period. I also developed an interest in Big Sur because of my frequent visits to our property there. I decided to combine these interests and write a book on the history of Big Sur, California, and I would begin with a chapter on the Spanish period.

I quickly learned that the European phase of Big Sur's history was minimal. It consisted of two things. One was the forlorn account of one Spanish soldier who had become detached from his unit and wandered into the Santa Lucia Mountains. Once he entered into the rugged hills of Big Sur, he became lost, and was forced to follow the ocean from high up in the jagged hills, going sharply up then steeply down one severe hill after another until he found a Spanish camp at the end of the range. The second historical factor was more mundane. The Spanish ships of exploration or supply that made their way along the California coast almost invariably mentioned the spectacular coast, and in particular Point Sur, a small high protrusion into the ocean that seems both from the land and the water to be almost an island.

I began to spend time in the California Collection Room of the San Francisco Public Library parsing out these general facts. Then in the first few months of 1968 I began to search out primary materials in translation, for I then was ignorant of Spanish, at the public library and also the California Historical Society's library, then located in a beautiful mansion on Pacific Heights. I passed many pleasant afternoons and evenings hard at work. I even spent an entire day, April 27, 1968, working at the Bancroft Library at the University of California, Berkeley, reading primary manuscript materials with the aid of a translator. I could not imagine then that twenty years later I would spend weeks at a time working at that marvelous place, and doing my own translation.

Working in a major research library or manuscript collection such as the Bancroft gave me a positive pleasure. I would determine what records I needed to see, working with a catalogue or finding aid. Then

I turned in a call slip at the circulation desk, and in short order the materials would arrive for me to take to my reading space. It felt as though I were in some sort of treasure house, and all I had to do was determine what particular jewel or ring I wanted to see. Then someone scampered off and fetched it for me. It was wonderful. It also felt good that I was working alongside other scholars, working hard in their own reading spaces, enjoying other gems of the treasure house.

By early April I had finished a rough draft of the Spanish period chapter of Big Sur history, and had even begun some preliminary work on the Mexican era, to be the following chapter. Through this research and writing I learned much about the range and substantial volume of printed primary sources of early California. The end results of my early historical scholarship were minimal, and they certainly did not prepare me for work with unpublished manuscript materials. Nevertheless, I did make substantially more use of primary sources, albeit translated and in print, than I had ever done at Dartmouth. I enjoyed their inspection, analysis, and comparison. This early work was the shaky foundation for much more substantial historical work that would develop over the next ten years. I polished that draft and ultimately fashioned an article on the Spanish period of Big Sur history and submitted it to the *California Historical Quarterly*. It passed the preliminary review but ultimately the *Quarterly* turned the piece down because it made little use of manuscript materials.

My San Francisco years, 1965-1968, were also a time of great friendships and many activities with friends. Stanley Siddle lived with me in the apartment on Washington Street, the Babylon Gardens, in the summer of 1962. We also shared the House of the Flag from my law school graduation in 1965 through mid-1967 when I moved to a flat on Greenwich Street. He was, and still is, a great friend. In those days we often had dinner together, explored some of the back roads of the Bay Area, and had numerous bridge games with David Palmer, and others. Ann Glashagel and her flat mate Susie Parker often came over from their apartment house adjacent to the House of the Flag for informal dinners and bridge games. We organized a few large-scale parties in the old house, as people were much taken by its elegance and spectacular views.

In 1966, Ann moved from the apartment she shared with Susie Parker to her own flat on Pine Street, a street that runs along the side of Nob Hill. It was a nice neighborhood. Her new apartment was across the street from a building that once was a brothel run by Sally Sanford, a well-known madam of the 1940s and 1950s. It was boarded up, and since there were no lights from the inside, the power was obviously off. Ann noticed one day that a side door was ajar. A few days later, fortified by a good dinner and a bottle of wine, Ann and I went inside that side door armed with flashlights. We spent about an hour exploring the distinctive design features of a bordello: a large and lavish open area to the front, complete with an elaborate fountain, and dozens of very small bedrooms to the rear and upstairs. It was fun, and probably not a burglary since the door was open. I am sure we broke a lot of other lesser laws, and it was certainly not the sort of thing either Ann or I would do later in life, without the invincible feeling that comes with being twenty-something.

Another dinner, another bottle of wine, and we hatched another crazy idea. We decided we would make a sociological study of bars in the working-class Mission District, specifically how the social class of the clientele related to the lighting and music of the establishment. Our methodology was simple. We would look at every bar on Mission Street between 16th and 20th streets. One night we went down to the Mission District and did just that. We worked our way up one side of Mission Street, from 16th to 20th and then back down the other side. The problem was that we could not just walk in, look around, and make our notes. No, we thought that would make us look suspicious. So we had to have a drink in every bar. We did not realize that there were so many, many bars on Mission Street. By the time we were done, we two young researchers were thoroughly plastered, and we each had to take a cab home.

Ann was truly a good friend. Until her untimely death from cancer in 2002, we were always able to be very open and relaxed with each other, and often confided our personal anxieties and aspirations, hopes and fears, in very candid terms. After I left the Bay Area, I would often return for conferences or research, and on every trip we would have dinner together and talk. In many ways, Ann was the sister I never had, and I was the brother she never had. I miss Ann very, very much.

My friendship with Gene and Adele Malott, the publishers of a small weekly newspaper in Hillsborough, down the peninsula, began to flourish during this period. We had begun our relationship as attorney-client only, but we quickly became good friends. I spent several evenings at their apartment in Burlingame, and after dinner and a lot of drinks I often spent the night. They also came up to San Francisco, and we had dinner together at several Italian joints in North Beach, near my flat, such as the Golden Spike, New Pisa, and Savoy Tivoli, where seven-course dinners could be had for $3.00 or less. The wonderful and atmospheric Iron Pot was only a bit further away, on Montgomery near downtown. Gene was especially fond of Basque food and there were several Basque restaurants in North Beach, of which the best were Elu's on Broadway between Mason and Powell and the Basque Hotel, named for its overnight Basque clients, on Romelo Alley off Broadway near Columbus.

In the mid-1960s, Ann Glashagel, my good friend from high school days, married John Schumacher. I remember many great charade games at John and Ann's apartment, but I will never forget the sauerbraten lunches with John, on Wednesdays at Breen's, 3rd and Jessie Alley just across the alley from the San Francisco *Examiner* building. When one walked in off 3rd, a long wooden bar sat on the right facing a row of booths on the left. Further back were tables, and at the very end of the large room was a serving line where one got food, with sauerbraten the special on Wednesdays. The sauerbraten was good, but the martinis were excellent, and *the* place to sit was at a booth where the bar was close by and the carrying distance not too great. This was necessary because the bartender filled the martini glass up to the very top lip. He skillfully laid in the olive with a toothpick resting horizontally along the rim of the glass, so that the olive itself displaced very little of the precious liquid beneath. Carrying such a completely filled glass was difficult, and it helped to have a booth near the bar. This bar and food operation was typical of downtown San Francisco in the late 1960s; there were dozens of these

31

highly atmospheric older places around. These pieces of old San Francisco are almost all gone now, replaced by sterile high-rise office buildings, devoid of character, which have no ground floor restaurants, and certainly none that are old and atmospheric. The old joints, and there were so many of them, are almost all now torn down in the name of progress.

I developed a taste for sauerbraten during those years, and when I worked for Dunne, Phelps & Mills, which was a downtown law firm, I worked out the pattern of restaurants that served sauerbraten so that I could, if I wanted, have the wonderful sour German beef any day of the workweek. There was a place on Market, name forgotten, that had sauerbraten on Mondays. It was the poorest of the lot, and I seldom went there, but it did, in fact, have sauerbraten every Monday. For Tuesdays and Fridays I could count on Schroeder's, a classic German restaurant on Front Street, a block from the financial district. Ladies were always admitted in the evening, but until the passage of the Equal Accommodations Act, lunch was for men only. Large round tables nearly filled the cavernous room, leaving only a few rectangular tables on the side. When one came in, a no-nonsense maître de seated you at a round table, where you ate communally, although everyone had their own service. Most everyone praised Schroeder's potato pancakes and sauerbraten, although I personally thought Breen's, mentioned before for Wednesdays, and Hoffman Grill, on Market Street, for Thursdays, were both better. Hoffman Grill had a beautiful female nude painting over the bar, perfect potato pancakes, and wonderful sauerbraten. This tile-floored, wood-paneled saloon, still with its beautiful Victorian fixtures, opened in 1891 and died in the 1980s, a victim of the greed and false notion of progress that have killed off so much of the old atmospheric San Francisco.

There were so many things to do in those years in San Francisco, aside from fabulous dining. There were the topless bars where one could watch braless young ladies gyrate around poles. Street fairs around town had a variation of the water dunk, where someone, often of prominence, dropped into a water tank when a carefully thrown ball hit a designated mark. In 1960s San Francisco, one bought chances to hit the mark with a ball for a different outcome. Buxom women stood by, and upon a successful throw of the ball, they would take off their bras and stand topless for a few minutes. I recall one such fair in North Beach that had a mother-daughter team. I was with Stanley, and when he struck the mark they both proudly took off their bras. They were both well-endowed, and we told them "very nice." Forms of toplessness were everywhere. Some restaurants in the downtown featured topless waitresses. I recall a shoeshine stand on Columbus just off Broadway with topless females who buffed your shoes while you sat above them in the traditional shoeshine stand seating.

Quite different were the few bottomless joints, where the young ladies "danced" to recorded music while stripping off all their clothing. Then they laid on the stage and by crossing and uncrossing their legs, and using their fingers, they gave all in attendance a total view of their private parts. These establishments did not serve liquor. The California Alcoholic Beverage Commission denied liquor permits to totally nude establishments on the specious reasoning that such exhibitions would cause men to drink excessively. The real reason was, of course, that they were just prudes.

Standing on quite another end of the cultural spectrum, well-stocked bookstores, both new and used, offered an endless joy of browsing. The best known of these was City Lights Books. Opera bars, operating in the same Broadway/Columbus area as City Lights Books, offered the real thing: operatic arias sung by enthusiastic young talent to the accompaniment of a live piano. Wonderful!

I remember Mr. Otis, a joint on Green Street that did not push for drinks but offered cool jazz, Earthquake McGoon's on Turk where Turk Murphy held forth with Dixieland, and two joints right on Embarcadero on the waterfront filled with sailors and good jazz – Pier 23 and On-the-Levee. Pier 23 was built over the water. Its toilets were in a separate but adjacent building and to reach them one had to step across a lengthy metal grating that passed over the water. Crossing over that grate was quite exciting in the frequent San Francisco fog. Jimbo's Bop City opened after hours out a way on Post Street. Jimbo, a tall, well-dressed black man, always wearing a cap, watched over his hangout personally. His joint *opened* at 2:00AM, and served cups of coffee at $6.75, the cost of about five alcoholic drinks at the average bar in those days. A good many jazz musicians jammed here, after leaving gigs at clubs with conventional closing hours. I believe all of these jazz joints are gone now. More substantial music ranged from *Messiah* at Trinity Church to Bach's *Mass in B Minor* in a church far off in the Richmond avenues on Sloat, right across the street from the Sigmund Stern Memorial Grove that sometimes featured Gilbert and Sullivan among its densely placed eucalyptus trees.

The Drinking Gourd on Union Street was filled every night with young people listening to folk music. Among the regular bars I favored, those without music or shows, my favorites included the Buena Vista, a popular bar and eatery in the Marina on Beach, at the end of the Hyde Street cable car line; Vesuvio's, on Columbus, just across an alley from the famous bookstore City Lights, filled with aspiring Bohemians sitting around in high-backed woven wicker chairs with wide arms, wicker thrones really, smoking strong Gauloises cigarettes; and the quiet yet lavish neighborhood bar, Yerba Buena, on Washington and Taylor high on Nob Hill, with its beautiful golden colored metallic bar mural of the San Francisco hills being overcome by the ocean's fog.

I went to restaurants, jazz joints, and bars with friends, dates, and my parents when they visited. However, one thing I seemed to do by myself, probably because it was so expensive, was the opera. I never had season tickets in these years; that was way beyond my financial means. On a few occasions I just showed up at the opera house and bought an orchestra section ticket, for $12. If I was going to the opera, I wanted to be reasonably close. I received a tip about a little bar where the opera singers went after performances. One Saturday night after seeing *Un Ballo in Maschera*, I tried out the suggestion. It was an ordinary kind of piano bar in an undistinguished neighborhood on Polk Street. About an hour after the last curtain call the two male leads did come in and began to sing along with the piano. After a few drinks they let loose with real power and the volume nearly blasted everyone out of the bar.

Another interesting opera experience, in November 1967, was a performance of *Barber of Seville* sponsored by the San Francisco Department Store Employees Union. Held at a much less exalted venue than the opera house and with only two pianos rather than a full orchestra, it also cost only $1.00 rather than the San Francisco Opera's $12.00. Apparently the tickets were given outright to the union's members and families, and the excess was then sold to the public. The singing was fine and the performance most enjoyable. I had read a local newspaper article that said this was the first time a union had sponsored an opera. Only in San Francisco.

Perhaps because I indulged in much of that nightlife, money was occasionally in very short supply during my San Francisco years. For lean impecunious times I had some creative ways to entertain myself. If I had any money at all, there was a double feature movie theatre on Market Street that changed movies every week and charged 50 cents. For the same price I could occupy myself for the same amount of time by the San Francisco Municipal Railroad, the name given to San Francisco's unique public transit. The city possesses four different types of street transportation: the famous cable cars, ordinary buses, buses with fixed routes and wires to an overhead power supply, and true trams that ran on rails. I managed to thoroughly explore almost all of San Francisco by riding its public transit on the cheap. When you paid your first fare, the driver or gripman in the case of the cable cars, handed you a slip of paper that showed the line originally boarded and the time. That paper ticket could be used as a transfer not just once but twice, provided the later uses were in the same direction as your overall journey. This was to prevent the transfer from being used as a return trip, for which the Muni, as the system was called, expected an additional fare.

A body of interpretation had built up over what travel in the same direction meant. For example, it could include a ride in a sharp angular direction, so long as it was not backward. I had a detailed map of the Muni system, and worked out routes whereby I could travel literally all over San Francisco and then return to my point of departure using only two fares and four transfers. These routes took me on weekends to obscure locations, through many different neighborhoods that most San Franciscans never visited. I had fun with my Muni map in my study in my flat on Greenwich Street, working out how I could best use transfers to take in the maximum amount of the city.

I cannot leave my discussion about my San Francisco years without saying something about the hippies. After all, I was there during the 1967 "Summer of Love." In 1966, at the beginning of the hippie influx into San Francisco, many locals confused the hippies with the beatniks. In the early days, one often saw signs saying, "beatniks not allowed," when the sign maker obviously meant hippies, there being no beatniks in sight. The beatnik movement came first in the 1950s, and centered in North Beach, near to the entertainment district of Columbus and Broadway. The hippies concentrated in the Haight-Ashbury district, near Golden Gate Park, in the period of late 1966 through 1968. The beatniks tended to be older, late 20s, 30s, than the younger hippies, 16-21. Beatniks were rebels and rejected society as it existed. Many were creative and some had real talent. Allen Ginsberg, Jack Kerouac, and Ken Kesey were all noted writers who came out of the beatnik tradition.

I recall the Haight-Ashbury neighborhood from late 1965 and early 1966, just before the invasion of the hippies and their Summer of Love in 1967. Before the hippies, the Haight-Ashbury area was bohemian, with coffee shops, art supply stores, and galleries. Spaced-out people had not yet filled it in 1965-1966, nor was it dirty. An East Indian restaurant called Connie's operated on Haight Street. Light and airy in the interior, and with wonderful food, it featured good lunches and complete dinners under $2.50. Across Haight Street from Connie's, the Juke Box gave forth great evening jazz. Within months after the hippies arrived, all these businesses plus the art supply companies and galleries were all gone.

There was an element of bitterness about the beatnik rejection of society. The hippies, on the other hand, were younger, but merely wished personally to "drop out" of a society they rejected as meaningless. There was no bitterness to the hippies. A common image was of hippies stuffing flowers into police or military guns. One poster common in the Haight-Ashbury District read "Smother the Police with Love." However, because the hippies were interested only in disengagement from society, they had little interest in bettering conditions or in creativity. They rejected the "should" and "should-

36

nots" of authority sources, parental or governmental, as part of the general pointlessness of life itself. The only thing that mattered, the hippies claimed, was to *be* and to *love*. Not surprisingly, the hippie movement produced no notable writers and the artists who drew the ubiquitous psychedelic art never claimed that their art was anything serious. Some beatniks used drugs, but the hippies did so universally and with greater intensity. By the time of the 1967 "Summer of Love," there were some 15,000-20,000 hippies in San Francisco, most living in the 30 square block heart of the Haight-Ashbury District.

The hippies were a colorful group to look at. They often danced to the beat of a drum in the Golden Gate Park panhandle. I stopped a couple of times by these dances, and the long-haired hippie girls drew me into the group dancing circles. I was never interested in a personal relationship with the hippies. They were younger than me, and whether lawyer or clerk at the Court of Appeal I was clearly part of the "establishment" from which they wanted to distance themselves. Further, there was a hygiene issue with many of the hippies. I looked at a hippie "pad" in the basement of a small Victorian house on Oak Street. The hippies had left, or been evicted, and the owner was selling the three unit building, including the erstwhile basement hippie apartment. The two occupied units upstairs were fine, but the hippie unit was filthy. The walls were streaked with excrement, the toilets stopped up, and the floors covered by litter and dirty clothes.

The hippies included an altruistic primitive-communistic element descended in a line from the utopian colonies of the 19th century. The "Diggers" was a loose element in the hippie community that provided free food daily in two locations, one in Golden Gate Park and the other in Washington Square in North Beach, and only two blocks from my Greenwich Street flat. It was not revealed until years later that the City of San Francisco, fearful of disease and disorder that might permeate a youthful horde, actually subsidized the food program. The Diggers also operated a "Free Store," in the Haight-Ashbury. I went there in May 1967. The Free Store was organized like most every department store; for example, it had a clothing section, a book section, an appliance section, and so forth. It was entirely self-service, and signs encouraged people to take only what they needed. There was no cost. Needless to say, almost everything was used and of poor quality. I found only one thing of interest, a "Colorado College Student Handbook for 1963." I took it, because I wanted something from the Free Store, and I sent it to my dad. Since he was a 1933 alumnus of Colorado College, I thought that he might enjoy looking at it.

I think of the years 1965-1968 as years of tremendous transition for San Francisco. I even sensed that at the time. When I arrived in San Francisco there was only one business building that was a skyscraper, the 44 story Wells Fargo Building. The business district was filled with modest buildings of two or three stories, some with only a single story. That made it possible for so many restaurants to be visible from the street. Some of these were businessmen's hangouts, the various bars and grills that were San Francisco classics: Tadich Grill, Sam's Grill, Jake's, the Fly Trap, Hoffman Grill, to name just a few. Even modest sandwich shops were at ground level and clearly visible from the sidewalk. With the advent of the multiple skyscrapers that have now taken over the downtown, precious few restaurants remain that are visible from the ground. True, there may be a coffee shop on the 34th or 35th floor of some gigantic office structure, but those add no atmosphere to the downtown as did the older style of grills. While the entire forest of skyscrapers was hardly complete when I left San Francisco in 1968, many had been built in the years 1965-1968, and the direction that future development would take was clear.

The old San Francisco was a very masculine place, and was filled with stores, grills, and bars that catered to older men's tastes. By 1968, San Francisco was well on its way toward catering more to young men and also young women. I offer one example outside of the array of masculine restaurants and bars already discussed: the second floor men's department of San Francisco's Brooks Brothers. In 1965 the men's department had heavy tables throughout, hunting and fishing sporting paintings on the dark walls, heavy leather board-room style chairs, and male employees to help with one's selection. When I left in 1968, the tasteful hunting and fishing paintings had been replaced with more modern paintings designed, I think deliberately, to have androgynous appeal, pastel colors predominated on the walls, and the attendants seemed to be primarily women. Some might applaud all this as opening employment opportunities for women and appealing to a younger and broader clientele. I do not feel that way and think it a loss in taste and quality emblematic of a general shift in San Francisco values and traditions.

Chapter 2

San Jose and the Beginnings of Scholarship:
Summer 1968-Spring 1977

My chosen colleagues, Bruce Christenson and Earl Hedemark, practiced law in a small converted house on First Street about a mile east of downtown San Jose when I joined them in May 1968. Bruce was in his early 30s, had an abundance of quick nervous energy and intelligence. He practiced civil law, and primarily represented businesses. Earl was 49 and had an interesting background. When the United States entered World War II, Hedemark served as a Marine corporal stationed in the Philippine Islands. After the fall of Corregidor in May 1942, the Japanese captured Hedemark and forced him into the infamous Bataan Death March. Many Americans did not survive that experience but Earl did. The Japanese military then incarcerated him in a prisoner of war camp for the duration of the war. He brought back with him some fascinating stories, many sad, but some humorous, particularly of his days in Japanese prison camps. Earl primarily practiced criminal law.

Bruce was a heavy drinker and Earl was a recovering alcoholic. In those years, liquor fueled legal culture. Many, many attorneys, including myself, headed after work for watering spots close to their offices, had a few drinks and shared stories with fellow lawyers of courtroom victories, wise or foolish judges, or their favorite new restaurants. When a client required urgent attention, for example, in drafting a temporary restraining order, or preparing a response to an immediately threatening government regulation, and certainly in the middle of a trial, then an individual attorney might work on after work hours until 9:00 or 10:00, or even later and, for a few days, miss this camaraderie altogether. We all understood this because we had all been in this position.

Earl had interesting politics. Left of center on most issues, he vehemently opposed the Vietnam War. Because of his prisoner of war background, the government supposed he was a good patriot, and appointed him to the local draft board. But in fact he represented many draft resisters, including some who lacked the means, for free, *pro bono*. He also brought lawsuits against the government, seeking in various ways to hinder or halt the draft system. As a member of the local board he always voted for individual exemptions or requests for reduced draft status. In one striking way of showing contempt he put the unframed original certificate of his presidential appointment to the draft board on his desk and used it, and invited his clients to use it, as a mat for their coffee cups. All of this caused great conflict with the military supervisors of the draft, whom Earl always called "the colonels" with a contemptuous sneer. The uproar and accusations became heated, even making it into the newspapers, and eventually Earl resigned from his board. He was never in very good health, because of his brutal treatment at the hands of the Japanese and added upon by his drinking. Earl Hedemark died in 1974 at age 55. Beneath a gruff exterior he was a kind and caring man.

The firm moved upscale a bit in the early 1970s, when we moved our offices from the house to the 10th floor of a downtown office building. We usually had a holiday party for the staff and ourselves at a local restaurant. However, this year we expanded it to an office-warming party for friends, clients, and spouses, probably the largest office party we ever held.

Bruce, Earl, and I took several short trips with our wives. I remember taking the "Fun Train" as a group to Reno. The Southern Pacific operated the Fun Train, and it was precisely that. A quite modest cost purchased round-trip transportation, leaving San Francisco in the early Friday evening and then leaving Reno for the return on Sunday morning. The price included accommodations at a first class Reno hotel for Friday and Saturday evenings, meals on the train, dinner on Friday and a brunch on Sunday. The Reno casinos provided many, many coupons to use to enhance a bet, for example such a coupon matched with one's own $5 would be treated as a $10 bet. The casinos also included coupons in the package for free drinks or half-off dinners. The train itself was nine or ten cars, and every third car was stripped of seats and provided with a bar at one end and a band at the other, so that passengers could use the middle space for dancing. Southern Pacific operated five or six of these Fun Trains every winter. No longer, of course, like so many good things that have been abandoned. My wife Bernadette and I took this train a couple of times by ourselves.

We held several office parties but the most spectacular was at my father and my ranch in Big Sur. Warner Brothers has just completed the filming of *Zandy's Bride* on the property, but the set, consisting of temporary structures appearing as a 19th century ranch house and barn, had not yet been demolished. All the partners, their wives, secretaries and boyfriends, associates who worked in our office, and their significant others, and children, all came to the ranch in Big Sur. We had a great barbeque on outdoor grills. Someone played a guitar and we sang songs by the massive fireplace in the log cabin. Some of us slept in the cabin, others in the barn, and still others outdoors under the stars. It was a good time. Most of our office parties with the staff were simply Christmas lunches that we held every year for the lawyers and secretaries in a nice local restaurant. We also had occasional parties for our clients that we held in our offices.

We acquired another partner, Don O'Keefe, a stately and friendly man a few years older than Earl and hence our oldest partner. The name of the firm changed from Christenson, Hedemark, and Langum to a more-stately Christenson, Hedemark, Langum, and O'Keefe. Some clients joked that we sounded like a railroad. Shortly after Earl's death we made our final move as a firm, this time to the end of the same floor, renovated and rebuilt with offices designed to our specification. Don O'Keefe left the firm to become the president of an insurance company at approximately the same time I left to become a law professor. Don died about a year later. I kept in touch with Bruce for many years after I left the firm, visiting him in San Jose at his new offices, then new homes in Los Gatos, Carmel, Lake Tahoe, and Reno. Every time I saw him I would joke that it really was good to see him, an allusion to the fact that we were the surviving two partners of our four-man partnership. Bruce died of pulmonary hypertension in 2011.

We had some wonderful secretaries, and in particular I remember three young ladies in their early 20s, Velma Bateman, Vikki Aranio, and Nora Roberts. They joined us in office picnics and parties. We were all friendly and palled around together, but no hanky-panky. I have stayed in loose contact with them over the years.

In 1970 I married Bernadette Williams Pucine. She had six children by her previous marriage and was necessarily a fulltime mother. When her children grew older, she worked for the Santa Clara County Transit District. Upon the birth of her youngest child, Bernie, as she was generally called, had a tubal ligation as she did not then want more children. After our marriage she underwent surgery to reverse the ligation, as she knew I wanted children. However, the surgery was unsuccessful, and the failure to have children created tension in our marriage. We divorced in 1978, and Bernie died of cancer, all too young, in 1995.

I was an active step-father with her children, participating in school work and activities, taking them to movies, dinners, and on many long trips for vacations. We had a good relationship and even now in 2020 I feel close to and visit with them. The step-children are, in birth order: Patricia, Eugene, Roberta, Dina Marie, Dean (goes by Dino), and William (goes by Willie).

I had a general civil practice, with an emphasis on business litigation and real estate. But I also took any civil matter that came my way, from divorces to bankruptcies. The criminal cases I had were generally either civil clients who later found themselves in minor criminal difficulties, such as DUIs, or a few criminal cases that in the nature of their proof were very similar to civil cases, such as a security fraud prosecution. I became real friends with some of my clients, such as Gene and Adele Malott who owned a weekly newspaper, *The Hillsborough Boutique*, which I represented from organization through disputes and litigation, and eventual sale. Through the sale of the newspaper I lost a client, but I had acquired friendships with the Malotts that endured for many years until the last of them died, in 2005. Bob and Sue Miller owned a tax service, San Mateo Tax Service, where I worked as a law student. I later represented them in litigation and eventually represented them in their firm's merger into a much larger tax service. I merged myself out of a client, but I retained two friends, Bob and Sue Miller.

Although I enjoyed some aspects of practice, and some clients a great deal, overall it was not working out well. One reason was that I probably did not charge what my services were worth, a point Bruce Christenson often made to me. The more basic problem was that I did not have enough clients. I am shy, always have been and am now, and it was very difficult for me to schmooze with prospective clients, at cocktail parties for example, tout my abilities, and bring in the clients. It was not that my work itself was bad; to the contrary my partners and my clients were happy with my work product. Even some judges intimated that my written briefs were excellent. I simply could not round up the business base necessary to thrive.

I was genuinely unhappy, I can see now in retrospect, during my ten years of law practice. I was unhappy in my marriage, and probably the drinking did not help. I engaged in all sorts of activities to mask this unhappiness. I began to write scholarly articles, and I worked on and obtained my M.A. degree in history. I also engaged in teaching law, at first just a matter of gathering some small sums of money to augment my impecunious position, but within a few years a source of pleasure and stature.

I taught at an unaccredited night law school, Lincoln Law School of San Jose. This experience offered me insight into another way, professional law teaching, that I might earn an income that would be sufficient so that I need not dip constantly into my capital that I had acquired by inheritance. Teaching also had the advantage that students presented themselves to the school and faculty for instruction without the need for the faculty to hustle them in as a lawyer does with clients. The idea of a full-time academic life first occurred to me at Stanford where I was doing some complicated legal research. It was a beautiful day with a gentle breeze and I was walking under the pine trees on the trail that goes from the art gallery to History Corner. I was admiring all this when suddenly the Hoover Institution bells burst forth, and that seemed to complete a perfect scene. I immediately thought how wonderful it would be to work in a serene setting like this.

Lincoln Law School was and still is a night law school, offering a four-year curriculum designed to provide the opportunity for older students who have full-time jobs to switch careers and become lawyers. It is now accredited by the State of California, although not by the American Bar Association, but in 1968 when I arrived it was totally unaccredited. However, students could sit for the California Bar examination if they first passed a preliminary test at the end of their first year. I'm not sure how I even heard of the school, but in the academic year 1968-1969, I began teaching Evidence, the rules of what can and cannot be introduced at trial. My salary was an insignificant $480.

This was my first law teaching, excepting the short Trusts course I had taught at San Francisco Law School. Lincoln seemed more like a real school, notwithstanding its meager facilities: two classrooms, library, reception desk, and an office for the Dean. The faculty came from local legal practitioners, and all were part time. Evidence was offered only bi-annually, so I did not expect that I would be teaching in the 1969-1970 academic year. By 1973-1974 the pay had risen to $1,000. From then on I taught at Lincoln every year until my departure for Detroit. I began teaching Torts in addition to Evidence, and I added Legal History. In my final year of teaching at Lincoln, I also taught classes at its branch in San Francisco, and my salary had risen to a more significant $6,300.

Even though the pay was always low, I discovered that I enjoyed teaching. Some students thought me gruff and that some of the questions I asked in class were confusing, but the student evaluations also concluded that I was well prepared and that they had learned much from my courses. For my part I enjoyed interacting with the students, who were generally peers in age, some even older than me. Law was still taught Socratically through questions about actual legal opinions that the students read in casebooks. Often that method broke down, and I had to resort to straight lecture about legal principles, rather than questions. But when it worked it was a joy for me to address a series of questions to a student and see the glow in his eyes as her understanding grew of the legal principle involved. The student had discovered it on his own, and that is the best kind of education, and a real pleasure to the teacher.

The California legislature enacted a new California Evidence Code to be effective January 1, 1967. The courts always have slightly modified procedural and evidentiary rules by their decisions. This judicial construction or modification of a statute is known as "judicial gloss." I thought in 1974 that enough time had run since the effective date of the legislation that it might be appropriate to consider in what ways the courts had judicially modified the legislation, and whether those modifications were justified or merely examples of judicial arrogance, or in the current parlance judicial activism. As do most law schools, Lincoln had a scholarly law review, and I published my research and reflections in the 1974 *Lincoln Law Review* as "Judicial Gloss and the California Evidence Code." It was a substantial article, 23 pages in print, and re-reading it now as a seasoned Research Professor with many books and dozens of articles to my credit, the piece reads well. It was the first legal article I had written since my student days with the *Stanford Law Review*.

In 1971 I purchased a Victorian house on Chapman Street in San Jose. This quiet neighborhood was "mixed" in the sense that there were some other older houses in the immediate vicinity, but also some newer structures from the 1920s-1930s. Unlike our two earlier homes in San Jose where nearby residents were mostly working class, our neighbors on Chapman Street were primarily professionals. Across the street lived an interesting couple, Franklin and Barbara Dalkey. They worked for San Jose State University, he in the photocopy department and she in the library as the musical librarian. Bernadette and I became friends with them, and we often had dinners together at ethnic restaurants or gatherings in our homes. I was particularly impressed by Barbara who I thought had a first class mind and was an interesting conversationalist. I still think that and have kept in touch with Barbara, now Barbara Jeskalian, over these many years.

At some of our earlier get-togethers, and with other people as well, I bragged about my determination that someday I would get a master's degree in history. After I had said this two or three times to Barbara, she quietly handed me the packet of papers needed to apply to San Jose State University. If I were vainly huffing about the someday master's degree, Barbara called my bluff. I filled out the papers, and began my master's studies in the fall of 1972, and ultimately graduated in December 1976. It took me longer than most master degree students for several reasons. I was practicing and teaching law, so my courses were limited to evening classes. In addition, I had to take two semesters of second-year Spanish to satisfy the program's language requirement. The Spanish was technically an audit, but I had to take and pass the final exams with a B or better. At least I was allowed to begin at the second year level because of my prior studies in Spanish.

I must admit with shame that I petitioned for an exemption from the language requirement on the basis that my precise dissertation did not require Spanish. The history faculty honorably stuck to its rules and voted to deny my request. My forced exposure to additional Spanish became very helpful later for my doctoral dissertation, where Spanish was essential for my research. The current San Jose State catalogue indicates that the language requirement has been dropped for students seeking a master's degree in the area of American History, as distinct from European, and that in my judgment is sad. My law practice and teaching at Lincoln Law School meant that I could only take a single class in any given semester. I elected the thesis alternative, rather than take additional courses and a final comprehensive exam. This meant fewer semesters of course work. For all these reasons the progress toward the master's was slow.

My general interest was in the history of the American West. However, my frequent trips to Big Sur and Monterey, my research into the Spanish period of Big Sur, and my fascination with Bernard De Voto's *Year of Decision 1846*, combined to make pre-American California my specific focus. I took Lawrence Lee's "Seminar in the Westward Movement," as well as Benjamin Gilbert's "History of California to 1849" and "Colloquium on California Cultural History." Gilbert served as my first reader for my thesis and Lawrence Lee as second reader. I audited "History of the West," offered by an outstanding young teacher, whose name I do not recall. I also took courses offered by another outstanding teacher, E.P. Panagopoulos, "Early American Republic" and "Colloquium on late 18th and 19th Century American History." I even took some European history courses, McNeil's "European Social and Intellectual History since 1800," and Irma Eichhorn's "Colloquium in Nineteenth Century European Intellectual History." All of my teachers at San Jose State were excellent, and I learned a lot from their courses. I must single out Irma Eichhorn who was a powerhouse and a great intellectual stimulus. I genuinely enjoyed the academic experience, and I recall walking around the campus wondering if I could work this into my life.

My thesis counted for 12 units and my coursework for 21. That brought me to 33 units, more than I actually needed for my degree. My interest was in Hispanic California, and my thesis concentrated on various images of Hispanic California in contemporary times and especially in later eras, with a study of how those images arose and how accurate they were. The title made a generic statement, "Images of Hispanic California," and the four chapters made them explicit: "Californios and the Image of Indolence," "From Condemnation to Praise: Shifting Perspectives on Hispanic California," "Californio Women and the Image of Virtue," and "The Caring Colony: Alta California's Participation in Spain's Foreign Affairs." It pleased me that I ultimately placed every one of these chapters as separate articles in scholarly publications. I did not require much help from my faculty readers for the research and writing of the thesis, as I already had a good working knowledge of Spanish and Mexican California, and even at this early date had a good-sized library of books dealing with Hispanic California's history.

Two of the thesis chapters were published while I was still in San Jose. One, "The Caring Colony: Alta California's Participation in Spain's Foreign Affairs," appeared in the *Southern California Quarterly*, fall 1977 issue. The other, "Californios and the Image of Indolence" came out in the *Western Historical Quarterly*, April 1978 issue.

At the time I began my master's program I became interested in an historical question concerning the westward migration along the Overland Trail. I wondered how bands of immigrants in wagon trains, constantly on a daily westward move, handled social disruptions. If there were a robbery, assault, or murder, did the overlanders attempt to try and punish the offenders? Any sort of formal inquiry would take time and interfere with the need to push forward and reach the westernmost mountains before the snow made them impassable. To answer this question I needed to read as many narratives written by the emigrants themselves as I reasonably could. In 1969 the leading historian of the Overland Trail, Merrill J. Mattes, estimated that there were approximately 700 primary accounts of the overland journey, in the form of diaries, letters, and reminiscences. By 1988 he had increased that estimate to 2,000 narratives written by overland travelers.

A great many of these narratives simply record daily movement of the wagon train and have no mention of any trials or punishments. Others are military accounts. The great majority are extremely short. Many are unpublished manuscripts languishing in state or country historical societies and with few guides to their discovery. However, publishing houses, sometimes obscure, have published many diaries as books, and state and national historical journals have as well. The San Jose State University Library had an excellent collection of published overland narratives and I also had access to many state and national historical journals. I plunged in and read approximately 300 printed overland diaries and reminiscences as well as some manuscript sources, focusing on those portions that dealt with offenses and their punishments, which I located with the use of an index if available or skimming the materials to find relevant matters.

I read and read, and thought and thought. Then I wrote it up in an article that ultimately reached 18 pages of print and 54 footnotes. I concluded that "only in the relatively rare situation of deliberate murder did the pioneers ever unite in a calm manner to effectuate judicial deliberation and punishment. Far more often trials were merely an opportunity for amusement and a break from trail monotony." For murder there were actual executions. However, other serious crimes, say robbery or assault, usually resulted merely in banishment—not much of a punishment as the miscreant could simply join up with the next wagon train to arrive, usually only a half to a full day's wait.

This became my first historical article, and I was anxious to see its publication. I sent out query letters to several state historical journals and national historical journals, imposing a 30 day deadline for their consideration. Some refused to consider the piece under that tight a deadline. Others thought it had too narrow a scope for them or that it was too legal in nature. However, the Wyoming State *Annals of Wyoming* accepted it, the editor, Katherine A. Halverson, writing on October 4, 1973, that my piece was "an unusually interesting and well-written article, and the bibliography indicates a substantial background of research on your subject."

I was delighted with the news. But three weeks later, on October 26, 1973, bombshell-like news arrived. The *Western Historical Quarterly* accepted the article, subject to minor editorial tinkering and the possible additional suggestions of historical experts on the overland companies. Now I was even more ecstatic. The *Western Historical Quarterly* is the premier journal for western history, and my publication there would mean my arrival as a scholar. However, I had to apologize to the Wyoming journal, and I did so, fully explaining my situation. Mrs. Halverson sent back a most gracious letter, saying, "I fully understand your feeling that you must take advantage of the opportunity to have it published in *Western Historical Quarterly*. The *Quarterly* is, indeed, one of the most prestigious of the western history journals, and you must be pleased and flattered that your article was accepted, especially since it is your first attempt at publication of historical material."

There remained some back-and-forth with minor suggestions for improvements, nothing more than usual in the publication of scholarly work, as I would learn in the years to follow. The article ultimately appeared in the October 1974 issue. I used the manuscript version of the article as my course paper for Lawrence Lee's Seminar on the Westward Movement, one of my courses for the master's degree. Lee was excited that my paper would appear in such a prestigious journal, but cautioned me not to mention this to any of my classmates. He worried that the news might discourage their own efforts. In December 1973, when the course had ended, all the papers turned in, but before the article's publication, Lee hosted a wine party for the class at his home. Then he gushed forth with pride about his student, me, having a paper in the *Western Historical Quarterly.*

In addition to my writing and studying history, teaching and practicing law, in my San Jose years I continued to read considerably into the philosophy of history, history outside of my specific field, and novels and plays. My reading was highly diversified and extensive in light of my other activities. My records are not as complete as would be desired, but I do know that in 1973 I read 31 books; 36 books in 1974; only 12 in 1976; and 28 in 1978.

In these years I engaged in all sorts of personal lawsuits, ranging from silly collection suits brought when I was too stubborn to pay a particular merchant up to Federal District Court litigation I brought against a company in which I had invested. Two lawsuits are particularly interesting, one involving so seemingly trivial a matter as a parking ticket, and the other a last-ditch effort to save an historical landmark from demolition for which a permit had actually been issued.

San Jose had a one year statute of limitations on prosecution of traffic tickets, but it had fallen far behind in its efforts to prosecute them. Apparently a parking ticket was placed on my car on April 23, 1973. Bernadette was driving my car at the time, but in any event I never saw the ticket. Then in November 1974 I received a written notice of the violation in the mail. If the original ticket constituted the "complaint," then the ticket could not be enforced after April 23, 1974, and the written notice came seven months too late. Parking tickets were still regarded as a very low form of misdemeanor. I filed a motion to halt the prosecution on the basis of the statute of limitations.

The District Attorney countered my argument, contending that the written notice was the actual complaint, not the ticket left on the car.

52

The trial court decided in my favor, ruling in January 1975 that if the city "does not process the citation and ascertain identity of the registered owner in a year's time, then prosecution is barred by the statute." But my little parking ticket defense had stirred up some controversy. The *San Jose News* for January 23, 1975 gave my case front-page treatment with an article headlined "TRAFFIC TICKET UPROAR IN S.J." It pointed out that San Jose had over 30,000 unpaid parking tickets more than a year old, and that the decision in my case could cause a substantial revenue loss to the city.

I was amused that I had thrown a small wrench into the maws of the city's bureaucrats, but they did not feel that themselves. Instead, the District Attorney appealed. This was a much more formal process than that at trial, and involved the preparation of written briefs and then a hearing on September 4, 1975. In December 1975 the city's appeal was granted, and the case set for further hearings to be held on January 6, 1976.

I may have lost the issue of the statute of limitations and what constituted the complaint for the purposes of that statute, but I still insisted on a trial. It was not my ticket, and in those days defendants were still permitted a trial on traffic tickets. In spring 1976 we had a trial. I testified that I did not drive the car that day. I called Bernadette as a witness, and she affirmed that she had had the car then, but did not remember any ticket. She also testified that in April 1973 she had been attending classes at San Jose City College. The written notice of violation described a location close to San Jose City College as the place of the overtime parking. The judge declared from the bench that it was obvious it was not my ticket and acquitted me. In those years I enjoyed tweaking the nose of authority, and I had enjoyed the entire three year ride from original ticket to acquittal.

The battle over the House of the Flag was more serious litigation. This was the Victorian house described before where I lived, 1965-1967, with three other bachelors, set high on Russian Hill with a fabulous view of San Francisco. After I left the House, I visited there with Stanley many times. Then I left for San Jose in 1968, and Stanley left temporarily for a year's sojourn in Hawaii, and I visited it less frequently. Between 1968 and 1973, when I again became very active with the House, several events had transpired. In the late 1960s, the San Francisco Board of Supervisors designated it as an official city landmark. The reason for this status was that during the fires that followed the 1906 earthquake, a large American flag flying from the roof attracted the attention of soldiers who raced to it with water that prevented the house from burning.

In the early 1970s, however, a developer desired to tear it down and build an apartment house. He obtained a demolition permit but the local historical ordinance provided for a delay before a locally designated landmark could be demolished. Interested preservationists had obtained a six month freeze, although not without vigorous opposition from the developer. Then they obtained another extension for an additional six months. Since no one had purchased the property or otherwise negotiated with the developer, and the year's delay provided by the historical landmark ordinance had expired, the developer was apparently free to destroy the House of the Flag. The local preservationists apparently believed they could do nothing further since the ordinance provided no further relief, and were content to let the landmark house be destroyed.

I learned about the House's plight only at this juncture, and decided I would make a last ditch attempt to save it. I filed a protest with the Board of Permit Appeals and urged that the developer should have first obtained an Environmental Impact Report, which requires the study of social and historical impacts as well as merely physical. The developer's attorney argued that the historical ordinance failed to provide for any discretion beyond the granting of a year's delay. It had done that, but now, after the year was spent, the demolition permit should be issued immediately. In a hearing before the Board of Permit Appeals on July 9, 1973, the Board called my case without merit and denied my appeal. Their rules provided for a single petition for reconsideration.

While the hearing for rehearing was pending, someone working on behalf of the developer did some preliminary work to demolish a portion of the House's roof. The roof that was injured was actually over a portion of the house that was unoccupied and did little damage. However, we alerted the media and local politicians and arranged with the tenants (Stan Siddle had by then returned from Hawaii and was the lead tenant) for a time when the media could view the damage. This was an effort to bring the threatened demolition to maximum public attention and also paint the developer as uninterested in following the legal rules by his premature activities. Bernadette was a great help in this phase, as she did all the calling of the media and offices of the Supervisors of San Francisco.

About 30-40 people showed up at the House of the Flag at the time designated, including one Supervisor, John L. Molinari, and several reporters and photographers. Stanley was there, of course, but we could not act as though we were friends, just a past acquaintance from when I lived there. Whatever the historical status of the House of the Flag, Stanley himself had no protected status, and could have been evicted at any time by the developer.

While Bernie was busy calling reporters for me, I was talking with several of the local preservationists who had obtained the year's delay in demolition, but did not see any way forward. I pointed out that after the Board of Permit Appeals denied my petition for re-hearing, we could take our legal claim to the Superior Court and contend that the house could not be demolished without an Environmental Impact Statement. We could try to obtain a writ of mandamus to direct the City and County of San Francisco to refuse a demolition permit until such a Statement was prepared, a slow process that would probably buy at least another year's time. Litigation would be costly, and I could use their help. These good liberal San Francisco preservationists sat around in their Russian Hill houses, talked earnestly with me on several occasions, wrung their hands, but in the end did nothing at all to help.

The Board of Permit Appeals peremptorily denied my application for a rehearing. It was time to cut bait or fish by myself alone. I prepared the massive amount of paperwork required to be presented to the Superior Court. Then, on August 7, 1973, I talked with the appropriate San Francisco judge, made my preliminary case, and received a temporary stay order, and an order that the developer show cause on a hearing to be held August 27, 1973 why a preliminary injunction should not be granted.

I also applied for and received a cease and desist order from the Zoning Commission prohibiting the developer from any further action on the House pending the litigation. With the reporters at the House, my allegations of bad-faith premature partial demolition, and the Cease and Desist order, both the House of the Flag and me personally began receiving a lot of media attention. Several reporters interviewed me, and newspapers carried several articles about my cause. The *San Francisco Sunday Examiner & Chronicle* remarked that it was strange that "of all people a San Jose man is trying to save it [*i.e.*, the House of the Flag]. The would-be savior is San Jose attorney David J. Langum. He has a sentimental attachment for the old house because he once lived there."

This large-scale litigation required a great deal of time. It took more than a dozen trips from San Jose to San Francisco, and I had the fast and non-stop, one hour bus schedule almost memorized. My motive for this was indeed a sentimental feeling for the House and also a feeling of outrage that a demolition permit had actually been issued for an historical landmark. However, I admit after being mentioned in so many articles, I began also to harbor a hope that this publicity might attract a client or two to my office. It never did. Not one new client came through my doors because of this litigation, notwithstanding fairly extensive media coverage.

Judge Ira Brown, the San Francisco Superior Court Judge who regularly heard motion cases, presided over the hearing for the Preliminary Injunction held on August 27, 1973. It went on for over an hour, as the attorneys for the developers and I argued our respective contentions over the requirement or not of an Environmental Impact Report. Finally, Judge Brown remarked that he had given us more time than the U.S. Supreme Court allows for lawyers arguing before it, that he understood the issues and legal arguments, and would consider the case, with an order to follow.

Before Judge Brown had reached a decision, the defendant [developer] asked the Court to continue the case under submission, "during which time we will further explore the possibility of developing the property while retaining the house." Then on

February 14, 1974 the developer and I jointly requested Judge Brown to retain the case under submission pending settlement negotiations. The only settlement offer I received from the developer was to put up a plaque about the House of the Flag on their new apartment building. I promptly rejected that proposal. Then on March 16, 1975 the developer asked Judge Brown for a ruling.

On May 30, 1975 Judge Brown issued his order. He *granted* the writ I had brought to set aside the decision granting the demolition permit, reasoning as I had contended that the developer should have prepared an Environmental Impact Report. I had won!! I was so excited, particularly when I remembered that this was the first time ever, that an actual demolition permit had been issued for an historical landmark, then for the landmark to be saved, and by me, at the 11th hour from the wrecking ball.

By February 1976 came talk of a sale to a new owner who wanted to retain the house, remodel its inside into 8 condos, and build a smaller apartment house next to and downhill from the House. This would destroy the eloquent interior of the grand old house and block off entirely the view of the downtown and the Bay. However, the landmark status protected only the exterior where the flag flying on the roof had attracted the attention of the soldiers. That would be preserved. The landmark status failed to protect the House's magnificent views or its elegant interior where in 1965-1967 we had enjoyed so many parties and eaten Martha's fabulous dinners. Even though the exterior would be preserved, there was no way to prevent the interior from being trashed.

The architectural plans for remodeling the House of the Flag into eight apartments were ready by June 1976, and the Planning Commission approved the plans on July 1, 1976. Because the new zoning preserved the historical aspect of the House's exterior, somewhat sadly I acceded to the developer's request and dismissed my lawsuit as moot, nothing left to litigate, on August 23, 1977, a little over four years since my initial foray into this magnificent and successful effort to save an historical landmark from destruction at the 11th hour. I felt quite pleased with my work, and I still do, something that my readers will probably sense.

In these San Jose years my dad and I did a lot of things together, including quite a bit of travel. In October 1968 we drove down the Fraser River Canyon in British Columbia. For eight days in July 1971 we paddled down the Missouri River, in its most scenic portions through the cliffs in mid-Montana, on a Sierra Club trip. We went on other western ramblings as well.

I realize that my investments are beyond the scope of this memoir. Yet I believe that an extremely brief discussion of them will be essential to convey how very busy I was during these San Jose years. I do not discuss any publicly-traded stock investments, since these required but little time.

In 1971, I purchased equity shares in Scenic Railways, Inc., a small company that was the operator of the narrow-gauge Cumbres & Toltec Scenic Railroad that ran for 64 miles from Chama, New Mexico to Antonito, Colorado. I was appointed to the Board of Directors and had to travel many times to Chama, New Mexico for directors' or other operational meetings. I became very dissatisfied about the work of the officers of the company, and through lawsuits I brought in state and federal courts and also the necessity to obtain releases to facilitate a stock issuance under ICC regulations, I was able to compel a settlement. It was much more complicated than this precis, but I recovered approximately 60% of my $40,000.00 investment. I recovered nothing for a huge investment of time, but it was well that I got anything back as Scenic Railways went bankrupt within a few years.

I bought a club car, the *Sarah Jane*, ex-Baltimore & Ohio, and had it transported on its own wheels to Antonito, Colorado, where my thought was to establish a cocktail lounge near the Cumbres & Toltec's station. I never could find an owner of standard gauge tracks willing to enter into a long-term lease. I tried to sell the car in *Trains Magazine* and other places. I obtained a contractor's estimate to refurbish the car, but nothing seemed to be working and ultimately I sold the car for scrap, for a net loss of some $3,000 plus a lot of time.

I bought a narrow-gauge boxcar, ex-Denver Rio Grande Western. My thought was I would refurbish it as a weekend cabin and then store it on and run it over a narrow-gauge railroad in the California Sierras. I paid $850.00 for the boxcar and had it hauled from Alamosa, Colorado to the West Side & Cherry Valley Railway in Tuolumne, California at a cost of $1050.00. A former logging railroad, the West Side was attempting to re-organize a small portion of its trackage for tourist use. The arrangement was the railroad would haul my car hooked onto a regular tourist train at a rate of ten times the regular single passenger rate, and I would guarantee two trips a year. The railroad had trouble getting its train service in operation, and we agreed I would pay $100 per annum as a credit toward the future fare, but with no additional present cost. I tried and could not find a carpenter to work at that remote location to refurbish the boxcar.

In 1972 I actually used the car. On a Saturday in February, my stepchildren and I, and a couple other dads and their kids, motored up to the railroad. We definitely looked at the box car, a real curiosity to all, but I think we also took a slow-moving flatcar out for a couple miles of the remaining track. Later that year in November, Bernadette and I, together with Barbara Jeskalian and her son Alexander went up there and rode in the boxcar "hobo style," with our legs hanging out the open door. The operator took us the entire length of its five or so miles of tracks. It was an exciting ride, but very slow due to at least six derailments. The engineer and his assistant got us back on the track easily enough, using a metal shoe, but it took considerable time.

Time passed by, and nothing much happened. I kept trying to get a carpenter to work on the boxcar, but without any luck. In 1976 I advertised the boxcar for sale in the *Wall Street Journal*. I thought surely some executive would think a narrow-gauge boxcar might make a great romantic escape. However, I received not a single nibble. I was told in October 1975 that the railroad was about to be sold, and I imagine that was the beginning of Glen Bell's (founder of Taco Bell chain) ownership. In May 1977 I sold the boxcar to the West Side & Cherry Valley Railway for $1,500.00, a slight loss on the money side, a lot of time spent, but then a couple of very fun excursions.

In August 1971 I purchased a motel directly across the street from the Cumbres & Toltec depot in Chama, New Mexico. I renamed it the Chama Station Lodge and for a little more than a year I tried to operate a motel by long distance from San Jose, California. The best local manager I could find was poor at the job, and may have, although I am not certain, actually purloined some of the cash rents. I bought the motel for $ 28,000.00, put in almost $4,000.00 of capital improvements, and sold the place the following year for $42,500.00, representing a significant gain.

Stanley Siddle and I bought a condo in Fairfax, California in 1976. I bought Stanley out a few years later, and then sold the place for a huge gain in 2011. I always kept rents on the reasonable side with the understanding that my tenants would take care of all relatively minor repairs. Therefore, this project did not require much time for management.

My dad and I bought a tract of about 27 acres of open land in Tucson, Arizona in 1971 and 1972 in separate transactions. I had to fly to Tucson for two different hearings, in a futile attempt to obtain denser zoning. We sold the property after the end of my San Jose years for a large profit of $112,000.00. I also bought 3-4 houses in San Jose during these years, and had a few landlord tenant problems. I recall one tenant who simply left all his belongings in the house, but then left without any explanation or rent payment for three months. I assumed he had abandoned the place for whatever reason, and moved all his clothes and furniture into commercial storage. A month later he showed up to a house I had partly refurbished and re-rented and found all his goods and chattels were in storage with a substantial bill for him to redeem them. Again, I wasted time on each one of the houses, without any significant gain.

My father observed all this activity of mine from a distance, but we talked frequently, and also Bernadatte informed him by their clandestine telephone conversations. He wrote me about this on September 19, 1971, and gave me some good advice, which like most parental advice I totally ignored. What he wrote me was right on point, however:

Somehow I have the feeling that you get side-tracked to matters of lower priority, both in your law work and in other things. The RR [i.e., Scenic Railways investment and directorship] is a fascinating personal venture. I know and can understand, but the time spent on it might better be spent on the law. You are a brilliant lawyer, Dave, and I hope you will proceed to the big time and not be bogged down in time-consuming, exhausting, and poor-paying legal assignments or other things.

In the summer of 1977 I became determined that I would be serious about scouting out the prospects for a full-time teaching job in legal academe. There were several reasons for this decision. One serious problem was that I was not making enough money from practicing law. My partners thought I did not charge my clients enough. That could be part of the problem, as I was timid in setting fees. However, the more basic problem was that I did not have enough clients. It was in no way a result of the quality of my practice. Many of my clients praised my work, and my partners who had read some of my briefs and motions thought they were well-reasoned and well-written. Judges are self-restrained in their opinions, but I had the impression that they thought my work good.

The main problem lay in my personality: my shyness and diffidence toward meeting new people. Lawyers get new clients primarily by schmoozing at cocktail parties, joining service organizations, and doing public work that gains publicity.

I am reluctant to go up to people and introduce myself. I have watched my father do that so many times, working a room by barging into conversations and introducing himself. I cannot bring myself to do that. I did join a local chapter of the Rotary, but my year's active engagement with it brought in only one client.

My most significant piece of public service during this period was the effort to save the House of the Flag from demolition. This ultimately successful lawsuit generated considerable publicity. Although my motivation for this work had little to do with acquiring clients, in fact it did not, so far as I could tell, result in a single additional client. Two other matters brought my name to the newspapers: the effort to void a personal parking ticket, previously discussed, and the successful litigation by a father to gain custody of his child from his ex-wife, unusual in those days. So far as I could tell, neither case brought in additional clients.

Another major motivation for my leaving the active practice of law was that I was increasingly enjoying my teaching at the unaccredited Lincoln School of Law. In fact I liked it so well that I suggested to the Lincoln administrators that they hire me as a full-time instructor to teach law and also history, for a salary of $18,000 per year, provided, and this was a major proviso, Lincoln increase that salary each year to match the current inflation. Lincoln University considered this, but ultimately decided it could not afford that level of commitment. I am glad that this arrangement never worked out, as my later institutional resources and time for research, and even salary, far surpassed what could have been available at Lincoln University.

Then too I was enjoying scholarship. By 1977 I had already published a major article in the *Western Historical Quarterly*, "Pioneer Justice on the Overland Trails," (1974) and another large piece, "Californios and the Image of Indolence," was in the pipeline. I had two book reviews published or in process, and I had a piece, "Californio Women and the Image of Virtue," ready for fall 1977 publication in the *Southern Historical Quarterly*. The "Pioneer Justice" article constituted a revised paper I had submitted for a seminar in my master's program at San Jose State, and concerned laymen dealing with crimes along the Overland Trail. "Californio Women" was a chapter in my master's thesis. Typically, new academic scholars begin with articles, and often from seminar papers or chapters from their dissertation. I also had a legal article "Judicial Gloss and the California Evidence Code" published in the *Lincoln Law Review*.

In 1975 I submitted a manuscript to *The American West*, a popular journal that concentrated on the history of the American West. They liked it and paid me about three hundred dollars, with which I was wildly pleased. The piece, titled "Californios and the Image of Indolence," another chapter of my master's thesis, described how American observers in the 1830s and 1840s had commonly described Mexican Californians as lazy and indolent, and that the general historical explanation for this was that these feelings were the product of then-prevalent American Protestantism, Manifest Destiny, and Anglo-Saxon racism. However, I pointed out that since Russian, French, German, Swedish, English, and even Spanish observers also noted in the same time periods that the Californios were lazy and indolent, the particular American phenomena of Manifest Destiny, American Protestantism, and Anglo-Saxon racism could not be the cause of the Americans' viewpoint.

I suggested that perhaps the increasing pace of life due to industrialization in the United States and all of these European countries might have caused their citizens to regard the Californios as lazy and indolent. The Editor of *The American West* in his letter of acceptance on March 25, 1975, gushed with congratulations: "You certainly write well – scholarly, accurate presentation but easily and fluently readable to the layman. This is exactly what we want but too seldom find."

Publication was to follow their acceptance, but after a long period went by and it did not appear in print, I began to pressure them for some definitive date. Eventually, on May 6, 1977, I received a letter stating that with a "good deal of reluctance" *The American West* would not publish the piece "in view of the controversial nature of the subject matter." I could keep the money and place the piece elsewhere, but they were not going to use it. These were the years of "Chicano Power," and several Mexican-American historians were interested in Mexican California. Although not explicitly stated, it was implicit in the editors' viewpoint that my piece could be read as calling the Mexicans lazy. I had, in fact, said nothing of the kind, but had merely attempted to explain why others had so characterized the Mexican Californians. Then in 1977 I submitted the piece to the *Western Historical Quarterly*, the same journal that had published the overland trail article.

It not only accepted the article, but awarded it their *Herbert E. Bolton Spanish Borderlands Award* for the best article of the year dealing with the history of the Spanish Borderlands in the Southwest. I flew up to Portland for their annual meeting and accepted with great pleasure the $300 check that accompanied the award. This was the first of many post-student literary awards I would receive. Even following more prestigious book awards I would later receive, the Bolton Award has always seemed special to me because it was the first. The *Quarterly* also promised a definite printing date of April 1978.

When my first big piece was published in 1974, my partners thought it wonderful that they had a "resident scholar" among them. However, when my scholarly activity persisted with the master's degree and other publications, they questioned whether this was a good use of my time that otherwise could be used in rounding up new clients for the firm. I felt this from a drop in their enthusiasm for my writing rather than anything said to me. Only Earl Hedemark ever said anything, and that was a questioning of my reasons for getting a master's degree when I already had a doctor's degree. Of course, he completely confused the formal name for the basic licensure degree in law, JD or Doctor in Jurisprudence, with a real doctorate that requires a dissertation. Falsely assuming the basic law degree, the one needed for a license to practice, as the equivalent to a real doctorate, he thought I was working on a lesser degree, a master's in history.

By 1977 I just could not help but think I would be happier in academe, where I could do the scholarly work I really enjoyed, and be rewarded in money by my bosses and open praise by my colleagues for what was received by my law firm colleagues only with hesitation and muted praise. Although I did not expect a large financial reward, I thought there would be comfort in a more steady and reliable income.

Overriding all these considerations was that I no longer wanted my life to be organized around the practice of law and its supposed making of money. I had experienced the satisfaction of scholarship and thought my life, at least the work-related portion of my life, would have more meaning if organized around research and writing than hustling clients and gathering fees.

The year before, in 1976, I made some desultory efforts to obtain a teaching job by sending out my resume and an offprint of my 1974 article to schools that had identified themselves in various legal publications as looking for faculty. However, I had learned that the real route for entry level law teachers was through the interesting procedures of the Faculty Recruitment Conference sponsored by the Association of American Law Schools. The way the process works is that applicants for teaching posts fill out a standard and much-abbreviated one page resume form which they send to the Association (AALS) together with a hefty registration fee.

The AALS then photocopies all the resumes (in many years numbering as many as 900 or so) and distributes them to every law school in the United States and Canada. The law schools' faculty recruitment committees then go over these resumes with care, judging their potential interest in terms of the merits of the candidate, his or her potential for scholarship, depth of academic preparation, and whether the candidate's interest in potential teaching subjects matches the school's own curricular needs.

The AALS organizes a huge weekend recruitment conference held annually at a major hotel, in those years varied among different cities. The schools usually have a suite, with one room suitable for interviewing. The candidates have their own rooms. After the schools have looked over the resumes and decided on which candidates are of interest, someone from the law school will call the candidate and schedule a time for an interview during the conference of about 20 minutes, now extended to 30 minutes. The candidates travel to the interviewing room of a school that has called them for the talk. In the 1970s these conferences were typically held in December.

It is a somewhat brutal process, where many egos can be crushed very quickly. What if very few schools call for an interview? What if the interviews go poorly? What if, at the cocktail hour, you notice an interviewer from the most desired school on your list, who barely nods hello to you, engaged in earnest conversation with a competing candidate? Even with all the anxiety, it is a terribly efficient method of recruitment. Every seller of a very particular service, entry level teaching at a law school, is right there, and in the same hotel are representatives from every prospective employer of that service, the law schools.

After the recruitment conference is finished, the various faculty recruitment committees meet to go over their impressions of the candidates they have interviewed. These are whittled down to one or two, sometimes three, for each position to be filled. This process varies among the schools. Sometimes the candidates are vetted by the faculty as a whole, and in some institutions, the faculty committee operates independently. However a decision is made, calls go out to the one or two top candidates competing for a position, inviting them to come to the school for a day or two, meet the entire faculty, perhaps teach a class or give a lecture, and talk with a select number of students, often the law review's student editorial board. Travel arrangements are usually made by the candidates and then reimbursed by the school; lodging is usually provided and reserved by the school. In any event, the expenses of the candidate's visit, all dining, sleeping accommodation, and travel, are picked up by the institution. At these visitations, the school is selling itself to the candidate as much as the reverse, so often two or three faculty members will take the candidate out to dinner.

After the visits are over, the faculty discusses the candidates and decides on which one or ones they wish to invite to become a colleague. That being decided, the dean of the school then calls the winning candidates to discuss the decision, and negotiates salary and moving arrangements. With some slight variations, this is the way all law schools go about hiring entry level faculty.

I received about seven or eight invitations to interviews at the Recruitment Conference, held in 1977 in St. Louis on Friday and Saturday, December 2nd and 3rd. I did not think I did terribly well at the interviews. I was anxious and slept very poorly Thursday evening at the hotel, the night before my initial interviews. Most of the interviewers were young faculty members, and it seemed notable that Detroit College of Law had only its dean and associate dean as the interviewers. In contrast to the young faculty who seemed keen on demonstrating their own sophistication to prospects, I thought John

Abbott and Jim Huddleston exemplified Midwestern traits of plain, clear talk.

In the event, I received invitations to interview at two schools, New England School of Law in Boston, and Detroit College of Law. The Boston trip was the more exciting since I was caught in a major snowstorm and had to stay an extra night after Logan Airport closed down briefly. I do not remember much about the Detroit trip. The school did not want the expense of an overnight hotel, and the visit was brief. The Boston trip was more formal, with set interviews by students, administrators, and faculty. Detroit was informal, and talks with faculty were brief and determined by who was in their offices as I was given a tour of the facilities. I do remember being taken to the nearby Detroit Athletic Club for an excellent lunch. In neither school was I asked to teach a class, nor asked to give a formal presentation on my current research, although my scholarly work was informally discussed at both.

The Boston trip was January 19-22, 1977, with an extra day there because of the storm. The Detroit trip was within ten days of the Boston visit. I did not have to wait long for the results. Within two weeks I heard that New England did not need my services, but at the same time Detroit College of Law would hire me, with teaching assignments of Evidence, Personal Property, and Legal History. It offered a low salary, $22,000, but I regarded the job as a first step into legal academe, and I accepted its offer. Then, of course, I had to find housing in Detroit. I spent a long weekend looking at various neighborhoods. Housing was cheap. I bought a house at 4111 Courville Street, on the eastside. My immediate area was mixed; I had a black neighbor on one side and a white neighbor on the other. My house was of reasonable size, but the neighborhood's lots were small, which made the houses very close together. However, the ambiance of the neighborhood was pleasant, the streets lined with tall trees and overarching limbs. I bought the three-bedroom house for $22,000 from a white minister who was moving to the suburbs in typical white flight.

Chapter 3

The Detroit Years:
Fall 1978 through Spring 1983,
Part One

My stepson Dean Puccini traveled out to Detroit with me. Then he stayed at my new house for several days and helped me considerably, moving things in, helping me with new furniture I had to buy and lug into the place, and lending a great deal of moral support. The house I had bought, at 4111 Courville, was spacious, with a kitchen, small living room, breakfast nook, separate dining room, den, and half bath on the first floor. Upstairs were three bedrooms, including the huge master bedroom with two walk-in closets, a full bath, and an outside deck to the rear. The front doors had beveled and leaded glass, and most of the other first floor windows were leaded. The basement had an old clunker of a furnace and a separate room that I used for storage.

I had bought the house in May 1978 at the price of $22,000, amazingly cheap by California standards. My salary the first year at Detroit College of Law was also $22,000. That left more than enough after income and employment taxes for me to pay my monthly house installment of $145.00 per month and all my other necessary living expenses. Truthfully in my first few years in Detroit I was constantly dipping into the proceeds from the sale of my property in San Jose, but this was caused by eating out almost constantly, a lavish social life, and very frequent trips back to California.

Detroit was not yet as blighted as it became in later years. True, there were many derelict buildings, abandoned and busted up houses and office buildings, in fact probably more in those years than later because the city government was then less aggressive in tearing down decrepit structures. But those tended to be on the fringes of the downtown and in particularly poor neighborhoods, for example along Mack Avenue closer to the core of the city. There were still perfectly decent neighborhoods, where houses were kept up. My immediate neighborhood was one of those. It was integrated. With lower-middle class families living in houses crowded together on postage stamp lots, it was far from affluent. It was safe, though, and I felt no danger at all in taking long evening walks about my neighborhood.

The commute from home to Detroit College of Law, always referred to by faculty and students as DCL, averaged about 25 minutes. The school had a half block of parking, an abundance. The primary structure was a large four-story building completed in 1937 and located at 130 Elizabeth Street, separated by an alley from an even-larger YMCA building. The complex sat at the edge of downtown, two blocks away from Grand Circus Park and Woodward Avenue.

A modern two-story annex sat attached to the original school edifice. The facilities were efficiently arranged. The law library occupied the lower floor of the annex and extended into a smaller space, the original library, in the four-story building. Faculty and administrative offices took up the fourth floor of the main building and about half of the second floor of the annex. Classrooms filled the third floor of the main building and half of the second floor of the annex. The bookstore, registrar, placement office, student association office, and so forth, lodged in the second floor and a mezzanine of the main building. The student law review office was on the second floor of the annex, and a student lounge occupied the basement of the original structure. Interior hallways provided smooth access between the two buildings. Both had elevators.

Detroit College of Law has since morphed into a more conventional law school as Michigan State School of Law. But in the years I was there, 1978-1983, it was a large, bustling urban law school. It had an evening division to serve the numerous older working students who wanted to become lawyers, as well as a day program that generally attracted younger students. As is true with all schools with evening programs, students took fewer courses than day students and attended for four years, rather than the traditional three.

With an evening school as well as day, DCL would be essentially running two separate schools, excepting that the American Bar

Association mandates that full-time law professors teach in the evening as well as day division to assure that there would be no substantial lowering of quality in the night work. But DCL did more to confuse matters. It also had spring admissions as well as the conventional fall admissions. In other words, some day and evening students began their studies in the fall, whereas other day and evening students began in the spring. Since required courses constituted most of the first two years of study, DCL was essentially operating *four* separate law schools, as only in the last year or two would students from the four annual admissions be in a classroom together. Of course, students who dropped a required course for illness or anxiety might find themselves thereafter in a class with another cohort of admittees.

DCL had a higher proportion of students who were re-taking courses than normal. That was because of a highly unusual procedure. Most law schools require students who wish to drop a course to do so at some early point in the semester. DCL allowed students to go so far as to actually look at the final exam, write a "W" on the exam book, leave the room and receive an Incomplete that could be made up the following semester with no penalty in grade point. That was called "walking the course," and resulted in a higher proportion of DCL students retaking courses than is normal. Still, this was relatively unusual and that meant most students for their first two years were in their separate four tracks determined by the fall or spring and day or night division of their admission. With a large number of required courses, and the need to have four sessions of each course for the four divisions, DCL needed a large faculty.

During the years 1979-1982, the school enrolled approximately 150 students to each of its seasonal admissions divisions, divided about equally between day and evening. With 300 entering the school each year, at any given time about 850 students would be enrolled, with regard for graduations and the longer evening program. Of course, the applications were nearly double the ultimate enrollments. A snapshot in time confirms these generalities. In September 1980, the day division held 398 enrolled students, and the night school held 450. With that number of students, hallways were generally crowded.

During my first year of teaching, academic year 1978-1979 and the summer following, my office was located in the second floor of the annex. Law schools generally are easy on first year teachers, to allow for acclimation and first time preparation for courses. In my case it was ridiculous how easy my first semester turned out. I was scheduled to teach two courses, Property I in the day division, and Legal History in the evening division. The school required a minimum number of students, I think six, in order for a class to be offered. My initial Legal History class did not "make," as it was called, so I was left to teach only Property I, which met for two academic hours, 1:00-2:40, on Monday afternoons. I mused on how easy it would be, expenses notwithstanding, to commute from California to teach this course. That way I could still live with my girlfriend Lucie, with whom I was deeply in love. My committee assignments at first were minimal. I was placed on the Financial Aid Committee that seldom met, and then doled out about truly low-level loans, $200-$400, to meet student emergencies.

The first semester of property was personal property – possessory actions, bailments, gifts, and the like – and was followed by a four unit course, Property II, which taught the more important real property. The teacher who followed me, older and venerable, used an antique casebook filled with nineteenth and early twentieth century cases. It was just awful and taught a lot of detailed old law that had little modern utility. If I had taught the entire sequence, I would never have considered using that book. Nevertheless, I did not want to force the students to buy two separate and expensive property casebooks, each offering the entire sequence, but one for use in Property I and the other in Property II. So I used the badly outdated book and made the best of it by bringing in discussions of modern law as I could.

When I taught that first term course, I was a bit anxious about my performance as a professor. Although I had taught for years at Lincoln Law School in California, that was only an unaccredited night school, whereas Detroit College of Law was the "big show," a fully accredited law school. I tried my best to emulate what I recalled from my truly talented professors in my days as a Stanford law student. That meant using the Socratic Method that I thought admirable as a teaching device if not carried to an extreme, albeit that I had despised it as a student. I think I came down too hard on the side of academic severity and over-reliance on the Socratic Method. In their end of term evaluations the students reacted to that. One called me "drastically too traditional," and many students noted the "numerous hypothetical questions." I guess that was not the norm at DCL, although it certainly had been my experience at Stanford. One student critique almost precisely described the Socratic Method: "at times so many questions were asked, which had no real answer, and many were posed and no answers, or suggested answers given," and another suggested I should give "hypos [hypothetical questions] and answers to where they go – don't give an example and leave class hanging for an answer." While one student thought I had "made a dull subject interesting," and two praised the use of historical discussion for the background of the legal rules, it was clear enough from the answers that the full Socratic Method did not work well among the DCL students, and I should lighten up on that approach.

I had a more normal load in the spring 1979 semester. I resolved to try to lighten up on hypothetical questions, but I do not know how successful that was in reaching the students, as my student evaluations are missing for that term. In those years DCL required its faculty to teach in its summer school for two out of three years, unless some other arrangements were made. I negotiated to teach two courses in the summer of 1979 and none in 1980 and 1981 in order to maximize the time available for research during the two totally free summers. Accordingly, in the summer of 1979 I taught two electives, a Seminar in Law and Literature and a Seminar in Evidence Problems. Because of their structure as seminars, the enrollment was low. Law and Literature required the reading of several books and both courses required papers. I gave the written work a line-by-line scrutiny that I think many of the students had never before received. One student was moved to write of the Law and Literature course, new to Detroit College of Law, that "a course of this nature should be included regularly in the curriculum."

There was a fair amount of social activity right there at DCL. The administration treated the faculty to elaborate luncheons at the nearby Detroit Athletic Club once every semester, and invited the faculty to its annual State Bar Reception. It held receptions with well-laden tables for each of the two annual graduations, and on other occasions as well. I became acquainted with several of the faculty members and friends with a few, especially Nick Revelos and Bradford Stone, and it was common for three or four of us to go out to one of the many nearby restaurants for lunch, and not unusual but less common for some of us to gather for dinner in the evening after class or for a drink.

I worked in Detroit to finish up the term and conduct my 1979 summer seminars. In late June after I finished grading my seminar papers, I visited my dad and his wife Sue in Elgin, Illinois, seeing a performance of *Swan Lake* in Chicago with them on June 26. I think it was at this time that Dad, Sue, and I attended one of the last performances of *Song of Hiawatha*, a classic that combined the reading of Longfellow's poem with the dancing and acting of local youth. It had been performed at the Boy Scout Camp Big Timber in Elgin for years, but with the declining years of its founder and director, Carl H. Parlasca, and the increasing disinterest in the young people of Elgin in playing Indian, the sponsor had announced that this would be its final season.

Then I pushed on to San Francisco, where I stayed with Stan Siddle. It was a crowded apartment that summer as mutual friend David Palmer and his new girlfriend were also there. In July 1979, virtually every weekday I took a local bus to the 16th Street Bart Station, and then the train to the downtown Berkeley stop. There, I crossed the street and caught the California Student Body connecting bus, "Humphrey Go Bart," that took me to a stop just uphill from the Bancroft Library. I worked there on reading expatriate and official papers from California's Mexican years, researching their legal affairs. On some days I would arrive slightly before the Bancroft opened, and I would sit for a few minutes in the miniature park under the Campanile and enjoy the relative quietude of that spot. At noontime I would generally walk by North Hall, where my father had his office in 1940-41 and which still housed the Economics Department, then turn right and walk down the campus past Sather Gate and Sproul Hall to pick up some takeaway lunch from among the many ethnic food vans parked on Bancroft Way. I would take a Japanese bowl of chicken and rice or a Mexican plate of burritos and beans, for example, back up toward Sproul Hall. Then I would find a place in Sproul Plaza along the concrete retaining wall opposite the Student Union, eat my lunch, and listen to the various folk singers, dancers, or other more spontaneous entertainment of the day. Bancroft Library was a pleasant place to work.

At the end of July 1979 I flew down to Tucson for a short visit with my dad and Sue at his ranch. What they were doing in Tucson at that time of year is beyond recall. After just a few days in Tucson I returned to California and began to look at the Mexican trial records held at the Monterey County Recorder's Office in Salinas. The purpose for this summer was not to make an extensive survey in these records, but rather to assay them, see how complete they were and whether they would support a full study of the Mexican California legal system for a book. I stayed for about four or five days in my stepson Gene Pucine's undergraduate "pad," and slept on a waterbed. I was 38 years old that summer, and it was an interesting experience living with four teen-aged college males, all athletes. I saw enough of the records of the alcalde, the local judge in Mexican California, that I was sure I could write a full study of the Mexican California legal system, using them and also the information gathered at Bancroft, plus other finds I was sure I would make. I took notes of the types of documents at Salinas, but put off their full examination until the following summer.

In terms of my intellectual growth and work, the academic year 1978-79 was primarily a time of laying preparation for longer range projects, as I was headed toward a book on the Mexican California legal system. I had been fascinated by Mexican California for many years, and thought it was time to apply my particular abilities of legal analysis to an historical study of the period. However, I did accomplish some other intellectual work during the year. I wrote a review of Sheldon Jackson's *A British Ranchero in Old California: The Life and Times of Henry Dalton* for the *Western Historical Quarterly,* and published in April 1979. I also researched and then wrote a paper on domestic relations law in Mexican California and placed it with the *Pepperdine Law Review.* This review did not actually publish the work until 1980, and I will discuss that troubled process later. In addition to my work in California on the book project, I also read the papers of some leading businessmen in Mexican California, the Stephen Reynolds Papers at the Peabody Museum in Salem, Massachusetts and the Bryant & Sturgis Papers in the Business School Library at Harvard. I attended conferences, "Humanistic Education in Law," at Columbia University March 30-April 1, 1979, and "Michigan Legislative Histories," April 24, 1979. In the spring of 1979 I did some pro bono research for Michigan State Representative Kenneth J. DeBaussaert, my girlfriend Laura's employer and at her request, on Michigan landlord-tenant law applicable to mobile home parks.

The most interesting writing project for the year involved an article published in April 1978 in the *Western Historical Quarterly*, before arriving at Detroit College of Law, and described earlier, "Californios and the Image of Indolence." The earlier journal that had rejected the piece, even after paying me, was correct in thinking its publication would be controversial.

David Weber, a leading name in Spanish Borderlands studies, wrote a rebuttal, received by the *Western Historical Quarterly* in June 1978. In September the editors decided to run the rebuttal in their November 1979 issue under the rubric of "Communications," and invited me to respond. I remember sitting in my office at DCL reading the letter from the journal in a state of considerable academic frisson. This was heady stuff for a newly minted academic, both because my writing had caught the notice of such a prominent scholar and because I had been invited to respond to his critique. David, who I later came to know on a first name basis, wrote that the hispanophobic Black Legend pervaded much of Europe and was the basis of most of these thoughts. In my very brief one page rejoinder to the rebuttal I pointed to many incidents of American thought regarding the Californios that could not possibly be related to any Black Legend. I thought that I had gotten the best of the discussion, and later private discussion with several California historians confirmed this.

Of course, I kept up with my reading. It was both extensive and highly diverse, including Lawrence Durrell's *Alexandria Quartet*, with its exquisite vocabulary and refined sensitivity. It was a curious series, in that I thought the first of the four books, *Justine*, was superb, and that the quality of the remaining three books, although excellent, steadily declined a bit, book by book.

I returned to Detroit College of Law in the fall of 1979, with an 11% raise in salary to $24,200, and greater teaching and committee responsibilities. That fall I taught day sections of Property I for two academic hours, Evidence for four hours, and in the evening Legal History for two hours, a full eight hour component. For spring 1980 I taught two Evidence sections at four hours each, one in the day division and the other in the evening. Compared with undergraduate faculty, law professors generally have far lower teaching loads and far higher salaries. The expectation is that this will facilitate two other generally recognized responsibilities of law faculty beyond teaching: public service and scholarly research and publication.

The Admissions Committee, under the chairmanship of Don Campbell, was an important committee to which I was appointed for the academic year, 1979-1980. In the spring of 1980, 75% of DCL's total income came from tuition, income from endowment and annual gifts being a relatively small component of income. So we had to be sure that we admitted enough applicants to yield a sufficient class size to pay our bills, but at the same time we could not ethically admit students we knew were probable academic failures. These are usual problems for most admissions committees at low-ranked schools and call for careful examination of the credentials of borderline applicants and also vigorous recruitment of candidates, precise advertising, and attendance at college career days and programs for collegiate prelaw clubs. Superimposed on the 1979-80 admissions committee, and ultimately on the DCL as a whole, was a running battle with the American Bar Association that was building to a head.

The approval of a particular law school by the American Bar Association's accreditation committee and its Section of Legal Education and Admissions to the Bar, is crucially important. Almost all states, excepting the very few such as California which have alternative accreditation plans, require graduation from an ABA-approved school as a condition for a prospective lawyer to sit for the state bar exam. In turn, the passage of the state bar exam is required for admission to the bar to practice law. In other words, there are several gatekeepers to assure the quality of persons permitted to practice law. Students have to attend and graduate from an ABA approved law school, and then pass the state's bar examination. That constitutes three levels of checks, the ABA approval of a school, the school's approval of the student by permitting graduation, and the passage of the bar exam. If a school loses its accreditation, its students cannot take the exam, and it would be pointless for almost all students to attend a non-accredited school.

Since 1978 the Detroit College of Law was under steady pressure from the American Bar Association and threatened with disaccreditation, which would have resulted in the closure of the school. The ABA's complaints included a high student/faculty ratio, and a weak library collection, but most emphatically that the school did not have a large enough minority enrollment. At the beginning of 1980 the ABA advised the DCL administration that it did not have a sound educational program, the basis for disaccreditation, because it lacked an affirmative action program. In 1979 minority enrollment was 5% of the student body, anomalous, perhaps, in an essentially black city. The entering class of spring 1980, admitted fall 1979, had 9% minorities. Minorities in the context of a school located in downtown Detroit essentially meant blacks.

In January 1980 huge pressure began for an affirmative action plan. Edward J. Littlejohn, a black law professor from Wayne State University, came on board as a consultant. I was a little skeptical and asked the simple question of what prompted this all of a sudden? What were the pressures upon us? The faculty was unaware of the correspondence back and forth with the American Bar Association that threatened disaccreditation. In fact, the ABA had scheduled a re-inspection for April 1980. I also raised the question of the impact of easier admission standards for black applicants, because even if it did not significantly lower the bottom line for admissions, it would certainly result in more students concentrated at the bottom line. Already in spring 1980 black applicants admitted to DCL had an average score of 461 on the national law aptitude test (LSAT) compared with an average for the entire entering class of 526. Since our experience showed that students near the lowest end of admissions generally had academic difficulties and often flunked out, if we kept our present grading policy, a substantial number of these special affirmative action admissions would likely flunk out. For years the DCL faculty had graded severely since it was understood that we had a liberal acceptance rate and often constituted a second chance for legal education for older students.

I proposed as an alternative a heavy emphasis on recruitment of black applicants and additional financial aid for minority students, but otherwise keeping a neutral admissions policy without advantage given to minorities. At a faculty meeting Don Campbell, our committee chairman, stated that mere financial aid and more active recruitment "would not constitute affirmative action in his estimation." So Detroit College of Law went along the path of so many law schools in these years by making it easier for blacks and other minorities to be admitted, beating out white applicants with better credentials. The irony of my opposition is that I was appointed to draft a proposed admissions formula for the ranking of applications, taking into consideration, of course, the newly minted affirmative action plan that I had opposed.

In my opinion, the ABA's insistence on affirmative action regarding minorities has eroded the quality of legal education, particularly at low-ranked schools. The ABA's pressure on affirmative action and for higher percentages of minority students in enrollment has caused law schools to accept poorly qualified minorities simply because their presence will improve the schools' percentage of minority students, and sometimes to reject non-minority applicants with higher credentials.

Turning to teachers, by no means are all minority faculty less qualified than non-minority. However, ABA pressure has caused low-ranked schools to hire some less-qualified minority faculty to increase their minority profile. It is difficult for a low-ranking school to compete with a Harvard, Stanford, or even a Notre Dame, for highly-qualified minority faculty. The less-qualified minority faculty that do enter low-ranked law schools may be good teachers, especially as they "relate" to the poorly-qualified minority students, but they often fail to adequately meet the traditional professional responsibilities of pro bono work and especially faculty scholarship, research, and publications. I acknowledge that these thoughts are only generalities and are not intended as blanket assertions.

The student evaluations for fall 1979 showed again that most students did not enjoy my use of the Socratic method, but many praised my preparation and organization. Typical of the negative comments were: "professor is pedantic and petulant," "be a bit more patient when answers to somewhat vague questions are not immediately forthcoming," "come down to our level," "conduct class more like a class and less like a cross-examination," "make questions and explanations more clear, concise and understandable," and "course should be taught by someone else." On the other hand, other students observed that "Professor Langum is by far the best instructor I have had to date! A truly outstanding teacher of interesting material," "overall – a good job," and "this course and Prof. Langum are one of the best, most well-organized courses & Professors I have had at DCL. I was particularly pleased with the fact that the Professor emphasized learning the material rather than his personal point of view on life. He avoided interjecting his personality into the lectures & gave us an objective presentation of the material."

Spring of 1980 once again showed the Socratic method was just not going over well. I was rated very, very high on knowledge of the subject matter, preparation, and organization, but low on ability to ask clear questions, courteous classroom demeanor, and respect for divergent points of view. There were some favorable comments including: "Professor Langum is the paragon of excellence for a law professor. His zeal for the subject catalyzes the students," "I liked course over all!," and "good class." Two students had trees planted in my honor, "in appreciation of your proficient teaching" under the Trees for Israel program. The bulk of the negative comments again related to the Socratic method: "don't go in circles – set for the general principle & go from there – not vice versa," "insure that questions are direct and pertinent," "talk down to the students more. I don't mind being led by the hand in areas I don't understand," and, right to the point, "decrease the amount of time spent on the Socratic method."

I enjoyed a faculty party in early October and a law review party at Nick Revelos's house in late August. That fall I also joined Mensa, the high I.Q. society, to attend its monthly meetings that featured very interesting speakers, and with the further object of meeting interesting people, especially women.

In May 1980 my old Lincoln collapsed. I resisted the need to spend money on a new car, and as a result I commuted between work and home by local bus for a couple of months. As a result I learned more about the local transportation system in Detroit. The city had been an early target of the so-called block-busting activities of the 1960s and 1970s. In block after block some realtors introduced a black tenant or owner, often of a lower class and undesirable sort, with the intention of deliberately scaring the other owners of houses on that block. Many of the white owners then panicked and sold their houses for very low prices, often to these same realtors who then sold or rented to other black customers at very profitable markups. This process left thousands and thousands of angry whites in the dozens of suburbs surrounding Detroit convinced that they had been "forced" out of Detroit.

As a result of these bitter feelings, the suburbs operated their own bus service, with morning pickups throughout the suburbs, and then running express without stopping anywhere in Detroit until reaching the central downtown. In the afternoon and early evening the suburban bus services picked up at several downtown locations and then ran non-stop to the suburbs. The suburban buses were new, air-conditioned, and seldom broke down. The city buses that operated within Detroit were old, lacked air-conditioning, and often broke down.

To take a city bus home at night, following an evening class ending at about 9:00PM, I had to walk several blocks through the darkened central city to a small and often empty square where my bus stopped. It let me off on Mack and Courville, and I had another few blocks to walk home. In retrospect, this seems like a dangerous or at least frightening situation, but I must say I was never, ever bothered. I was often the only white person on a bus, but I never felt any sense of anxiety or even discomfort.

I went to California at the end of the first week in July 1980 and settled into the same house in Salinas at the edge of the Hartnell College campus as I had stayed in the summer before. The house was intended for Hartnell's student athletes, and had several bedrooms, a large living room, kitchen, and a nice lanai outside. Since I was there for more than a month this year, compared with just a few days in 1979, I had my own room and paid some rent into the house kitty. Every weekday I walked along Main Street past John Steinbeck's childhood home to and from the Recorder's Office, from early July through mid-August. Norman Borchert, the Assistant County Recorder, kindly provided me with a desk in a private area and freedom to access and use documents without any restriction. I read the Mexican judicial records for lawsuits in the Mexican period, 1821-1846. I worked really hard, and made detailed notes about the names, factual issues, and the judgments proposed by the conciliators. Although these records were only conciliation hearings, the recommended judgments resolved almost every lawsuit in Mexican California.

But when not working I had fun. I went to Bach's *Mass in B Minor* in San Francisco with Stan Siddle and David Palmer. I took my stepdaughter Dina Marie to *Guys and Dolls*, and I saw by myself a few plays performed at Hartnell College in Salinas or in nearby Carmel. I attended the California Rodeo, held in Salinas, with my stepson Gene, and some of his roommates and their fathers.

Although teaching was my major work at Detroit College of Law in academic year 1979-1980, I did other intellectual work as well. I attended the annual conference of the American Society for Legal History, held in Williamsburg, Virginia in October, and participated as a commentator at the Great Lakes History Conference, about two weeks earlier in Grand Rapids, Michigan. Detroit College of Law generously paid all my travel expenses. I wrote a lot of poetry in the fall of 1979 and spring of 1980. One group of four or five poems focused on my relationship with a girlfriend I lived with in the summer of 1978. I called the collection, somewhat pretentiously, The Lucie Poems. Other poems were on more serious philosophical or political topics, "The Sophomore Studies Social Science," about false dichotomies in political reasoning, and "Reflections Upon a Western Sunset Viewed from an Airplane Window," about the decline of Western civilization and the possibilities of nuclear destruction. I tried without any success to have these published, submitting them to small literary reviews, many journals, and poetry magazines. I had too much pride to travel the self-publishing route through the subsidized poetry journals.

I had two research assistants in the spring term working to check the accuracy of my citations for an article, "Expatriate Domestic Relations Law in Mexican California," that was to be published in the *Pepperdine Law Review*. Eventually it was published, actually in 1980 but carrying a date of 1979 on its cover. Everything was delivered to the student editors of the *Review* in meticulous condition, all quotes, citations, and spelling checked for accuracy. Then these student editors at Pepperdine thought fit to edit, and produced page proofs for my approval that were replete with literally hundreds of errors. It required a telephone call of 1½ hours going over the piece line by line to put it back into proper shape for publication. I was so irritated. This article was based on original Mexican sources later republished in English translation. A similar chapter in my later book on the Mexican legal system relied on many of these same materials but taken from their original archival sources in Spanish. In a sense this earlier article was a precursor to that chapter.

The most significant thing I did in 1979-1980 to extend my intellectual horizon was to apply to the University of Michigan Law School for admission to its LL.M./S.J.D. Program. I had checked the credentials of all the directors of the American Society for Legal History and the Editorial Board of the *American Journal of Legal History* and noted that most of them, a large majority, had either a Ph.D. or an S.J.D., a research doctorate in law, to their credit. I decided that to be taken seriously as a legal historian I too needed a doctorate, and that the fastest route to a doctorate would be through the S.J.D. Program. Michigan was not only an excellent law school, but nearby in Ann Arbor. So I filled out all the paperwork and applied in

December 1979, using as references John P. Reid, a distinguished legal scholar who knew my work; Bradford Stone, a colleague at Detroit College of Law and who was a graduate of the University of Michigan Law School; and Ben Gilbert, my master's dissertation advisor at San Jose State.

Michigan accepted me at the end of February 1980, and not only accepted me, but gave me a full tuition waiver. Only one problem remained. Michigan Law School wanted its students to be in "full time" residence, which did not mean they had to be there constantly, but did mean they could not have full time employment elsewhere. The problem was that I needed my salary from DCL to live on. I asked the law admissions people at Michigan whether part-time employment would be acceptable. They said yes. Then I inquired if teaching a couple of evening classes and perhaps something in the summer would be okay. Yes, that would be okay. Then I asked John Abbott, the Dean at DCL, whether for 1980-81 my teaching could be limited to two evening sections of Evidence plus two electives in the summer of 1981. John agreed to this with no reduction in salary, thereby making it possible for me to participate in the wonderful Michigan doctoral program in law. Behind a gruff exterior, John Abbott was a very kind and helpful man. When I told him how Michigan had offered me a full tuition waiver, he remarked that it did not surprise him at all.

In the spring of 1980 I had to choose my fall courses at Michigan. The course requirement was minimal: two seminars. But I wanted more than that. After I advised him of my acceptance and thanked him again for the reference, John Reid wrote and suggested that I take as many theoretical classes in history as available, as that was something he missed in his own work. So I signed up to officially audit Rebecca Scott's seminar in the History Department on "Studies in the Comparative Method of Historical Inquiry," the closest thing available in fall 1980 to theory. I had noted a course called "Anthropology of Law" in the Anthropology Department, but Thomas Green, my advisor, countered with a course he thought would be more helpful and also offered a course I could then teach, Peter Westen's seminar on "The Law of American Slavery." So I abandoned the anthropology and signed up for Westen's slavery course. Additionally I arranged with Tom Green to informally audit, through just showing up, Green's introductory course on English legal history.

In the spring 1981 semester I would be required to take another seminar. I would have to meet periodically with Tom Green to discuss my dissertation, its scope, methodology, and my work thereon. For my first year, 1980-1981, the two seminars plus substantial progress on the dissertation would be all I needed for the award of the masters in law degree, LL.M., and with it admission to candidacy for the doctorate. Substantial progress meant a couple of chapters, perhaps an outline. I then had five years to complete the dissertation and extensions could be arranged. The big requirement, rising above all others, was the publication requirement. Whereas most doctoral programs require that an accepted dissertation be of publishable quality, Michigan Law School required, perhaps uniquely, that for its dissertations to earn a doctorate they had to be of such quality that they were in fact published, either in a series of law review articles or, if a book, in a university or other legitimate press. This requirement considerably raised the bar to be hurtled for the doctorate. The book itself, let alone its publication, was beyond the horizon in the spring of 1980, but the two seminars at Michigan and two chapters of the book were coming up fast as the academic year 1979-1980 ended.

Following Dean John Abbott's kind approval, my course load at Detroit College of Law was limited in 1980-1981 to two evening sections. That made it possible for me to attend Michigan Law School, technically on a full-time basis, to work on the master of law degree, the first step toward the doctorate. I took my two seminars, both excellently taught, "The Law of American Slavery" offered by Peter Westen, and, in the spring of 1981, "The History of Criminal Law," given by Thomas Green, my dissertation advisor. I also attended Tom Green's lecture course on the history of the English law, and formally audited Rebecca Scott's seminar in the History Department on "Studies in the Comparative Method of Historical Inquiry." I even sat in on a few Evidence courses to see how much more high-powered professors than I handled a topic I taught so often. For the slavery seminar I wrote a paper on "The Role of Intellect and Fortuity in Legal

Change: An Incident from the Law of Slavery." Professor Westin was kind enough to say that the piece was more sophisticated that most of the work he saw at Michigan. It later became an article in the *American Journal of Legal History.* For Tom Green I wrote a paper on criminal law in Mexican California that, later much improved and strengthened, became a chapter in my dissertation and in my first book.

The University of Michigan is in Ann Arbor, about 40 miles by I-94 from Detroit. The terrain is flat between the two cities, and while the drive is easy enough, it is tedious. My teaching schedule in Detroit and my commitments in Ann Arbor made it desirable to stay overnight in Ann Arbor at least once a week. I roomed at the Lawyer's Club, a small section of the law school quadrangle that had comfortable but basic rooms to let. It was cozy in a room at the Lawyer's Club Lawyer's Club, especially in the winter months when much snow nestled the buildings, and I enjoyed myself there, especially with a glass of sherry that I brought in with me. It was a convenient location as well, since I could take breakfast in the baronial style dining hall with its massive stone walls, arched ceilings, and high windows. It was only a two minute walk from sleeping room to dining hall, and then another two or three minute walk across the beautiful quadrangle to library or classroom.

Although I tried a bit to fraternize with the law students at Michigan, nothing came from the attempt. I turned 40 that fall of 1980, and even then I felt a little "old" compared with the law students, most of whom were in their early 20s. I found a fellow graduate student, Christina Murray, with whom I was comfortable socializing. She was a law professor from South Africa, younger than me but older than most of the law students. We became platonic friends, and I often took her to lunch either at the Gandy Dancer Restaurant or at a good buffet place downtown and five or six blocks from the law school. It felt good to have someone to talk with, especially as we had a mixture of somewhat similar but also somewhat dissimilar interests and circumstances.

My advisor's field was English medieval legal history and, within that, a specialty in the history of the law of crimes. It is about as far as possible from my work in the Mexican California legal system and how American and British expatriates were treated within it. I was somewhat curious as to how he was going to supervise me, given that disparity of interests. I imagined that Tom Green was curious as well. His solution was interesting. About two weeks into the fall term he took me to a small coffee shop near the law school. After the coffee was on the table he led me on a tour of California northward from San Diego. He stopped at each town on our progress northward and asked me who were in the 1830s and 1840s the leading merchants in that town, what were their chief products of sale, and what problems they encountered in their businesses. He reasoned, I assume, that if I were working on the legal system of Mexican California I had to be familiar with her leading businessmen and their work, because they were likely to be involved with the legal system. About halfway up the California coast Tom said "alright!" We moved on to more general topics and finished our coffees.

Thereafter Tom never questioned me about the historical facts or figures about whom I was writing, and confined his critiques to my legal analyses. Those critiques were very helpful to me, and made my final dissertation and book into a much more polished product. They led me into a more analytical direction, and I began to ask different questions of my assembled materials, such as why did the Anglo-American expatriates strongly dislike the Mexican California legal system even as they were well-treated by it, and what does the answer to that question tell us about the differing expectations of a legal system by the Anglo-Americans compared with the Mexican Californians.

I enjoyed my work at Michigan. I was amazed at the resources of the University of Michigan Law Library. Books that I needed, even obscure Mexican works published in the 1830s, were almost always available in house right there. Tom invited me to join his legal history colloquium for faculty and graduate students. This met every Wednesday to discuss a new book or an idea. It was very intellectually stimulating. I received the LL.M. in May 1981. My dad, Sue, and my new wife, JoAnne, whom I had married in early 1981, attended the ceremony. I had five years from the LL.M. to complete my dissertation and obtain a publishing commitment, and I ultimately completed the work a year early and received my doctorate in 1985. But in the interval I became anxious over the dissertation, just as I think every doctoral student must. At the end of November 1982 I wrote in a letter that I was worried that the book was not coming along as rapidly as it should, even to the point where I thought I would stay in Detroit for the summer "to force myself into my office to sit down and <u>do it</u>." Three weeks later I was a bit depressed because I had so much to do, so I thought, stacks of exams to grade, committee reports, errands, etc. that I was not getting much writing done. Those circumstances would change very soon.

Chapter 4

The Detroit Years:
Fall 1978 through Spring 1983,
Part Two

During the academic years fall 1980 through spring 1983, Dean Abbott and the faculty of Detroit College of Law were engaged in a major program of institutional improvement. The components of this program included an effort to substantially increase endowment and rely less on current tuition for support; more rigorous evaluation of students in academic trouble; the improvement of scholarly output among the faculty; more strenuous recruitment of prospective students; and an increase of faculty compensation.

During this time period current tuition had risen to 86% of DCL's revenue. This sharp dependence on "gate receipts" was both unstable and also had the inherent vice of encouraging the admission of ill-prepared students because their tuition dollars were vital to institutional survival. However, by 1983 the school had hired a Director of Institutional Advancement, fund-raiser in plain English. The Dean began an aggressive program of speaking before Alumni groups all over Michigan, and the percentage of alumni donating to the school increased from 11% to 27%. The endowment stood at $1,750,000 and the hopes were to increase that to $4,000,000 by 1987, and to significantly reduce the percentage of tuition support of the school's operations.

DCL's grading policies had always been vigorous, but they were paradoxically accompanied by several variance and re-admission procedures that permitted some students, seemingly designated as academic failures, to stay on, or at least be later re-admitted. These procedures did not go away in these years, but they were considerably tightened. Increasingly, appeals of flunked out students for re-admission were denied. I was a member of the Variance

Committee for 1981-1982 and I personally observed that the number of variances granted to students for various relief from academic requirements was dropping.

Scholarly output among the faculty was increasing. Computers were starting to be a significant factor, and DCL had installed a Lexis program enabling word search through much legal and non-legal material. Although computer-assisted research techniques became ever more sophisticated in future decades, even this early computer facility greatly facilitated the research necessary for scholarly legal writing. I acquired my first computer in 1982. The Internet was many years away, and I used it for word processing only, but what a magnificent improvement over older methods of manuscript preparation.

Other encouragement given for scholarly activity included the school's financing of research assistants and two trips for professional meetings or research each year. Faculty could hire a student research assistant, for course credit or cash, up to ten hours a week, thirty weeks a year. Very generously, DCL gave full reimbursement of travel expenses and lodging, without limitation, but refused to reimburse any meal expenses. I thought that strange at the time, but have changed my mind after experience at other schools. Reimbursement for meals adds considerably to the number of receipts to save or lose, and sometimes has involved discussions with administrators as to the size of the bill or whether any *verboten* matter, such as wine, is disguisedly included.

I was on the admissions committee in both 1979-1980 and also 1980-1981. We were a hard-working group and made detailed considerations of individual application folders in our meetings. Members of the committee personally interviewed many of the applicants, and all of the high-credentialed ones. We went off to college recruitment fairs, and I was dispatched to a Boston College law school fair in October 1980 and another at much closer Western Michigan in Kalamazoo in March 1981. Much of this heavy lifting was new to the school, which had had a somewhat more passive relationship with admissions in the past. In contrast, we were now doing our best to lasso the best and the brightest for Detroit College of Law.

Abbott began a campaign with the DCL Trustees to increase faculty salaries as early as 1981. The problem, I believe, was that the Trustees regarded faculty as their employees. The faculty realized that they were technically employees of the school, true in every law school. However, because of the freedom given university faculty in the organization of their courses and the direction of their research interests, law teachers, probably all university faculty, regard themselves as independent contractors. At Detroit, the dean really did stand as a mediator between faculty and trustees. By 1982 salaries at DCL were very low on a comparative basis. According to one survey the national average salary for full professors of law in 1981-1982 was $46,310, whereas at the same time the average DCL full professor earned only $33,900. Locally in Michigan, the median salary paid by DCL for all law faculty was next to the lowest of the five Michigan law schools.

In the spring of 1983 Dean Abbott announced a new plan that the Trustees had approved to give more weight to years since receipt of first professional degree to the salary formulae. The median of salaries would increase by $4,000. My own personal salary had increased to $30,000 for 1980-1981, $32,400 for 1981-1982, and $34,080 for 1982-1983. It was scheduled to increase substantially in 1983-1984 to $41,500. Other financial benefits came to the faculty. Summer courses, previously required two out of three years, became entirely optional for faculty. A new sabbatical plan allowed one each seven years, at 80% of base salary less any earned income during the time of the sabbatical, with an individual's option of one year or one-half year duration.

I became a member of the Faculty Self-Study Committee in 1981-1982 and then Chairman of that committee for 1982-1983. All law schools prepare a self-study in the year that the ABA visits for renewed approval, usually then every seventh year, now every tenth year. Generally, the self-study reports are long and ponderous affairs, filled with statistics and heavy analysis. However, DCL prepared mini self-studies every year, with a fuller report co-incident with the ABA inspection. The mini-studies noted what progress if any had been made toward meeting the goals of the last major self-study.

At a meeting in early March 1983, just prior to the promulgation of our report, Dean Abbott had announced a seven point program of long range goals that he would present to the Trustees. In addition to scrutiny of progress on previous faculty recommendations, our self-study committee approved those goals and then went on to respond to the Dean's query as to whether DCL ought to investigate the many inquiries as to our interest in affiliation with another educational institution, and added another long range goal of creating some particular areas of expertise for which DCL could become well known. We suggested labor law, ideal for Detroit, and trial skills, and added the shorter term goals of regular faculty pedagogical retreats and an enrichment of the academic program that would require students to complete more written work.

We had two troglodyte-like professors on our five-man committee. One had taught at DCL since 1958, while the other began teaching at DCL in 1939, a year before I was even born. For the most part, we all agreed on the extent to which the 1980 goals had been met. But on affiliation and our shorter academic goals there was sharp disagreement. In separate reports the majority concurred that some sort of affiliation would be desirable, but with adequate financial safeguards to prevent a diversion of funds. The younger of our dissenters reported that some sort of affiliation "might be desirable," whereas the dissenter who had begun his teaching career in 1939 reported that "affiliation would be undesirable." As matters developed, Detroit College of Law a few years later did form an affiliation with Michigan State University in East Lansing, and is now known as Michigan State University Law School. As to the majority's recommendations of faculty retreats to improve teaching and more writing requirements, these same troglodytes reported in dissent that they did not think faculty retreats were necessary, and that they also believed that it was undesirable to increase students' written work in the school's course offerings. I think the reader can imagine how contentious our committee meetings were.

Part of the arrangement with Dean Abbott through which I had the two evening courses for fall 1980 and spring 1981, essential for my going to Michigan, was that I would teach two summer electives in 1981. Accordingly, I offered a "Law and Literature" seminar and another, more innovative, "The Influence of the Frontier on the Development of American Law." Then in the fall of 1981 I settled into a pattern of courses, Evidence, Property I, and American Legal History, taught in different combinations within the four different curricular tracks. By the fall of 1982 I had reached agreement with the faculty teaching Property II on a new casebook, so I no longer had to use the old monster book for my course in personal property.

During spring 1982 I developed a long series of multiple choice exam questions for Evidence, some that I made up, some from various states' bar exams, and some from faculty at other schools. I had about 200 questions, that I mixed up in various combinations over the years, some of which I continued to use right up to my retirement from teaching in 2005. For many years I treated these questions as crown jewels, and I devised many stratagems to make sure the exam booklets containing these questions were returned to me at the conclusion of the exam. In later years, beginning somewhere around 1995, I adopted a different approach, and put my entire portfolio, still of perhaps 200 questions, on reserve in the library. Then I promised my students that whatever questions I put on the exam would be drawn from these questions, which were fairly representative of the entire law of Evidence. I could tell from the library records that these questions were highly studied. And why not? The students knew that their own exam questions would be taken from these very questions on reserve. If the value of testing from a teacher's point of view is merely to force students to study and review, so as to learn, then surely throwing those questions out to the students was one of the best teaching devices I ever thought of.

That spring of 1982, when I first used the multiple choice questions, was also the first time I used the "evidence cartoon," inserted as its own page within the test booklet. It shows two robed judges walking down a corridor in their chambers portion of the courthouse. One is talking to the other, who has a shocked look on his face. The speaking judge is asking the other, "Did you ever have one of those days when you don't give a damn about the rules of evidence?" I thought a spot of levity would help reduce stress, and I used this cartoon for the balance of my teaching career.

One further matter on my professional career in Detroit. In February 1981 I was appointed as the faculty advisor to the *Detroit College of Law Review.* Although I think I was paid some slight amount for taking the assignment, it was truly a labor of love. In every law school in the country the brightest and most interesting students are always on the law review. It is a remarkable thing that the primary vehicles for professional legal writing are edited by students, albeit the students with the highest grades. The self-learning these students receive from their editing and also their own writing of scholarly notes is among the best available at law schools. I had little to do for DCL's Review. A law review advisor's job is primarily to buffer the students on the journal from undue pressure from faculty members who have the ill grace to attempt to publish in their own school's Review.

Faculty normally should not publish in their own school's law review since "outside" publications add to the faculty member's and the school's prestige. Then there is the danger that a faculty member who has written a poor article might attempt to foist it on his own school's review. The norm is to use another school's review because of the implicit pressure put upon students by their own faculty's submissions to take their piece, whether good or not. The editors must feel free to refuse publication and should not have to stand up against their teachers. Then too the advisor sometimes becomes a buffer between the student editors and the administration itself, when, for example, a dean is upset by an article that questions the legality of activities of a company controlled by a trustee or a major donor.

However, I don't recall encountering any such problems in Detroit, although I did later in Birmingham. The Detroit students wanted me to sit in on the interviewing and voting for the next year's officers, to assure the level of discussion remained professional and not personal. I did attend those annual sessions that sometimes lasted too many hours, but I really do not think my presence made any difference. I was asked my opinion on an editorial matter or two, but for the most part, my participation as advisor to the *Detroit College of Law Review* was to attend their parties. Since the students on the *Review* were almost all literate, articulate, and bright, their parties were a delight.

In the summer of 1981, I took a small *pied-a-terre* at Pebble Beach, California. From there I worked in the Mexican Archives in Monterey, a short drive away, wrote a book review, and prepared and sent out proposals for a compilation of readings on the influence of the frontier on American law, for teaching in law schools. That latter project was turned down by many publishers for lack of a significant market.

An important event of my Detroit years was my marriage in early 1981 to JoAnne Adams, a casework supervisor, stationed in Detroit for the state's social service system. We had two children: Virginia Eileen, born October 9, 1981, and John David, born August 23, 1983. From a very early age Virginia demonstrated keen intelligence and fierce independence. She earned her A.B. from Trinity College, Dublin, graduating with first class honors. She then obtained a M.A. in Journalism from Columbia University and worked a year as a reporter. However, she returned to her first love of literature and earned a Ph.D. in English Literature at Cambridge University. Thereafter she has taught Medieval Literature at the University of Umeå, Sweden, and has published widely in scholarly channels, including her book *Medicine and the Seven Deadly Sins in Late Medieval Literature and Culture* (2016).

John was not so fortunate. He was born with severe birth defects and suffered from cerebral palsy. He was paraplegic and non-verbal. He could raise and lower his eyes, but that was the extent of his voluntary movement. Because of a substantial malpractice settlement, we were able to obtain several specialty wheelchairs, vans equipped with lifts and tie-downs for chairs, computers adapted for access through head switches and eye gaze, specialty tutoring, and the best medical care available. But it was to little avail. JoAnne and I had always to provide every service to John, from feedings, diaper changes, to movies, readings, and other amusements. In his teen years John developed seizures and began aspirating his food, necessitating surgeries. JoAnne and I had to feed John through a tube connected to his stomach and to provide enemas, as well as to change diapers. All of this took time and caused emotional turmoil for both JoAnne, especially, and for me. John died in 2001.

JoAnne and I separated in 1986, and we divorced in 1989. JoAnne died in 2009.

Shortly after DCL had restarted in fall of 1981 Mary Kershner, a colleague, invited four couples, including JoAnne and myself, to form what we later named "Mary's Dinner Group." The idea was that we would meet once a month at each other's homes on a rotating basis for dinners based on specific nationalities. The hostess would select the theme of the dinner and prepare the main entrée. She would photocopy recipes for starters, side dishes, and dessert, and send them as assignments to the other wives. The husband of the home-of-the-month had to select and purchase all the wines needed for the various courses. It was a fabulous success. We ran through not only the typical French, Italian, and Japanese cuisines, but we also had dinners centered around more exotic foods, such as Szechwan, Indian, and Swiss. JoAnne and I hosted an Italian dinner in September 1981, a Spanish dinner in March 1982, and a Czech dinner in February 1983.

The Christmas dinners were always the most elaborate, held at the Kershners' home, and were on the theme of Christmas in Vienna, featuring roasts, such as a pig or a goose. Most of our gatherings were informal, but we dressed to the nines for Christmas in Vienna. The women wore cocktail dresses, the men wore tails, not tuxedos. We feasted on oysters on horseback and other traditional starters, standing, in cocktail party fashion, listening to Strauss, before sitting down to table for dinner. Word spread about our doings, and for the Caribbean dinner in April 1983 a reporter and photographer from the Detroit *Free Press* joined us. Soon we were written up in a feature article with a group photograph. JoAnne and I enjoyed this wonderful social activity until we left Detroit.

Even while commuting to Ann Arbor, attending classes at Michigan, writing lengthy seminar papers, and teaching at Detroit College of Law, I still squeezed in personal reading. For example, in 1981 my personal reading consisted of Elaine Pagels, *The Gnostic Gospels*; Herman Melville, *Billy Budd* (a re-read); Frederick Kempin, *Historical Introduction to Anglo-American Law in a Nutshell*; William Strunk and E.B. White, *The Elements of Style* (a re-read); Jean Anouilh, *Antigone* (a re-read); William Nelson, *Dispute and Conflict Resolution in Plymouth County, Massachusetts, 1725-1825*; Carl David and Richard Boyle, *Collecting and Care of Fine Art*; Evan Connell, *The Connoisseur*; Jacques Barzun, *Clio and the Doctors: Psycho-History, Quanto-History and History*. In preparation for the big event of early October 1981 I also read Donna and Rodger Ewy, *Preparation for Childbirth: A Lamaze Guide* and Joan Beck, *How to Raise a Brighter Child: The Case for Early Learning*.

In 1981 I made a determination to read the entire Bible, cover to cover, and sequentially. My motives were partially religious, but mostly cultural. So many of the people of the nineteenth century I admired had been very conversant with the Bible; that was once the norm of Western civilization, and I wanted to be familiar with it as well. I began with *Genesis* and in 1981 read through *Deuteronomy*. Although my 1982 records are lost, my 1983 Biblical reading started with *Isaiah*. By the end of spring 1983 I was up through *Mark*.

Of course, I also read several books for which I had been commissioned to write a review. For the period fall 1981 through spring 1983 these included Jeffrey, *Frontier Women: The Trans-Mississippi West, 1840-1880* and Faragher, *Women and Men on the Overland Trail*, the joint review of which appeared in *Nebraska History* for fall 1980; Hall, *The Politics of Justice: Lower Federal Judicial Selection and the Second Party System, 1829-61*, review published in *Detroit College of Law Review*, fall 1981 (the distaste of publishing in one's own school's law review does not extend to shorter book reviews); and Reid, *Law for the Elephant: Property and Social Behavior on the Overland Trail*, with review published in *The*

American Journal of Legal History for July 1982. In the spring of 1983 I had my first need to actually turn down a writing opportunity, although this would become more frequent later. Chris Fritz, an aspiring young legal historian, asked me to write a chapter in his forthcoming book on the California federal courts. I thanked him for his offer, but declined. It was not really my historical period of expertise, I wrote him, and in addition I had very little time and must use that to concentrate on my dissertation.

During these years, I was also busy presenting papers at scholarly conferences, as all aspiring junior academics do. In November 1980 I gave a favorable commentary to Chris Fritz's paper, "A Raid on the Federal Judiciary during the Civil War: Judge Ogden Hoffman and the Chapman Privateers." This was at a maritime history conference held at San Jose State, so I had a chance to visit with Ben Gilbert, my former M.A. advisor, and Ted Hinckley, a faculty friend who was also the conference director. I had lunch with Ted, my former partner in a failed attempt to establish a Westerners Corral in San Jose, and had the opportunity to learn about his recently completed teaching sojourn in San Salvador. I attended another Great Lakes History Conference in April 1981 in Grand Rapids. I proposed some remarks on the research use of legal materials for general historians, but instead was asked to comment on a paper titled, "Justice William O. Douglas and the Right of Privacy."

I made a presentation of a paper on "Resolving American Commercial Disputes in Mexican California," at the Western History Association Conference at Phoenix in October 1982. This was my first major conference paper, as distinct from a comment, and it was a big deal to me. Doctoral candidates working on their dissertations commonly deliver conference papers based on one or more of their chapters. This is an informal vetting process, through which the candidates receive feedback and criticism while their work is still in progress.

I was gratified by several favorable audience comments, and even more so by numerous requests for copies. I explained to those making the requests that my paper was an amalgam of thoughts from three different chapters of the book I was writing, and I preferred to hold off until the book was published. JoAnne came with me to the conference. Afterwards we drove to Tucson, spent a couple of days at my father's Diamond T Ranch, and toured Tucson together. My dad's place was the heart of an old dude ranch and had not been particularly well maintained. I remember that JoAnne remarked that it reminded her of the newspaper photos of Charles Manson's ranch in Southern California.

About this same time, John Wunder was sparking a panel at the American Historical Association meeting in December 1983, composed of former members of a 1982 NEH summer conference for law professors. I was pleased to be invited to participate and sent in my proposal for a paper, "Americans in Trouble: Expatriate Experience in the Criminal Law of Mexican California." I worked on that paper, which set out the themes of yet another dissertation chapter, during the spring of 1983.

In these years I was regularly attending annual conferences of the American Society for Legal History, the Western History Association, and the Association of American Law Schools, the costs for all of which were generously supported by Detroit College of Law. I especially recall the meeting of the ASLH for 1980 held in Philadelphia. It straddled my 40th birthday, and my father and Sue attended, both to have dinner together on my birthday and also because my dad wanted to attend a couple sessions to learn what this legal history was all about.

I attended some other miscellaneous conferences and workshops during this time. In May 1982 I went to Washington, D.C. for an extremely useful four day conference sponsored by the National Archives on the use of archival materials. I learned a great deal from the presentations. I was still toying with my poems, and in the fall of 1982 attended a mini-course on poetry. I have forgotten the sponsor, but the six or seven hour course met once a week at the Detroit Institute of Arts.

Academics are often asked to help with the process of vetting articles submitted to journals and book-length manuscripts submitted to university presses. The publishers request a specific professor to read a manuscript, identified by title but with names of authors withheld. Journals usually offer little else but thanks, but university presses generally offer a payment of a few hundred dollars in books or cash. The presses ask the readers, or referees, to comment on the manuscripts, and identify strengths and weaknesses, to search for works already published on the same themes, and so forth. Junior academics are generally offered journal manuscripts to vet, and more senior scholars receive the book manuscripts. During the period covered by this chapter, the *Western Historical Quarterly*, which had already published two of my articles, asked me to comment on two manuscripts. I suggested that a 1980 manuscript on law in the west during the progressive era was too legalistic and doctrinal as it stood; the author spent too much space informing us of *what* the courts had said, but with very little writing on *why* the courts had taken various actions. Regarding a 1982 paper, I made a detailed analysis of a major point of confusion in the manuscript, but suggested that after clarification it would make a publishable article.

The most interesting and satisfying vetting task came in an April 1983 request from Michael H. Dougherty of the Los Angeles County Counsel's Office. The Clerk's Office had discovered some old documents in Spanish, but no one was sure what they were, although they thought they were Mexican period court records. Dougherty enclosed several photocopies as examples and asked if I could identify them. Within a very short time I replied that they were the alcalde court (judicial) records for Los Angeles, for the approximate period of 1835-1845. I sent him some pages from a reference work on Southwestern Hispanic records that showed their provenance and exactly how they came to the County Clerk's Office. I told him these documents were priceless, and recommended that they microfilm the papers and then transfer the originals to the Huntington Library. Dougherty thanked me, but said the originals would probably go to a public institution, the Los Angeles Natural History Museum, which, despite its name, has a large collection of Mexican period artifacts and papers.

The primary measure of an academic's contribution to scholarship rests upon his or her own publications. Within this time period, fall 1980 through spring 1983 I was beginning to make my mark, although I wrote journal articles at a faster pace later and books were still on the horizon. In the fall of 1980 I published "The Caring Colony: Alta California's Participation in Spain's Foreign Affairs," in the *Southern California Quarterly*, yet another chapter of my San Jose State master's thesis. It described the loyalty of California to Spain during the war for independence, 1810-1821. I also briefly turned to some straight legal writing. Michigan had for years used common-law rules of evidence, those written only in court opinions arising out of specific cases. The Michigan Supreme Court had recently issued a printed body of the rules of evidence to replace the former vague law drawn from cases. I was convinced that these Michigan Rules of Evidence did not cover everything and left some uncodified former case-made common-law rules still viable. I wrote up my thoughts in "The Hidden Rules of Evidence: Michigan's Uncodified Evidence Law," and the *Michigan Bar Journal* published the piece in May 1982.

I thought the same could be said of the Federal Rules of Evidence which, in my view, left a lot of earlier common-law rules of evidence alive and not included in the newly-promulgated United States Supreme Court rules. So I wrote up a companion article changing some sections of the Michigan piece around by addition and deletion, of course using only federal court opinions to support my conclusions. *Willamette Law Review* published this federalized version of the same proposition as "Uncodified Federal Evidence Rules Applicable to Civil Trials" in summer 1983, just as I was in transition from Detroit to Reno.

My purely legal writing is inferior to my later writing, less sophisticated in analysis, less thought-through, in short a country cousin to the later historical and biographical writing in which I have more pride. These were my last pieces of legal scholarship, and subsequent legal writings were merely short commentaries. However, the evidence pieces cannot have been that bad. Professor Marcus Plant, an evidence professor at the University of Michigan, wrote me a note on June 7, 1982 "to express appreciation for the benefit and stimulation I experienced in reading your article [the Michigan "Hidden Rules"] . . . It is a highly valuable contribution and will undoubtedly attract wide readership." The "Uncodified Federal Evidence" piece won some appreciation as well. It was reprinted in

1984 by the *Defense Law Journal*, a journal for defense, insurance, and corporate counsel.

As mentioned previously, in the summer of 1981 I created an 843 page compilation of materials drawn from 35 articles, books, and cases that I tempted several legal publishers to bring out for law school use under the title *Readings on the Influence of the Frontier on the Development of American Law.* All rejected it, but by personalized letters rather than forms. The publishers all noted that their perception of a lack of market demand was the basis for their rejection. One other literary matter during this period is that in 1983 the Sunflower University Press selected me as the editor of a forthcoming *Law and the West.* This press publishes material first in its own magazine, and then in softbound book form. I was to select the authors, edit their pieces, and contribute an introduction. My editing experience and Sunflower's publication came in 1985, and are discussed in the following chapter.

Two other major things became a part of my intellectual life 1980-1983. The first was a December 1980 trip to Guatemala, mentioned earlier, for more intensive Spanish study at the Proyecto Linguistico Francisco Marroquin in Quetzaltenango. The second was a National Endowment for the Humanities summer seminar on American legal history for law professors, held at Stanford University in Palo Alto, July 7 through August 10, 1982.

My purpose in going to Guatemala was to improve my Spanish, hopefully making easier my reading of the many Spanish language documents needed for my doctoral dissertation. I had been to Guatemala before, with Bernadette in 1974. The country was now at war, essentially a civil war between a radicalized element of the Guatemalan Indians, who comprise the overwhelming majority of the country's population, and the militarized government. The Indians were mostly in the countryside. Security was tight and police checkpoints were everywhere. On a 3½ hour drive before beginning my studies, from Guatemala City to Xela, an affectionate name for Quetzaltenango, the military stopped our bus three times at checkpoints. No real problem developed on these mainline buses. The officers just stuck their heads inside the buses, looked over us over, and studied the passenger manifest list. However, deeper into the countryside, security was tighter. I took a local bus one day from Xela to attend a local market at San Francisco de Alto, and out in the middle of nowhere, the military had set up a barrier to stop all traffic. Every man was forced out of the bus and patted down for weapons. Perhaps a result of their machismo culture, the soldiers did not require women to exit or be searched. That women might carry weapons was beyond their comprehension.

Security was heightened even in the cities. The insurgents made regular threats on national leaders, murdered national policemen, and in Quetzaltenango, for example, gunfire sounded from the hills surrounding the city many evenings. The urban police seemed much more militarized than they had been in 1974, wearing battle fatigues and carrying submachine guns. I always said good morning or good afternoon as I passed these policemen on the streets. Regardless of the politics or what group was doing what, these individual policemen were young, 18-21 years old, and all of them appeared to me not as macho bullies but more as frightened kids.

Quetzaltenango was a fascinating place that combined different cultures. For example, when I attended the Roman Catholic Cathedral, located on the central plaza where I also lived, I was surprised by the richness of the European music in the service—a hymn based on Beethoven's *Ode to Joy* in his 9th Symphony and a processional based on Bach's Toccata and Fugue in D. Yet during this same service, Indians gathered in a back corner of the cathedral huddled around a large bowl in which they cooked some strongly-scented material. They were both attending the Roman Catholic service and practicing some older pagan ritual at the same time.

Since it was December, the religious processions and celebrations were numerous. I remember watching one procession in early December that was almost surreal. Dozens of Indians led the way carrying lighted candles. Next came drummers, then banner bearers, followed by a truck carrying an image of a young Mary surrounded by neon lights and emitting incense. A portable power generator pushed by an old man followed Mary's truck, and supplied power for her neon lights. A blaring band concluded the procession. As the feast day of the Virgin of Guadalupe approached, a Mexican saint but revered in Guatemala as well, the sounds of marimba music, drumbeats, and many dozens of men singing a haunting melody came up from the central plaza. As Christmas approached processions of some type appeared every evening. The candles and caroling of *las posadas*, firecrackers, rockets, the carrying about of various Nazareth scenes, streets and parks filled with humanity—all these scenes were repeated nightly. All were colorful and enjoyable, excepting the firecrackers. The Guatemalan use of firecrackers is to throw them at others, and then artfully dodge out of the way of incoming firecrackers.

I recall a conversation with Sven, a Swede also studying Spanish in Quetzaltenango. We talked about the poverty and obvious health hazards from piles of garbage and filth in the streets. Sven said that if Xela were in Sweden the government would shut down the entire town. Yet we both agreed that the locals all seemed to have a lot of fun. Well, perhaps not *all* of them. I recall one day while on a walk I passed by a tacky brothel and bar with window doors on the front. I saw a man passed out on a table, when suddenly a fight between a different man and a prostitute caused the table to tip, and the inebriated man slid down to the floor without waking up. The two combatants went outside where the whore grabbed a beer bottle, smashed it against a stone wall, and stood ready to take the man on with the bottle's ragged edges. It was at that point that I thought it prudent to leave.

The school arranged residential facilities for its students. I was a guest of an upper middle class family. Jorge, the local manager of the Bank of Guatemala, had a large apartment over the bank, right on the plaza. He was very kind to me. Jorge took me to Zunil, a beautiful hot springs and spa. It was an idyllic spot in the mountains with ferns and tropical trees overhanging the pool and poolside bar. He also played lots of chess with me and a couple games of ping pong, and he beat me consistently. He even bought me a wonderful steak dinner at his private club.

I did improve my Spanish in Quetzaltenango, but I concluded that even if I were proficient enough to read Spanish, and I felt I was close, I never was going to be very good at speaking it. I ascribed that to a combination of shyness and being afraid to make a mistake. I had had enough study. I also was sick much of the time. It was not constant, but often I was very cold and trembling during the afternoon and hot at night. My medication did not prevent diarrhea. Yet these conditions were not always present and not debilitating. I decided to cut the Spanish study short by a few days and see Belize, a country I had never visited.

I only spent three days in Belize, but I formed a favorable impression. It has a different culture than neighboring Guatemala. Blacks comprise the majority population, descendants of slaves who logged the mahogany forests of the former British Honduras. English and Spanish are both official languages, and although one hears Spanish, most of the inhabitants speak a creole English. Belize felt more like a Caribbean black culture than the feel of Hispanic and Indian in Guatemala. Houses were built on stilts for miles inland from the Atlantic. Still further inland thatched huts prevailed, some firmly constructed and others not. Fewer police appeared around towns in Belize than Guatemala, and those police did not carry weapons. What policemen were visible had a very British bearing, as they walked erectly and looked very proud, unlike the Guatemalan police who are much less formal and austere but who do carry guns.

Generally speaking, the people in Belize seemed healthier and better nourished. Primitive as it was, Belize seemed somehow cleaner than Guatemala, although there was considerably more dust in the interior. There was less rubbish lying around, less mess in the buses, although in Belize City there was quite a bit of filth outside the central area. The wealth of Belize, such as it was, seemed more evenly divided than in Guatemala, not so much disparity in the distribution of goods. Walking around Belize City, Dangriga, and San Ignacio, everyone in sight seemed to be in the lower middle class, but their clothing was clean and not tattered as I often saw in Guatemala.

I spent two of my three days in Belize traveling around the country. I took a bus from Belize City to Stann Creek Town, known also as

Dangriga. We went through a slow rise of land from swamps near the coast, then sandy land, and then a high plateau. On the way, the bus passed through Belmopan, the new capital. In 1980, Belmopan consisted of a few concrete bunker-style buildings, an open air market, a couple of gas stations, a very few houses, a movie theatre, a store or two – that was it. The terrain changed dramatically between Belmopan and Dangriga. We threaded our way among ranges of high hills, jungle foliage, and flashing rivers. It seemed like a very empty land. This then gave way to a flatter region of citrus fruit that led into Dangriga, a small town with two or three blocks of a main street, with stores, bars, a couple of restaurants, and a theatre that showed movies twice a week. Houses and most "downtown" businesses were on stilts. I had dinner at the Chinese restaurant, generally a good choice when traveling in unfamiliar locales, and went to bed very early as the only bus out of the town left at 5:30AM.

I changed buses in Balmopan to reach San Ignacio in far western Belize. The terrain going to San Ignacio opened up and cattle and sheep ranches appeared here and there. Many Mennonite farmers have come into this region. A large British base is located nearby because the Guatemalan border is only a few miles beyond San Ignacio. Guatemala contends that Belize belongs to it, and on many occasions has threatened to invade it. The British troops are stationed here to guard against that threat. San Ignacio itself is a small, very dusty jungle town. I explored it in twenty minutes. There is absolutely no catering to tourists here as the only tourists were young backpackers. I returned to Belize City that afternoon, and spent the next day walking all over. A guard let me in to see the judicial facilities, including the Supreme Court courtroom. The law library appeared to be very inadequate, filled with older and very tattered books. I saw the British governor walking near the governor's house. He was very friendly and we exchanged greetings.

It seemed that Belize had benefited from being colonized by the British. Two concrete examples of civilization and civility caught my attention. One was in San Ignacio. This small town on the edge of the jungle had a bookstore. To my delight and amazement that bookstore carried Shakespeare, Dickens and almost the entire canon of classic British literature, the books kept more or less dust free by heavy plastic strips running down over the display cases. In the absence of any significant tourist trade, these books meant there were local readers in this tiny town who read Shakespeare and the rest of the British literary canon. There would be nothing comparable to this in an equivalent Guatemalan town. The second example came from Belize City, where I purchased a few books from a government store. I went on my way when suddenly the government sales clerk came running after me crying out, "Your receipt, sir! You forgot your receipt!" The rectitude of that civil servant came straight from British colonization, and would not be found in most places of the world, including the United States. I have learned, unfortunately, that since 1980, as Belize has moved further away from its colonial past, widespread corruption and in some cases incompetence has entered its culture. That is a shame.

The second miscellaneous yet major event in my intellectual development during the years 1980-1983 was my participation in a National Endowment for the Humanities summer seminar at Stanford in the summer of 1982. Lawrence Friedman, one of the most renowned of American legal historians, was the director. I applied and was fortunate enough to receive his invitation to participate. There were 15 of us, all law professors, and we each received a modest stipend from the NEH that helped defray the cost of housing and transportation. JoAnne was quite put out with me for my failure to consult with her in advance, but was able to come out for three of the five weeks with 1½ year-old Virginia. We lived in an old double trailer, situated an easy walk from the law school, in a place on campus that held several. John Wunder was the only participant whom I knew before the seminar, and since he and his family were also living in our "trailer park," we socialized a bit during those five weeks.

The seminar was extremely helpful to my understanding American legal history, and in particular I learned much by observing and talking with Lawrence about his teaching methods. The summer was also a lot of hard work. We met as a group weekdays from 9:AM to 12:noon. Then we had at least 100 pages of materials to read each day, drawn from cases, legislative reports, and to a lesser extent from secondary sources. In addition to preparing for the daily discussion, we each had to prepare individual reports and give a talk on our own areas of research. The federal government sent out an inspector toward the end of our seminar to check up on us, make sure the funds were not wasted on liquor or riotous living, and that the director was giving us the governmental money's worth. This officious little man wanted to take as many as wished to go out with him to dinner, but we participants in the seminar were so put off by the inspection process and the presumptuousness of the thought that we had to be checked up on that none of us were willing to have dinner with the fellow.

In the spring of 1983 I was worried about my progress toward the completion of the dissertation. Actually, I was in reasonably good shape. I had spent much of the 1979-1981 summers in California, working at the Bancroft Library or the Monterey County Recorder's Office where the Mexican archives were then maintained. Perhaps 85% of the research was complete. I had a tentative but skeletal outline of the entire book, and I had finished first drafts of two chapters, and outlined a few of the remaining eight chapters.

In March 1983 I noticed an ad in the *Chronicle of Higher Education* seeking a dean for a new law school in Reno, Nevada, curiously named Old College School of Law. I had never lost my desire to return to the West, and although California specifically was my place of desire, the California state line is only 12 miles from Reno and San Francisco itself only a four hour drive. I was also enthusiastic about helping to mold a brand new law school. I responded to the ad, but still thought that nothing would come of it. However, I soon received a telephone call inviting me to go to New York City for an interview with John P. Leary, the Jesuit president of Old College. Shortly thereafter I flew to New York and talked with Leary. I must have made a favorable impression as shortly thereafter I was invited to come to Reno at the school's expense, for further interviews and for me to see their institution. It makes for a good story with a New York-as-center-of-the-universe theme, that a man from Reno would interview another man from Detroit about a job in Reno, each traveling eastward to New York to do so.

JoAnne joined me on the trip to Reno, her parents minding Virginia. I was delighted with the prospects of once again living in the West. I was too naïve to ask hard questions about finances, the certainty of promises of major donations Leary so vaguely mentioned, the capacities and willingness of the trustees to take an active hand in the school's governance, and even the supply of prepared students. I also underestimated the insistence of the American Bar Association on a large capital cushion in any new school that obtained its approval. I failed to question the background of Fr. John P. Leary. I might have learned, although it was still concealed, that he had been essentially dismissed as President of Gonzaga University and later forced to leave a school he had founded in San Francisco, New College. Instead, I was blinded by what I thought was a great opportunity in the West.

In Reno, JoAnne had told me that it looked as though I had the job if I wanted it. And soon enough I had a call from Leary offering the deanship at $60,000 annually together with a tenured faculty position. I insisted on a letter from him granting autonomy to the law school, allowing it to form its own curriculum, hire its own faculty, and prepare its own budget. I accepted his offer subject to those conditions, which he accepted. I advised my colleagues at DCL of my resignation on May 9, 1983, "with a great deal of tenderness and mixed emotions." In my letter of resignation that I circulated to the Detroit faculty, I told them that "my experiences here have made possible a significant amount of professional and personal growth, and I have enjoyed my work with you," but cited the opportunity to help mold a brand new law school and a return to the West as overriding. Several colleagues took me out for a farewell lunch and gave me gag gifts for my use in Reno, including, as I recall, a hand warmer for the winters and mosquito spray for the summers.

Almost immediately some ominous shadows appeared. When I told Dean Abbott about my decision he wished me well, but advised that it would probably be necessary to raise $10,000,000 for the new school to satisfy the ABA. While my agreement with Leary made it clear that I was not responsible for fundraising, I wondered if Leary were up to that Herculean task. I had asked John P. Reid, another outstanding American legal historian and one who knew my work, to write Old College a letter about me. I had already been hired, but Leary wanted to fatten the file by getting reference letters. Reid sent Leary the requested letter, but then wrote me that he "should write to congratulate you, but as in all honesty, as I cannot for the life of me guess why anyone wants to be a dean, I don't know what to congratulate you for." We hosted a farewell dinner party for Detroit friends. One of them raised a glass and toasted us with "Westward ho!" JoAnne immediately replied, "Westward woe."

In any event we were off to Reno, for better or worse. We rented a moving van, then hired professional movers to pack and load our goods and chattels, including my growing library. My parents took Virginia for a couple of weeks and returned her in Reno. I rented out the Detroit house. JoAnne and I then drove across the country with our little dog Perry in a container.

Chapter 5

The Reno Interval:
Summer 1983 – Summer 1985

When John Leary hired me as Dean of Old College School of Law, Nevada's first law school, he gave me the mandate to bring the school up to the standards that would be acceptable to win the approval and accreditation of the American Bar Association. Technically, the American Bar Association (ABA) does not accredit law schools; it approves them. No real difference because almost all American states including Nevada require that those who sit for its bar examinations, and thus become eligible for admission to the bar upon passage, must first have graduated from a law school approved by the American Bar Association. If a particular school is not approved by the ABA, there is little inducement for any students to attend, since they cannot sit for a bar exam and become lawyers.

The chokehold of the process is the Accreditation Committee of the ABA's Section of Legal Education and Admissions to the Bar. It promulgates and amends Standards for law schools along with written and informal interpretations. It arranges for site inspections, generally conducted by academics from other institutions, to determine facts. Finally, and crucially, it issues findings as to whether the institution meets its Standards, relying on the facts found by the site inspectors. All of this is required before even provisional approval of a new school, and indeed the ABA requires a re-inspection of each American law school every seven years (now ten years).

Leary opened the law school in the fall of 1981, and for its first two years, Old College School of Law operated with local Reno lawyers serving as part-time adjunct teachers loosely governed by another local lawyer serving as a part-time dean. No one supervised registration to assure that each student carried a minimum of nine credit hours, as the ABA Standards provided; no one compiled student grade point averages; and no one put any student on probation or expelled any student for consistently poor grades. The ABA forbids the continued enrollment of students whose academic performance clearly indicates they will fail the bar examination. It is akin to theft to collect tuition from students clearly bound for failure. Not only did Old College encourage the continuation of poor students, it also made no effort to screen the students it admitted. For its first two years it had open admission.

Since I was mandated to bring the school to the proper level for accreditation, I had to tighten all this academic looseness in the quickest time possible. This emphasis on the Standards and the catch-up process bruised many student expectations. Students with poor academic records were shocked to learn that the new Dean had expelled those below 1.5, and placed on probation those between 1.5 and 2.0. Dilettante students who had wished to drift through law school with one or two courses per terms were upset to learn that the American Bar Association's Standards mandated a minimum of nine credit hours per term. Even some faculty members, although a minority, accustomed to coming in to teach and then leaving, were dismayed to learn that a clear standard of the ABA and sustained by the legal academic community required that they engage in scholarly research and writing.

The process of tightening academic standards began with my arrival, and was always presented as a need to conform with the ABA Standards that we had to meet for accreditation. One might have expected that students would have reacted to the reforms by rallying around the clear community of interest – the accreditation of the school. Some did, but in general most followed their own individualistic interests. Almost every step I took to correct past ineptitude and move the school into the well-charted waters of mainstream legal education were greeted with student howls of indignation directed at me: "I was promised I could take only one course a term; I wasn't told I had to take the Law School Aptitude Test; It's more convenient to take that course in a three hour session and only come down here once a week; What do you mean I have to get my college transcripts?; Why can't I continue on with my 0.39 grade point average?"

In addition to its academic deficiencies, which I could ameliorate, there was a larger deficiency over which I had no control: finances. Among the ABA's Standards are requirements that an approved law school must possess sufficient financial resources to assure that its program is adequately supported. The Standards include this general requirement and also specific requirements that the budgets projected over five years provide for adequate faculty salaries (the ABA has since dropped adequate salary requirements in light of an anti-trust challenge by the Department of Justice), staff support, library funding, and student scholarships. Old College, both the modest undergraduate program and the law school, lacked significant funding, and operated on tuition, the gate receipts.

When a law school was first proposed for Old College in 1980, Leary had been able to attract many prominent lawyers and judges, including Hon. Proctor Hug of the Ninth Circuit Court of Appeal, to form an advisory committee. After Leary announced on February 20, 1981 that the law school would accept students for that fall, many of the members of the advisory body resigned, citing inadequate planning. Leary did hire a legal academic to consult on finances. His report was dated December 15, 1982, a year after the first class had completed its first semester. The consultant emphasized the need for adequate resources, and recommended as a guideline toward accreditation law school budgets of $790,000 for 1983-1984 with six faculty members and $1,391,150 for 1984-1985 with twelve faculty members (the informal Standards required a minimum of twelve, although the formal Standards required only six). Leary cavalierly wrote on the face page of his copy of the report that "there are estimates, costs in this report with which I strongly disagree," and then proceeded to ignore it. He did not show it to me when he recruited me as dean.

These facts were leading to a crisis since some students had entered the law school in fall 1981 and were due to graduate in spring 1984. The school would need to schedule an inspection examination in the early spring of 1984 to assure even provisional accreditation by June 1984. Without taking this step the first graduating class would be unable to take the bar examination in any American jurisdiction.

Leary led a fund-raising drive in the fall of 1983. It raised only about $10,000 of actual donations. It had more success in obtaining letters of credit, about $600,000, from businessmen in Las Vegas who were essentially willing to stand surety to Old College's proposed $1,000,000 bond issue that I believe never materialized. I did not think the ABA would be impressed by an effort to garner the needed resources by borrowed money that ultimately would have to be paid back.

I invited Dean James White to informally visit the law school. Dean White was the consultant to the ABA Accreditation Committee and had great influence in the accreditation process. He came in September 1983, and we held a large reception for him to which we invited dozens of state and federal judges, and leaders of the bar.

White met separately with John Leary and with me. To me, he referred to the discussion with Leary as "Father Leary's homily." We had dinner with many trustees (all were invited) in a private dining room of a leading restaurant. White made it abundantly clear that the ABA would impose national standards on Old College's quest for accreditation, and not make any exceptions for a small state such as Nevada. Although he framed the thought in language less harsh and more polite, the message was clear that no backwater, ill-financed law school would win national accreditation unless it met the national standards of the ABA.

By the beginning of the spring term 1984 many students were alarmed. For many this was the time when an inspection had to come if they were to take the bar exam. I had given up hope and was beginning to explore a process whereby graduating students might be permitted to take the Nevada bar under permission of the Nevada Supreme Court. Yet Leary pushed on with his happy talk, assuring students that the fund drive had been successful, and accreditation was just around the corner. I held a well-attended meeting of students on the accreditation process, and explained why we were not ready for an inspection. I felt strongly that only ill feeling and significant costs would result from calling for an inspection. Leary posted an optimistic memo in late January to the effect that the fundraising had gone well and we should be ready now for an inspection. I replied with a single page memo I posted on January 23, 1984. I succinctly stated that "in my opinion the probability that we will be ready for an ABA inspection during the spring of 1984 is zero. I don't wish to arouse or sustain any false hopes. I think, however, the effort to raise funds is just as important as ever so that we can be ready for an ABA inspection this fall or next spring."

Even though we had disagreements throughout the fall term of 1983, Leary and I remained on good relations personally. During the Christmas break, JoAnne and I invited him over to our home for dinner. He sent a very gracious thank you note in which he commented on my work as Dean:

> Thanks much for all the hard work you do here. Your commitments are high & your resolves earnest. Thanks also for educating me. Don't mind a few disagreements. We'll resolve most of them.

A month later Leary fired me. What had happened? I think Leary's anger at me arose from his embarrassment at being publicly called out and his assurance that accreditation was just around the corner exposed as a pipe dream. My memo to the students mentioned above certainly did that, but even more forcefully did my remarks to the Trustees at their meeting of January 27, 1984 that immediately preceded my firing.

The trustees had not met since May 1983, although some of them may have been in informal contact with Leary. When I was hired as Dean, I negotiated for and obtained a right of the law school to submit a separate budget to the trustees, and in the weeks before the meeting I did mail to every trustee a proposal for a tenure policy, a very modest retirement plan for faculty, and most importantly a proposed annual budget for the law school. There was a general understanding that the school would pursue a $1,000,000 state bond, with the ten letters of credit as surety, and that these funds would be used for the construction of classrooms, theatre, and offices, together with significant retrospective law library acquisitions. The real battle of the budgets concerned law school operations. I recommended a dramatically higher budget so that we could hire the additional six faculty members needed for the twelve that the ABA then considered adequate, provide for a 5% employer match for a proposed retirement plan, and increase the pitifully small amount available for scholarships. I always took care never to criticize the Trustees' or the President's efforts at fundraising, instead advising what in my judgment was needed to obtain approval by the American Bar Association. I advised the trustees that the proposed $1,000,000 funding for capital items of construction and library acquisitions was probably enough for provisional ABA approval. However, I warned the trustees to the contrary regarding the operational budget. In my letter of January 11 I wrote:

> I realize that the proposed budget contemplates an operating deficit of $450,860 for the law school. In the final analysis, finances are a trustee responsibility, and I don't know how the shortfall will be financed. But I do think I must warn you of what I feel is the adverse consequence – a failure of accreditation – of spending less.

President Leary responded with what he called an "austerity budget," proposing to let go three of the six law faculty and demanding a 20% salary reduction of those remaining. This of course made for a lively discussion at the trustees meeting. I defended my position and additionally proposed that the Trustees establish committees to take charge of fundraising and an additional committee become apprised of the law school's operational difficulties. I pointed out that Leary's proposed cut in faculty would be a step backward, and that it would halt any chance of accreditation.

In light of all my warnings, some public but mostly private, about the amount of resources needed for ABA accreditation, why did Leary persist almost to the end in his optimistic talk that accreditation was imminent? I am not sure of the answer, but there is a clue in his prior professional history. A few years after leaving Gonzaga University in Spokane, where he had served as president, Leary founded "New College" in San Francisco. Initially only a liberal arts college, it began a law school that became *state accredited* under Leary's watch. California has its own plan for accrediting schools that are not ABA approved. The California accreditation permits its graduates to sit for the California bar, but none other. Schools that are approved by the ABA are exempt from the California state requirements and inspections because the ABA standards are higher.

The California State Bar operates the California accreditation process, and it is much less insistent on library requirements, number of faculty, and generous financial resources than is the American Bar Association. There are many state accredited law schools in California that operate with small law libraries and no full time faculty at all, with local lawyers teaching a class or two a week at very low pay. These schools possess weak resources, and the ABA would never approve them. Most of these schools are free-standing institutions, but those that are connected to a university generally operate at a net surplus that benefits the overall university. I believe this model is what Leary had in mind, and that when he began the law school at Old College he was clueless about the significantly higher costs involved with ABA-approved law schools. For an educator he was a slow learner.

On January 31, 1984 Leary sent me a seven page letter, specifying details of my deficiencies as an administrator as he saw them. Included were many matters, but the thrust of the letter seemed to be Leary's categorization of my correspondence with the trustees, my conduct at the meeting, and my memo to the students as insubordination. He gave me one day to resign or be fired. As soon as I received his letter I called an emergency meeting of the law faculty, asking them to decide, in my absence from the meeting, whether I still retained their confidence. A separate ABA Standard requires a dean to resign if he has lost the confidence of the school's faculty. I gathered faculty to meet at short notice, excepting one who I was unable to locate. They voted to express their confidence in me and recommended conciliation between Leary and myself. I accepted their suggestion of mediation or conciliation under either the faculty's or the Trustees' auspicious, but Leary did not.

Simultaneously I prepared my own seven page letter, rebutting Leary's allegations point by point, but more generally insisting

The school was founded with inadequate academic fiscal planning, and has been sustained by a considerable amount of inappropriate optimism on the part of President Leary. The law faculty and myself have engaged over the past six months in a terrible race against time in an effort to tighten our standards so that if the necessary resources were forthcoming we would be an institution worthy of ABA accreditation.

I have never criticized Leary's fund raising efforts. I applaud them. I have simply been insistent on the level of resources that accreditation actually requires and have refused to lead students on.

I made copies of Leary's letter and my response and posted them for a week in a glass cabinet designed for notices, locked and for which I had the only key. The next day, after I refused to resign, Leary sent me a dismissal note. I turned back to my scholarship and began searching for a new job. I think most of the students did not feel involved with these disputes, and I had in fact alienated some by my tightening of standards. However I did receive some thanks for my work from some students. Most of the faculty commiserated with me. Reporters interviewed me, probably Leary as well, and newspaper articles and local television coverage reported the story. I insisted that I was being punished as the bearer of bad news, and that Old College School of Law was probably never going to become accredited in the absence of significant changes in resources and attitudes.

Leary expressly continued me on as a faculty member since I had tenure as a professor. Administrative positions, such as a deanship, never come with tenure. However, deans are always hired with dual status as tenured professors, to protect them against the sudden displeasure of a president or provost, just what happened here.

In my first response to Leary after receipt of his resign or be fired letter, I told him that I would hold Leary and Old College liable for the difference between my decanal salary and the professorial level of $41,500. Through the balance of my two year contract as Dean, the differential was $23,700. We had a series of agreements about that contractual claim. In the first agreement, February 3, 1984, immediately after the firing, Leary and I agreed that this was the true difference between my decanal salary and the professorial salary that I would continue to receive. We referenced negotiations underway to compromise and settle this claim, and I agreed not to file a lawsuit while good faith negotiations were underway.

At the end of February I sent the President another memo, citing his refusal to entertain any settlement and my notice of intent to file a lawsuit. I engaged a local attorney to sue Old College. However, Leary and I continued to talk settlement, and our discussion focused on a sabbatical period in exchange for a release of my contract claim. My primary interest was time to work on my book, and, in any event, I thought it unlikely that I would actually collect a judgment against either Old College or Jack Leary. Several students had asked me to teach American Legal History as an elective and I agreed to do so for the fall term 1984. It would not take much preparation, and when students request me to teach my personal specialty, I am always receptive.

While that course was underway in the fall of 1984, Leary and I entered into a document I drafted, an executory accord, whereby, if I received my regular professorial salary through June 30, 1985 and the school made no further demands on my time, then upon the last of my monthly salary, Old College would be released and discharged from any claim for unpaid decanal salary. I thought this would be a good solution. The spring term of 1984 had already begun at the time of the firing, so I had the balance of that term to work on my book. I was teaching only a half load in fall 1984 with the American Legal History course, and I would have the spring 1985 term for writing.

Deans often teach a single course. It helps the faculty understand that the dean is one of their number, and it allows the dean to better understand the students. In the fall of 1983 I taught the first half of the two term course in Property. The student evaluations for that course were similar to those I had received in Detroit. Some students were quite enthusiastic: "asked very good questions"; "outstanding!"; "excellent consistent presentation"; "terrific lecturer – really knew his stuff"; "his enthusiasm is contagious!"; "he obviously enjoys his courses and we enjoy him." On the other hand, several students felt overpowered by my personality or intimidated.

When I reached agreement with Leary, I expected that American Legal History would be the extent of my additional teaching at Old College. But I discovered that the students already in the law school had received a very poor training in Evidence, one of my core teaching areas. I volunteered to teach a remedial course so that the students who were about to graduate would be able to pass the Evidence portion of the bar exam, assuming they would be allowed to take it. The remedial course concept floundered because we could not give credit for remedial study. I proposed to teach without additional compensation a new course called Nevada Evidence, but all who took it understood it would be basic Evidence. I really did not have to teach such a course, as our contract expressly called for no further teaching or other requirements. But I felt sorry for the students who really needed better training in Evidence, a subject always tested on the bar examination. It was a course I had taught many times before and teaching it once again salved my conscience as the students genuinely needed it, and it would not cut too much into my writing time.

I have no teaching evaluations for American Legal History or Evidence, but I must have done reasonably well as the student members of the Old College chapter of Delta Theta Phi, a law fraternity, voted me a "Professor of the Year for 1984-85." I also gave two talks to the members of the Washoe County Bar Association, one in October 1983 about the law school and our aspirations, and a second in March 1985 on non-statutory rules of evidence in Nevada, a talk for which attorneys could obtain credits for their continuing legal education.

The saga of Old College School of Law of course did not end with my decanal departure, and I would like to offer a brief epilogue. In 1984 the President changed the name from Old College School of Law to Nevada School of Law. I approved of this because the new name was more distinctive and would market better, although I had nothing to do with the decision. For a few months after my firing at the end of January 1984, the law school carried on under a temporary dean, but later that same year Leary hired a new permanent law dean, a questionable fellow named Morris Wolf. Wolf's administration seemed to be most noted by his absence from the school, as he was away for weeks at a time, allegedly doing fundraising, none of which materialized. When he was present Wolf was very quixotic, and antagonisms quickly developed between dean and faculty. I recall one faculty meeting in late 1984 when Wolf excoriated the faculty for their allegedly negative attitudes toward Nevada in general and Reno in particular. He went on and on. For the next faculty meeting I wore an "I Love Nevada" tee-shirt, with a large button proclaiming the virtues of Reno.

Many of the students developed antipathy toward Wolf, I think primarily because he was not around to answer questions about accreditation or anything else. One morning in January 1985, I saw Wolf when we both were walking on the foot path around Virginia Lake. I stopped to greet him and warned him that this was dean-firing season at Old College. He seemed quite assured of his position, but in fact Leary fired Wolf that same month. Wolf had negotiated a much more detailed contract regarding his deanship, and it provided that if Leary wanted to fire Wolf as dean, a Decanal Review Committee had to be formed to review the legitimacy of the firing. Apparently the contract said nothing about Wolf's position as a tenured faculty member, and after Wolf's termination there was considerable turmoil and contention as to whether a separate effort had to be made to terminate his faculty tenure. By this time almost every constituency at the law school wanted Wolf gone, but it eventually took a $20,000 payoff in cash to make him leave. A much more capable man, Felix Stumpf, retired Academic Director of the National Judicial College, replaced Wolf as dean and served as the law school's final dean.

In 1984 it became apparent that the law school would not be accredited before June 1985, when its first class was due to graduate. Old College hired outside counsel to bring a petition before the Nevada Supreme Court. It sought a waiver or modification of the Court's rule that required persons seeking to sit for the Nevada bar examination and become licensed as lawyers in Nevada to have graduated from an ABA accredited school. In January 1985 the Court denied the petition for a general waiver, but did give Old College graduates some limited relief. It ruled that the graduates of newly renamed Nevada School of Law could take the bar examinations. Further, if the law school obtained ABA provisional accreditation (the initial first step toward full accreditation) prior to August 31, 1988, then all graduates of Nevada School of Law could join the Nevada Bar, subject to bar passage and character fitness. The order kept the accreditation fire to the school's feet, as it were, as no graduate was eligible to join the Nevada Bar until the school was ultimately accredited.

Someone discovered that Old College's immediate location was in the middle of a poverty zone, and on this basis, in 1985, the school received a $1,000,000 grant that it used to construct additional law faculty offices, new classrooms, and a theatre in the building's vast cavernous area that once housed the printing press for the Reno *Gazette-Journal.* In 1982 that newspaper had given the unused building to Old College to operate its undergraduate and law schools.

The turmoil involving Leary had finally mobilized the trustees to act. In the spring of 1985 they asked Leary to resign, which he did. They then brought in a new President, Alan De Giulio, whom I met in my final few days in Reno. He seemed earnest and I thought he was probably a better administrator. I heard from former colleagues that turmoil continued, however.

From the summer of 1985 to summer 1986, the law school went on a frenzy of activity. During this period it raised the number of faculty to twelve full-time professors, completed several new classrooms, increased the library collection from 34,000 hardbound volumes to 71,854 hardbound and microfilm volumes, and hired a full-time library director who held both a law degree and a library science degree. Thus fortified, the law school applied for provisional ABA accreditation in September 1986.

The ABA inspection team, consisting of volunteer legal academics and attorneys, inspected Nevada School of Law in November 1986 and reported its findings to the Accreditation Committee for the Section of Legal Education and Admissions of the ABA in March 1987. On April 28, 1987 that Committee denied the school's request for provisional accreditation. That spring the law school held its third and final graduation ceremonies. Having seen the report of the inspectors, the administration could no doubt foresee the result, and from April to June 1987 made a concerted effort to give the law school, the undergraduate school, and all their physical assets, including the large building, by now improved with academic facilities, to the University of Nevada System. The Board of Regents of the University of Nevada system was worried about Old College's substantial debt, $3.8 million, and its large and continuing operating losses. Additionally it felt hampered by its own bureaucratic procedures for required reports and consultations preceding new programs. On June 4, 1987 it turned down any affiliation with or acquisition of Old College.

The Old College Trustees then voted to close the entire school, undergraduate and its Nevada School of Law, but with a ten month "wind-down" period. The law school taught a few courses during this wind-down, but the principal activity was to persuade ABA-approved schools to accept the Nevada School of Law's students, many of whom were only a year from graduation, as transfer students so that they would then graduate from an ABA-accredited school and be allowed to sit for any bar examination. The administration achieved a fair amount of success in this placement.

In spring 1988 Old College and Nevada School of Law closed their doors. Nevada was once again without a law school. It would remain that way for ten more years, until in 1998 the University of Nevada System opened a state-sponsored law school in Las Vegas, the William S. Boyd School of Law. With adequate and state-guaranteed funding, the school was quickly accredited. In naming the new school to honor William S. Boyd, a notable gambling executive, I wonder if any noted the irony that Boyd had previously been a trustee of Old College, home of Nevada's previous and first law school.

This left the 1985, 1986, and 1987 graduates in limbo. They had already taken the Nevada bar, and most had passed. But they could not obtain their law license until their erstwhile law school became accredited, and it was now clear that would never happen. Nor could they transfer to an accredited law school because they had already graduated and taken the bar. Over 50 of those in this category petitioned the Nevada Supreme Court for a waiver of any requirement that they graduate from an ABA accredited school on the theory that Old College/Nevada School of Law had been for them the "functional equivalent" of an ABA-accredited school.

The Nevada Supreme Court pointed out that ten of fifteen of the conclusions that the ABA Committee made in denying accreditation related to the lack of financial stability. It then looked one by one at the remaining conclusions and found that they looked toward probable future difficulty. The Court noted that the school's bar passage rate for 1985-1987, averaging 69%, was higher than several ABA-accredited schools in California, commonly attended by Nevada students. The financial difficulty in attracting good faculty looked to the future, whereas for now, the examiners rated the faculty's classroom performance "good to marginal," but in no respects inadequate. The inspectors' concern with the library involved future needs, but in the here and now, the school's 71,854 volumes exceeded the libraries of the Nevada Supreme Court and the National Judicial College.

The Court concluded that the education received by the Old College/Nevada School of Law graduates of 1985-1987 "has been functionally equivalent to that received at schools accredited by the ABA," and for these graduates only waived the rule requiring graduation from an ABA-accredited school. It ordered all of the Old College/Nevada School of Law graduates to be admitted to the Nevada Bar upon their satisfaction of the other usual requirements (bar exam, Multistate Professional Responsibilities Exam, and character review). The net result of the Old College/Nevada School of Law was to add approximately fifty worthy graduates to the membership of the State Bar of Nevada. Some of them have become judges in Nevada, and most hold other responsible positions within the legal community.

John Leary, S.J., the man, died in December 1993, but his saga continued on posthumously. The most interesting epilogue to the Old College story came in 2006, when the Oregon Providence of the Society of Jesus (Jesuits) made a startling announcement. Almost forty years earlier, in 1969, the Spokane police had notified them that if they did not get John P. Leary, then President of Gonzaga University, out of town within 24 hours, they would arrest him for pedophilia. Leary, a member of the Oregon providence that includes Washington, had been accused of molesting a boy earlier in 1966. But upon Leary's strong denial, the authorities dropped the investigation. Additional allegations had emerged by 1969 to the point where the police were ready to arrest him. However, the Jesuit order accepted the police offer and moved Leary to the east for a while, then back to Utah, and eventually to the Bay Area. When he resigned as President of Gonzaga University, in haste and one step ahead of arrest, he announced that he was in poor health. In 1971 Leary founded a liberal arts school in San Francisco named New College that contained a law school as well as a liberal arts curriculum.

San Francisco's New College stumbled near insolvency for several years, being liberal to the point where some students thought they need not pay tuition. The New College trustees gave Leary an ultimatum in 1974 that he had to broaden the fundraising base and fire the most radical of the faculty or resign. Leary resigned. Apparently poor fundraising and administrative skills caused the firing, and there is no evidence that molestation entered the picture. A few years thereafter Leary began the Old College undergraduate program in 1980, with the law school to follow in the next year. The Old College Trustees asked Leary to resign in spring 1985, apparently by unanimous vote. The real reason was Leary's administrative ineptitude, but the public announcement cited health concerns. No solid evidence exists of any molestation during his Reno years, although I have a doubt. The indications are that Leary had about a dozen targets in the 1960s. The Oregon Providence of Jesuits has paid out approximately $500,000 to settle claims brought against it by Leary's victims.

My scholarship began to blossom while in Reno. While never reaching the intensity of my book writing years later in Birmingham, what was accomplished in Reno constituted a promising start. I made my greatest effort on the dissertation that became my first full book. But I also published shorter pieces during the Reno years.

I had an article scheduled for publication just around the time I became Dean at Old College. The idea behind the piece was doing for the federal system what I had already done for the Michigan Rules of Evidence, examining rules of evidence that had not been included in the newly written codes of evidence but which were still practiced in the federal courts. "Uncodified Federal Evidence Rules Applicable to Civil Trials" was scheduled for publication in the *Willamette Law Review*, and to maximize its public relations value I had to work quickly to change the footnote concerning my affiliation from Professor at Detroit College of Law to Dean of Old College School of Law. I ordered 200 offprints of the article, and I had them on hand when I arrived in Reno. I sent a copy of the article accompanied by a personalized letter to every judge and every prosecutor in Nevada, state and federal, as a kind of introduction for myself and a modest piece of promotion for Old College to a state bar that was somewhat hostile toward Old College. It certainly did no harm to either Old College or myself as I received replies of thanks and best wishes from dozens of judges around the state. In 1984 the *Defense Law Review* reprinted the article.

Another piece that was in the pipeline when I left Detroit for Reno was an article, "The Role of Intellect and Fortuity in Legal Change: An Incident from the Law of Slavery," published in the January 1984 issue of *The American Journal of Legal History*. I had completed the article while in Detroit, and it was based on a paper written for Peter Westen's seminar during my LL.M. program. I was once again adapting and improving my earlier academic papers for later use.

A chronicle of the efforts at publication and various edits demonstrates how even articles take a perilous path to publication. I submitted the original seminar paper on December 2, 1980. In 1981 and 1982, with very little revision, I submitted it to 40 different student-edited law reviews, all of which rejected it, largely on the basis that they wanted cutting-edge modern law discussions, not historical studies. Two historical journals also declined. In December 1982 I tried a journal specializing in legal history, where I probably should have begun. The *American Journal of Legal History* responded in late January 1983 and indicated interest in the piece but only if I made certain significant revisions their outside reader had requested.

The ideas for this major revision appealed to me, and I hurried to re-write the piece, re-submitting it in early March. Their outside reader then accepted the article with minor caveats, and I agreed to most but not all of the minor revisions now suggested. The *Journal* then accepted the article subject to my making the final revisions I had accepted. I got those in by mid-May 1983, and the article then appeared in print in January 1984. This search for a publisher and then the give-and-take of revisions is typical of scholarly article publication.

The idea of this article was to examine very closely a change in an important extremely detailed aspect of liability for loss of a slave during times when slaves were leased out to free persons or corporations. I wanted to show that this change, accomplished through a new written civil code, was the product of the code's author, who individually believed that one legal route was better than another. It was offered as a small scale assault on the reigning theory of American legal history that law changes as a result of a clash between social and economic interests, and not through intellect or reasoning.

I sent an offprint to Lawrence Friedman, the director of the NEH Legal History for Law Professors seminar at Stanford in 1982, and in many respects my mentor. Lawrence is one of the leading American legal historians to promote the instrumentalist viewpoint, that law is a function not of intellect but social and economic forces. Since I was saying the opposite in this minor example, I was sure he would be interested. He responded:

> I read it with great interest. I don't say that I disagree with your approach, and I certainly like the general idea. ... it may well be that "individual intellect and fortuity" make a shortrun difference. Perhaps it is more important to note that the <u>kind</u> of problem presented is determined absolutely by social conditions. How could it be otherwise?
>
> At any rate, your piece was thoughtful and useful. The world of deanships may be worse off, but no doubt legal scholarship will be better off for your recent change of status.

During the period of my deanship at Old College, summer and fall, 1983 and continuing on to late January, my scholarship stalled. I had too much work to do, egos to be stroked, all as described earlier. Once fired as dean, I was completely free for the balance of that semester, not having a course to teach that term, then the summer, and with another year thereafter, 1984-1985, with a very light load. So I turned back to scholarship.

My most immediate deadline was the January 1985 issue of *Journal of the West*. The magazine had appointed me in February 1983 as the guest editor of the themed issue on "Law in the West" that would appear first as a magazine issue and then, with one additional article that I would not be concerned with, republished in book form. By the time I left Detroit I had solicited contributors for articles, but their writing did not begin coming in before I was in Reno. The last of the articles did not arrive until January 1985. Some of the pieces were in good shape, but most appeared to be throwaways from earlier work and were in wretched editorial condition. I did a great deal of editing and had substantial correspondence with Robin Higham of the *Journal of the West*. Only two of the eight authors I shepherded in this process had submitted graphics or even thought of illustrations, so I had to think over possible photographs, and badger state historical societies for reproductions. In the case of the Tombstone, Arizona courthouse, I hired a photographer to take some pictures. On top of all this, I needed to write the introduction.

The magazine issue appeared a bit later than its scheduled January 1985, but the book appeared on time, in July 1985. The production involved a lot of work, at least for the editor. In my judgment, the final product was not worth the effort. The problem was that the actual articles themselves were beyond my control. Massive editing was needed, and I did it, but I could not re-write entire articles for which I had not done the research. I resolved never to edit another book, and I have not.

Late in my time in Reno the editors of *The Californians* asked me to contribute an article. This journal, owned and edited by Michael and Jean Sherrell, was an earnest attempt to publish real history in a popular format. It solicited articles on California history from historians, high school history teachers, and amateurs who had a concentrated interest in California's past. Jean Sherrell scouted out appropriate graphics to accompany the articles and even had the text fact-checked by competent historians. It was a real shame that a serious journal so conceived and directed toward a popular audience could publish its bi-monthly issues for only 13 years, 1983-1996, before failing financially. The Sherrells worked to keep it afloat, offering pre-paid subscriptions, various printing services, and soliciting donations, yet it unfortunately failed.

I welcomed their request for an article and decided on an abbreviated popularization of my book chapter on domestic relations law in Mexican California. This ultimately appeared while I was in Birmingham as "Sin, Sex & Separation in Mexican California: Her Law of Domestic Relations." I did some research beyond what I had already done and found a formal separation agreement in the Mexican California archives that I wish had been available for the book. I did this additional research and some initial writing for this article while still in Reno, but at least half of the work was done later.

Work on my first full book constituted the major writing project of my Reno years. Before beginning the push in January 1984, I had prepared incomplete written versions of two chapters, together with a vaguely sketched outline of the book as a whole. I had the paper that I had used for Professor Green's seminar for the LL.M. degree, which was to be the basis for the book's chapter on criminal law in Mexican California, although it needed much work. I also had the law review article on domestic relations law, although it also needed work. Most importantly the research was complete, or very nearly so. I had all of this done when I left Detroit for Reno.

As soon as my decanal career ended, I galvanized myself into a writing mode. I had all my research papers and notes with me, and the first thing I did was to decide what order of chapter writing made the most sense. The logic of the evidence and a desire not to repeat observations combined to dictate an order to the chapters and also a logical order in writing them. I also made a list of what *specific* matters I still needed to research. For me, as for most scholars, the research is much more enjoyable than the writing. This explains why some 50% of doctoral candidates in history complete all of their course requirements and oral examinations yet never complete their dissertations, to become known as ABDs, all but dissertation. It also explains why so many university professors jabber on about the book they are writing, except they just need to do a little more research, then end up dying with no manuscript ever written. Determined not to fall into this comfortable trap, I charged myself to articulate precisely the exact matter on which I needed to take away any of my valuable writing time for additional research. I had plenty enough data, and the desire for anything more carried the burden of persuasion in my allocation of time.

Then came much more detailed outlines than I had made before on exactly what was to be covered in each chapter. I seized on each chapter as I was writing it, and made detailed work plans. I prepared day-by-day charts of what concepts I would write on that day, keyed to the detailed outlines. I put dates for each day's writing in the order of the provisions of the outline, and alongside the dates I had a separate column in which I wrote in red ink the actual date in which I had written the material allotted for that date. I could thereby see at a glance how far ahead or behind I was to my plan. I made such a chart for each chapter. Looking back at these charts, some of which I kept, it was clear that while I never got ahead of my plan, I seldom was very far behind. The charts served as wonderful discipline.

I worked steadily and calmly, in slow increments, and made my way through the chapters. I made no dashing charges into the writing, but worked at the pace of an ordinary day's work, and the chapters seemed to build themselves. I had so often in college dashed off papers in an overnight rush, but I learned in 1984 how much more productive I could be through steady and calm work habits. By early summer 1984 I knew it was time to begin thinking of publishers.

I sent out inquiry letters to the University of California Press and the Stanford University Press and received their form rejection letters, saying that my project did not appear to be within the needs of their current list, or similar nonsense. Then I thought of the University of Oklahoma Press. It enjoys an excellent reputation for publishing good western history. I sent five completed chapters plus a one-page summary of the book as a whole to Oklahoma in mid-July 1984. That I had five complete chapters says much about the progress I had made in the six months since I was fired as dean.

Within a few weeks I heard from John Drayton, Oklahoma's Editor-in-Chief. He said they were impressed by what I had sent and were prepared to send the completed chapters to outside readers if I could assure them they had an exclusive on the manuscript, pending the reports of the readers and the contract itself. I thought that was fair if they were going to the trouble and expense of sending it to their outside readers, and I agreed. By early fall the first reader's report was back. John Drayton told me that it was the finest first review, almost glowing, that he had ever seen. The reviewer noted in part:

> I think the scholarship is excellent. I was very impressed with the detailed research which the author has obviously done into Mexican legal documents which are difficult to locate and which require an excellent knowledge of Spanish. I was also impressed with the breadth of scholarship evidenced by the author who is clearly familiar with a great amount and range of American legal history. ... I greatly enjoyed reading the manuscript. I found the text and footnotes to be easily read and easily understood. ... The style of the manuscript is uniformly excellent. I definitely would publish this manuscript. I think the book is excellent in every respect. I was just tremendously impressed with the manuscript.

The second reader's report was not negative but was critical and requested many changes. Drayton sent it to me and asked me what I thought. I sent back an eight page letter, accepting a few of the suggestions, but on the whole attacking the premises from which many suggestions were derived. Drayton replied that I certainly had not been sparing in giving him what I thought, and he was happy I could defend my position so heartily. The contract arrived in early February 1985, and I sent a signed copy back to Oklahoma on February 10, 1985. I signed it over dinner with JoAnne at Reno's finest French restaurant. I had been writing during the back and forth with Oklahoma, and by spring 1985 had eight completed chapters. I lacked only two things: the domestic relations chapter, although I had a preliminary version published earlier in 1979, and the concluding chapter.

At this juncture, spring 1985, Tom Green, my dissertation advisor, telephoned to make an offer I could not refuse. He was off to a Stanford think tank for academic year 1985-1986, and if there was any way we could do it, he wanted to accelerate the process of the dissertation and award me the S.J.D. degree that spring, even if this was before the book came out. Tom had looked at and approved of the chapters as I finished them, going back to the earliest days when I was working on the LL.M. right to the present. He knew what I had and what I needed. He suggested that I write the conclusion forthwith and then submit the version previously published in *Pepperdine Law Review* as the domestic relations chapter for the dissertation. That, plus a very informal oral exam with two other law school faculty, my dissertation committee, would be enough for the degree. I could finish the incomplete domestic relations chapter later for the book, and I need not worry about submitting it for approval, even if I made changes, as Tom thought I had matters firmly in hand.

In early May, JoAnne and I went back to Ann Arbor with our children. I had a very easy oral examination, after which, pursuant to custom, the committee took me to a pub near the law school for a congratulatory drink. On May 10, 1985, I received my doctorate from the University of Michigan.

In addition to scholarly articles, the editing of the *Law in the West* book, and my dissertation, I also participated in scholarly conferences. I delivered a talk at the American Historical Association's annual conference in San Francisco, December 29, 1983, on "Americans in Trouble: Expatriate Experience in the Criminal Law of Mexican California." John Wunder, a co-participant in the 1982 summer National Endowment for the Humanities seminar at Stanford, organized a panel based on the borderland legal developments of American expatriates, Asians, Indians, and other minorities. He recruited me and I prepared a talk that was a broad-based cultural analysis of why the American expatriates in Mexican California regarded the local legal system so negatively while at the same time they were treated so favorably. I adapted and shortened my criminal law chapter of the dissertation and book to prepare the talk. Like most graduate students writing dissertations, the talk based on a dissertation chapter was designed to elicit critique and feedback that I might consider to make my dissertation as sharp as possible.

I delivered a short paper on the general topic, "The Mexican California Legal System," at a conference held at California State University at Long Beach, November 2-3, 1984 based on the equally general topic of "Rancho to Resort: Two Centuries of Diversity and Development in Southern California." Again, the paper was an abridgement of the civil law chapter on the Mexican legal system from the dissertation.

I served as a commentator for two papers presented at a session on "Constitutionalism in the American West," at a conference of the American Historical Association's Pacific Coast Branch, August 15-18, 1984, at the University of Washington, Seattle. In addition, an invitation arrived from Joseph McKnight of Southern Methodist University to give a paper at a panel he was organizing for the fall 1985 meeting of the American Society for Legal History. The theme of the panel was "Legal History in the Spanish Borderlands." I accepted, and although I did some of the work on this paper in Reno, the delivery itself and most of its preparation took place while in Birmingham.

As an advancing junior scholar, during the Reno years I received commissions for book reviews, and wrote and published four short book reviews, 1983-1985. I read a fifth and wrote a review in Reno, but publication came later. My personal reading suffered in Reno as a result of time being lost to hassles with Leary at Old College, doctor appointments and other care for my son John, and difficulties at home with JoAnne. Nevertheless, I did get in some reading summer 1983 - summer 1985.

Over that two year period I read five books of legal history including Thomas A. Lund's *American Wildlife Law,* a superb study of the social, economic, and political forces that have changed American wildlife law and shaped it over the centuries. I also read many complete books as research for my dissertation.

This left a small number of books that I read simply for my personal edification. After four years I achieved my goal of reading the Bible cover to cover. Of course, I also read many other books in those years. I count having read the complete Bible as one of my highest personal accomplishments, right up there with fathering my children, obtaining my doctorate, and writing my books. I also read: Robert Adams, *Decadent Societies*; Gustave Flaubert, *Madame Bovery*; Joan Haslip, *The Crown of Mexico: Maximilian and his Empress Carlotta*; Kenneth Roberts, *Boon Island*; Isaac Bashevis Singer, *The Spinoza of Market Street*; Stephen Spender, *The Year of the Young Rebels Revisited*; Kenneth Coil, *A Comprehensive View of Freemasonry* (I became a Mason in Reno, primarily because I was asked); and Benjamin Hart, *Poisoned Ivy*. It is a short but very diversified list. During the first half of 1985, while I was bearing down hardest on my dissertation, I read not a single book for any purpose.

One matter remains concerning my intellectual development during the Reno years. It was in these years, 1983-1985, that I began to form my hostility toward "political correctness," and began to regard it as an affirmative menace to intellectual integrity. In June 1984 I received a personalized letter from the regional chairman of the Dartmouth Alumni Fund, pointing out correctly that I had not been exactly constant in my giving to Dartmouth and expressing the hope that my check would be in shortly. I replied:

> I'm responding to tell you why you will not receive an annual gift this year. In short, I'm disgusted at the witch-hunts the Dartmouth administration conducts against those who disagree with its trendy liberal thought.
>
> I hold absolutely no brief for the Indian symbol, fraternities, ROTC, homosexual groups, or the merits of the other current controversies at Dartmouth. I simply do not have strong thoughts on these subjects. But I do vehemently object to the administration's attempts to willfully suppress the traditional, conservative viewpoints toward these issues. These actions are not only unworthy of Dartmouth but are antithetical to the

very essence of a liberal arts college and its function to provide a free and open examination of ideas.

By now the student-written and conservative *Dartmouth Review* has been accepted, and the administration is not as oppressive. But Dartmouth remains committed to extremely liberal positions on almost all issues. I have backed away from my not-one-penny attitude and have donated to Dartmouth alumni fund drives, yet not nearly as liberally as to Stanford Law School to which I feel a greater sense of gratitude.

After I was fired as Dean by John Leary, the President of Old College, I immediately began a search for a new job. He could not fire me as a faculty member, as I was tenured as a professor. However, I thought it was very likely that the school would never become accredited, and there was no point to staying on to the bitter end. After all the turmoil over John's birth, JoAnne's critical attitude toward Reno, and my disgust with Leary's attitudes and actions, I wanted to leave as quickly as I could. I took a three-pronged approach in the job search.

First, I contacted the legal academics I knew best, Tom Green at Michigan, Lawrence Friedman at Stanford, and John Reid of New York University. All said they would keep their eyes open for any available positions, but frankly, nothing came of those contacts. The second approach was to contact my old employer, Detroit College of Law, to inquire whether it might have an opening. I advised both Clarke Johnson, a former colleague who had become Associate Dean, and also Dean John Abbott, of my situation and my hope to return to DCL. Abbott responded that the hiring for 1984-1985 was complete, but there might be an opening for the 1985-1986 year and beyond. The hiring process for law faculty is so slow, explained earlier, that when I was fired as Dean of Old College School of Law in January 1984, I assumed that the earliest I could get another job would be beginning in the fall of 1985. So Abbott's response was not troubling. Johnson and other former colleagues favored my return and lobbied Abbott to that effect, but by the fall of 1984 he decided that DCL would not be hiring anyone for 1985-1986.

The third approach was to go through the faculty recruitment conference of the Association of American Law Schools. I had been following this alternative all along, as I could not necessarily count on success with the first two. I had my paperwork filed by August 1984, and attended the Faculty Recruitment Conference, December 7-8, 1984 in Chicago. I stayed with my father and Sue in Elgin with my family, and commuted into Chicago for my interviews.

I thought the interviews went much better than my earlier attempt to get a teaching job at the St. Louis conference in 1977. I was less nervous, and I had a more solid record behind me. I was invited on callbacks to two institutions, New England School of Law in Boston and Cumberland School of Law in Birmingham. I had already been in Boston dozens of times, and I even had a general sense of what to expect at New England School of Law as I had been called back to interview there in 1978. Birmingham, on the other hand, was new and really surprised me. I expected flat land, an industrial version of Plains, Georgia. Birmingham would be Detroit south, flat and with factory smokestacks sticking up here and there. But, no. Most of the old steel industry was closed, the air was clean, and the terrain was not at all flat. I discovered that Birmingham is surrounded by high rolling hills with abundant pine and oak trees. The campus of Samford University is in one group of those hills and has a sweeping view. And I discovered that Cumberland School of Law had neo-Georgian architecture, as did the entire Samford campus, and had a beautiful wooden interior, a good library, and wonderful facilities.

My interviews at Cumberland went well. I received several questions about my scholarship and publication interests, and there was quite a bit of interest in my forthcoming book with Oklahoma. It seemed apparent to me that the school wanted a productive scholar who was active in writing and publishing. I was delighted in discovering this as it meant that there would likely be financial support and encouragement for my work. What impressed me most about Cumberland, however, was the spirit of calm and peace that pervaded both the law school and the university, so very different from the chaos in Reno. I was therefore not slow to accept the offer I soon received for a tenure track position in the fall of 1985. I would keep my rank of full professor, and although the university had a policy against new hires coming in as tenured, I would have a fast track of one year before tenure consideration. The tenure delay did not bother me in the slightest, and the prospect of moving to Birmingham delighted me. JoAnne, so often critical of my decisions once they were made, actually thanked me for getting the family out of Reno.

Chapter 6

The Early Years in Birmingham:
Summer 1985 – Summer 1990

When I left Reno, the University of Oklahoma Press had already accepted my manuscript, *Law and Community on the Mexican American Frontier: Anglo-American Expatriates and the Clash of Legal Traditions, 1821-1846*, but the actual text was not quite complete. Specifically, the domestic relations chapter had to be re-written from the form originally published as a law review article. It needed tightening and some slight alternations, and the citation of the original Mexican documents had to replace the translations I had used as citations in the law review piece. Additionally, the concluding chapter needed reconceptualization as the version submitted to Michigan for the dissertation requirement had been slapped together to meet my dissertation advisor Tom Green's time requirements. I worked on these during the fall, and then sent the revisions to Oklahoma, which forwarded the manuscript to the copy editor. She spent two weeks making several grammatical and stylistic changes, some of which I accepted and others, especially where they changed my intended meaning, I rejected. It required close working with the proposed changes and my responses.

I sent the copyedited manuscript back to Oklahoma sometime in February 1986. At that point, the managing editor at Oklahoma decided that the manuscript looked clean enough that it could go directly to page proofs and skip the galley sheets process. In those days it was not so easy to make changes to page proofs, whereas there were few costs involved with changes to galley sheets. I had given a close read to the changes the copy editor proposed, but had not yet proofread the entire manuscript. When I received the page proofs for final proofreading I spent many nights in the law library going over the manuscript. I was aghast by what I saw: hundreds of printer's errors and worse, hundreds of my own errors. My own errors were a genuine burden. The publisher, University of Oklahoma Press, could require the printer to correct the printer's errors, but the cost of correcting my errors, about $250, was later charged to my royalties.

The last of my corrections after proofreading left for the publisher in the spring of 1986. Then came the long wait for the printing and binding. Most university presses send two copies of a published book to the author by first class mail, and the balance of the complementary copies, usually ten in total, by UPS or parcel post. Eventually my first two copies arrived on March 23, 1987. I was so thrilled! It was my first real book, as I came to consider the work published as *Law in the West*, neither really a book nor mine. It was only a short 81 page paperback in magazine format, and therefore questionably even a book. It was not really my own, either, since I had only done editorial work, albeit heavy duty, and had myself written only an introduction. But *Law and Community* was all mine, and I could not hold myself back from showing it off to friends, family, and colleagues.

Reviews of scholarly books unhappily take about a year from publication of a book to appear. In my case it was worth the long wait since the reviews were stunning. Most of the reviewers caught my central point that while American and British expatriates in Mexican California were treated fairly under the Mexican legal system, the expatriates still hated the Mexican California legal system, not because of any deficiencies in it, but simply because it was different in several respects from the common-law system with which the Americans and British were familiar. The Californio system's chief concern was the reconciliation of the parties to a dispute, and the common-law system's chief concern was with clearly defining winners and losers and providing efficient methods to collect precise judgments.

The book received favorable reviews in the two leading general journals of American history, *The American Historical Review* and *The Journal of American History*. It also received some absolutely glowing tributes. *The Midwest Book Review* called *Law and Community* "excellent. Good writing, well presented, profoundly interesting; these are justly earned words of praise for work this outstanding." Theodore Grivas, in *The Pacific Historical Review,* wrote that "the welcomed appearance of this impeccably researched and skillfully written study by David J. Langum has filled a glaring void in the history of legal institutions in Mexican California. ... One can only be impressed with this monograph." Christian G. Fritz in *The Western Historical Quarterly* wrote that the book "is a marvelous work of legal history and provides an excellent model for future studies of this type. [A] richly informative and insightful study." He went on to praise my "extensive research in legal archival materials." Of course the actual reviews were all much longer and more analytical than the conclusions I have quoted.

The reviews that pleased me most were the gracious comments of the leading historians in this particular field. John Phillip Reid, one of the leading American legal historians and also with much experience in western legal history, wrote in the *Law and History Review* that "David Langum introduces a new discipline to western historiography ... by asking questions that can be answered only by researching sources peculiar to the settlement of the west. ... This book makes ... stunning contributions to western history." In fact, in his introductory remarks at a session of the Western Historical Association on October 12, 1989, John made the kind yet audacious claim that *Law and Community* was *the best* book on western legal history. David J. Weber, the leading historian of the Spanish and Mexican Borderlands, and the fellow with whom I crossed swords only a few years before over the "Californios and the Image of Indolence" article, had high praise for my book. He wrote in *The Hispanic American Historical Review* that "building his explanation on an assiduous analysis of court cases, Langum has produced the best study that we have of frontier legal practice in any region of the Mexican borderlands."

In addition to favorable reviews, the book went on to garner not just one but two separate book prizes. The first was the Hurst Prize, named in honor of the premier American legal historian James Willard Hurst, and awarded to me by the Law and Society Association. Lawrence Friedman kindly alerted the Association's prize committee to *Law and Community*, as I was told that Oklahoma had failed to submit it to them for consideration. Cumberland Law School paid for my travel expenses to Vail, Colorado, to receive the prize and accompanying honorarium at the Society's annual conference, and make a few remarks. I believe that the new Cumberland dean,

Parham Williams, was so generous with travel funds because of his commitment to nourishing and increasing scholarship at the school. The Hurst Prize is the leading book award available to legal historians, and although my books went on to win six additional prizes, this first one, the Hurst Prize, has always seemed very special to me.

Law and Community won a second book award, this one from the California Historical Society, its J.S. Holliday Award. Dean Williams offered the funds to travel to the Society's annual meeting, to be held at the Ahwanhee Hotel in Yosemite. I thanked him but declined, advising him that I would have some research trips to take in connection with the next book, and it might be prudent to save that money for the new project. Instead, I asked Harlan Hague, with whom I was collaborating on the Larkin biography then underway, to accept the award on my behalf. He was pleased to do so.

It was only after I received the actual certificate from Harlan that I noticed the commendation was specific to the book. Most book prize plaques or certificates say that they are awarded for some general reasons, such as the Hurst Prize's statement that I was being honored for "Outstanding Scholarship in Legal History." On the other hand, the California Historical Society's certificate stated I had won the award "for excellence of scholarship in the area of 19th-century California history, having provided a new interpretive approach representing a significant achievement in historical research." I was pleased that they recognized the enormous research involved in its writing.

In this period, summer 1985 to summer 1990, I wrote only four mostly insignificant articles, fewer than I had for a comparable period of time five years earlier. That was because I was busy with two books. Likewise, in the following ten years, 1990-2000, I wrote three books and very few significant articles. From 2000 to 2020, when I wrote three books but over 20 years, I had the time to return to more significant articles.

In 1988 my 9 page biographical sketch plus bibliography of historian Herbert Eugene Bolton appeared in John R. Wunder, ed., *Historians of the American Frontier: A Bio-Bibliographical Sourcebook*. This was an encyclopedia entry, and although longer than many I wrote subsequently, it is hardly a significant article. During the 1970s-1990s, scholars often wrote entries for a burgeoning number of historical and legal-historical encyclopedias. The Internet has made these largely obsolete. The next year *Cumberland Law Review* published my remarks made at its annual banquet, "Autonomy and the *Cumberland Law Review*," again not a significant work but of some interest because of controversies then swirling about the *Review* that will be discussed later in this chapter. I re-wrote the domestic relations chapter of my *Law and Community* into a more watered down popular form for publication in *The Californians*, in 1987.

I was so fascinated by the Mexican notion of mandatory conciliation as a precondition of a formal lawsuit that I thought I would write an entire book on conciliation, as introduced into Spanish law and into the Spanish Borderlands, and then as continued on in the Mexican jurisdictions of California, New Mexico, and Texas, and then finally, roughly set aside during the American period. I began gathering documents on the use of conciliation in Texas and New Mexico, as well as the background for conciliation into Spanish law, in the Cadiz constitution of 1812. I remember explaining my new project to Joe McKnight, the leading legal historian of Hispanic Texas. It was at some historical conference held at the Biltmore Hotel in Los Angeles, and we must have had a couple of drinks, because after my detailed explanation, Joe remarked that my proposed book would be of great interest to about five people.

That set me to thinking that perhaps an entire book on conciliation would be too narrow and of little interest. However, I had already gathered all I needed for what I had planned as an introductory chapter. So I worked on that as a separate article that I published as "The Introduction of Conciliation into Modern Spanish Law and its Practice in the Spanish-American Borderlands," in Manuel J. Peláez, ed., *Studies in Roman Law & Legal History* (Málaga, Spain: University of Málaga, 1989). It was my first piece published abroad, and that pleased me. That was also the only article for this entire five year period that I would personally call significant.

Scholarly journals increased their requests for me to author book reviews. In the ten years from 1975 through the summer of 1985, I published nine commissioned book reviews. For the next five years, half of the previous time, I was commissioned again to write nine book reviews. So my rate of commissioned book reviewing had precisely doubled in 1985-1990. Many of these new reviews appeared in fine journals such as the *Pacific Historical Review,* *Hispanic American Historical Review, Southern California Quarterly* (twice), and the *American Journal of Legal History.*

Cumberland assigned me to teach courses in Equity and also Law & Society, or some similar name, for the fall 1985 term. The Law & Society was no problem as I could incorporate a lot of American legal history into that. I had never taught Equity before and had to spend considerable time preparing for class. I learned much more about equitable remedies than I ever knew before.

After this unusual fall term, my teaching settled into a pattern for the remainder of this period and for the rest of my career. Property at Cumberland was then a 6 unit course and included both personal and real property, i.e. land law. That constituted half of my teaching load. Evidence was a 3 unit course that I also taught every year. An elective in American Legal History filled the remaining 3 units, about half the years as a survey course with a casebook and half the years as a seminar with varied themes. 12 units per year is the standard load for law teachers, meaning 4-6 teaching hours per week for each of the year's two semesters. Law faculty typically teach half the load of undergraduate faculty and earn nearly twice as much.

These three courses, Property, Evidence, and Legal History, constituted a good combination for me. American Legal History is my personal field, and Property requires some discussion of 16th and 17th century English legal history to understand the development of Property law. I love Evidence because of its complexity. It is a code course, meaning that a thorough understanding of the Federal Rules of Evidence is more important than the particular cases we study. The Rules are intricate, with many exceptions and qualifiers to a general rule, and even exceptions to the exceptions. I always told my Evidence students at the beginning of the term that their essential job was to hear the Federal Rules of Evidence as discussed in class and then read, mark, learn, and inwardly digest them.

I spent much time with my seminar students, having an hour's conference over each stage of the course: selection of topic within the theme for the course, bibliography, detailed outline, and first draft. I helped the students find materials they had not thought of, critiqued outlines for typically not having enough detail, and spent hours on the first drafts, making extensive editing and organization suggestions. The papers needed to be at least 30 pages in length to satisfy a school policy that every student had to write a 30 page research paper at some point in their law school career. Many students told me that in their undergraduate work they had never been required to write such an extensive research paper.

Student evaluations were mixed. Some students thought I was condescending and critical, or worse; some thought I was an excellent teacher for those who were prepared. Almost all agreed that I was well-prepared and very knowledgeable about my subjects. I think as a general matter the better students liked how I taught. I recall once meeting a former student at a jazz club. He told me that I should never change anything about the way I taught Evidence. He had recently received his marks on the bar examination, and his highest score on the entire multi-state bar exam, the part given across the country, was in Evidence.

Another former student took me to dinner at the Highland Bar & Grill, Birmingham's premier restaurant, to thank me for what I had taught him. It is only hearsay but a lady bartender at Joe Bar, a sophisticated watering hole frequented by Cumberland Law students, told me that several law students had commented to her about what a good professor I was. I got along well with most of my students. I occasionally saw them out and about the town, from grocery stores or restaurants to night clubs, and we had a good rapport. Every spring the freshman class put on a show, the Freshman Follies, in which they spoofed or criticized the faculty, sort of an institutionally channeled pay-back time. Some of my colleagues refused to attend these shows, too thin-skinned to view even a mild parody. I think they were worried about criticism. However, I attended regularly. The student cast went out for drinks afterward, and I always joined them briefly, bought a few pitchers of beer, and congratulated them on their performance, all in a sincere effort to show them that I did not take their critiques personally, and in any event I had a thick skin.

I served on several faculty committees, as do all faculty members. During these years I was at various times on the committees for student recruitment, faculty recruitment, and rank and tenure. Faculty recruitment is now held annually in Washington, D.C., and the year I was there for that grueling process I decided I would stay away from the standard hotel, even though I returned there for our interviews with faculty prospects. I had never stayed at the Cosmos Club, an exclusive traditionally male urban club. I could use their facilities because my own club, the University Club of Chicago, has a reciprocal arrangement with the Cosmos Club. I mention this because I was fascinated by the severity of understatement the Cosmos Club exhibits. Large portraits of its most illustrious members hang on the walls of the anteroom to its dining room, men such as former Presidents Wilson, Taft, and Hoover. A nameplate beneath each portrait gives the life span, the years of membership in the Cosmos Club, and their occupation. Here is where the understatement appears. All three of these men had been President of the United States, and in addition William Howard Taft had been the Chief Justice of the United States. Yet Taft's occupation in the nameplate is stated only as "lawyer." The occupation for President Hoover is given as "mining engineer," and the occupation of President Wilson is rendered as "political scientist."

The committee I was most pleased to be on was the Policy Committee. This committee meets directly with the dean and has a quasi-administrative role in dealing with controversies and setting policies, with academic policies being subject to the ultimate control of the full faculty. I think the Latin phrase *primus inter pares*, first among equals, best describes the position of the Policy Committee. It is the only faculty committee that is elected by the faculty as distinct from appointed by the dean. I was pleased that several colleagues asked me to run for election to this committee, and that my colleagues as a whole held enough confidence in me that I was elected three consecutive times for the annual terms. I did absolutely no politicking for my election, although I did have opponents. After my second term I was asked by various faculty members to stay on the Policy Committee for an additional term, and I agreed but on the express condition that this term would be my last for a while. Later in the 1990s I again served on the Policy Committee.

Law faculty are expected not only to teach and engage in scholarship but also to be involved in some aspect of public service, *pro bono* work as it is called, short for *pro bono publico*, or the good of the public. I was not particularly strong in this field of work, but I did do some and in later years much more. In the late 1980s I talked before several parent support groups on estate planning for parents of severely disabled or retarded children. These children are probably destined for group homes, following the termination of parental caretaking through death or disability, and also, for the less disabled, the desire for some peer socialization. Unless a parent is exceedingly wealthy the cost of group living will inevitably be borne by Medicaid, which provides minimal care. Within certain limits, however, parents may establish support trusts to provide extras for their disabled children in a group home, for example additional clothing, a television, and the like. I had a certain amount of credibility, not just because I was a law professor, but because I was also a parent of a severely disabled child with cerebral palsy. I spoke before groups of parents who had children with cerebral palsy, Rett Syndrome, mental disorders, and so forth. In addition the dean and I spoke at a local ladies' literary club one time in late 1989. I've forgotten what Dean Parham Williams spoke on, but I talked about the abolition of trial by ordeal and the rise of trial by jury in the 13th century.

In 1990 Alabama was in the midst of codifying its rules of evidence, converting them from a system based on accumulated court decisions into a written code. A member of the lawyers' committee charged with drafting this code, who was a former colleague, asked me if I had any thoughts on reforming Alabama's rules of evidence. I said yes and convinced him of the desirability of simplifying Alabama's rules on evidentiary presumptions. He himself then convinced his committee, and ultimately the reform I originally brought forward, modest really in the larger picture, was made law in Alabama. It was satisfying that I personally could make a very slight but still real difference.

Also satisfying were the tutorials I held with a young lady, Jane Wang, from mainland China who, somehow and for some reason unknown to me, became a student at Cumberland School of Law in Birmingham, Alabama. She came to my office in the spring of 1989 and told me she really wanted to learn about the history of the American legal system, but could not fit my course on American Legal History into her schedule. I arranged for her to meet with me in my office for some very informal tutorials. I gave her readings in advance, and then we would talk for an hour about various aspects of American legal history. This continued on for about 10 weeks. It was a remarkable situation. She received no academic credit for her work with me. She did her reading and talked with me for the sole reason that I had some knowledge that she wanted to learn. How could any teacher resist putting in some extra, uncompensated time to help such a student?

During these five years there were two separate tenure battles. The first was within the law school itself. Prior to 1986, Cumberland School of Law did not have a real tenure policy. If a faculty member taught for several years and generated no significant controversies, the dean simply granted tenure. The new dean, Parham Williams, who arrived in 1985, the same year I did, viewed tenure as one of his many means to increase the level of sophistication and scholarship at the school. Within the first year of his administration, acting through faculty committees, he proposed a more specific tenure policy for the law school. The proposal required two major published law review articles or their equivalent for tenure as a full professor, and one major article for advancement from assistant to associate professor.

This would not seem to be controversial, yet there were "old boys" among the faculty who opposed it. Those already having tenure would not be affected by the new plan, but there were a number of faculty who had taught for three or four years who did not have tenure, and they would be required to publish in order to obtain it. Many faculty who did not have tenure had friends among the tenured faculty who were disposed to oppose the proposal to help their untenured friends. It seems incredible today, when Cumberland is in the mainstream of legal education with a frequently publishing faculty, but in 1985 very few Cumberland law professors published anything. It was just not expected, not a part of their job duties. After a great deal of wrangling in several confrontational meetings, the law faculty adopted the writing requirement for tenure by a narrow margin.

Two years later the university itself adopted a tenure policy. It was much lighter in its writing requirements, but with very little fuss the central administration agreed that individual schools within the university, such as the law school, could adopt more strenuous policies than those imposed by the university.

At the end of the 1980s a more significant issue arose as to what tenure at Samford meant. As a generality, when an academic institution grants tenure to a faculty member it means that he or she cannot be terminated without cause, generally limited to sexual improprieties, demonstrated incompetence, or persistent insubordination, for instance refusing to teach courses assigned by the dean or department chairman. Furthermore, such misfeasance must be specifically charged, a hearing held, with a neutral party making the ultimate determination. In short, faculty members cannot be fired because an administrator is angry with them, or is unhappy with their performance, without being specific about what is wrong.

When Samford University adopted its tenure policy, the central administration placed it in the faculty handbook, with specifics of how tenure was obtained and how tenure could be revoked only with cause, and through procedural safeguards. However, that same faculty handbook also clearly stated, and at the beginning of the faculty status section, that the trustees could alter the handbook at any time, that the handbook was not a contract, or "a promise of employment for a definite duration." From spring of 1989 through that fall, the law faculty engaged in a struggle with the central administration. We felt that this clause in the handbook effectively nullified tenure. What could tenure, not revoked for cause, mean if it did not entail a promise of employment until death, retirement, or resignation? Its essence was guaranteed and sustained employment over a long term. If the trustees could just vote to nullify the handbook or just nullify the tenure provisions, what real meaning was there behind a grant of tenure?

We gradually persuaded the undergraduate faculty to at least informally endorse our view. After two fruitless conferences with the Provost, I suggested to him that the law school appoint a small committee of two or three full professors, and that this committee meet directly with President Corts to see if we could resolve this issue. The law school tenure negotiating committee met with Corts in his office on September 1, 1989. He was kind and courteous, a true gentleman. Even more important he genuinely understood our concerns and the underlying issues. He was candid enough to say that most of the university trustees owned or managed businesses and it was difficult for them to think of faculty as other than employees and it was equally difficult for them to think of employment as being other than at will, where an employer could terminate an employee at any time. Corts suggested that perhaps we could add to the non-contractual language in the handbook a clause such as "except as affected by tenure."

I thought that was a real breakthrough, although some law faculty felt it was not sufficiently clear. The law faculty reluctantly agreed to such language as being probably the best we could get. Many individual undergraduate faculty thanked the law faculty for making a stand that they felt powerless to make. The law faculty has always felt more empowered because of the firm support of the ABA and the Association of American Law Schools, and also the ability to jump ship as it were, and work in an alternate profession outside academe, the actual practice of law. The general non-contractual and always-subject-to-trustee-amendment language has remained, but the limiting proviso has expanded and now reads that "nothing in this handbook shall be construed as limiting the rights of tenured faculty members."

Dean Parham Williams made great strides over these five years to promote scholarship among the Cumberland faculty. He did that in several ways. The most obvious was to hire faculty who were committed to research, writing, and publication. Most of the new faculty hires under Williams turned out to be true scholars.

Another way Parham promoted scholarship was by salary enhancements. Those faculty most involved in scholarship received the largest raises. In my own case, I began at Cumberland with a very modest salary of $43,000 for the academic year 1985-1986. In four years, 1989-1990, with two books written as well as a modest number of articles published, I was up to $74,000. That is an average salary increase of 18% per annum. Salary information is confidential at Cumberland, but I have no doubt that several others who were publishing widely were receiving similar increases.

Parham was liberal in paying the costs of attending conferences. During this period I attended the conference of the American Society for Legal History annually and most years the Association of American Law Schools annual meeting, and Cumberland paid all my expenses to these conferences regardless of whether I was presenting a paper or not. I also gave papers at conferences of the American Historical Association, The Western Historical Association, and other historical societies. Cumberland paid for all my expenses for these other conferences at which I gave a paper. Parham also caused the school to pay for all my expenses on two separate trips, one to Vail, Colorado and the other to Denver, Colorado, to accept book awards for my writing. Most generous of all, although after this time period, Cumberland paid for my air flights to and from The Netherlands to attend a conference where I had been invited to present a paper. Of course, it was not me individually that was being recognized by this level of generosity, it was scholarship. He also paid my colleagues generous travel grants to meetings.

In my own field of legal history/biography, and I think probably in other fields of legal scholarship as well, a book, a monograph of the type published by a university press, requires at least one, usually two, and sometimes three research trips to an archive, manuscript collection, or, in the case of a biography, to various locations to interview key friends and colleagues of the biographical subject. Parham was most generous in research grants, which would be over and above conference expenses. I am certain he was equally helpful with other scholars needing assistance for research trips.

Some non-producing Cumberland faculty complained that their class schedule interfered with their ability to research and write. That is a sad excuse in that the American law professor teaches an average of only 6 hours per week. If one makes generous allowance for committee work and class preparation, a law professor has a 20 hour workload. That provides an ample amount of time for scholarship. However, to obviate any silly excuse for lack of faculty scholarship based on teaching pressures, in late 1989 Parham instituted a scheduling plan under which each Cumberland professor would have one day a week designated as his or her "research day," in which they would be guaranteed not to have any teaching responsibility. My subjective impression is that these "research days" did little to promote scholarship. Those of the faculty who wanted to write found plenty of time outside their minimal teaching, preparation, and committee responsibilities. Those of the faculty who did not want to research and write, or were simply unable to do it, found a thousand excuses not to engage in scholarship.

The newly formed law school tenure policy was also promoting scholarship, by weeding out those who were unwilling to engage in the life of the mind in this significant manner. After the requirement of publication for tenure became effective in the fall of 1986 through 1990, two non-writing professors came before the Rank and Tenure Committee, in one case for tenure at the rank he held of full professor, and in the other case for advancement from associate professor to full professor and tenure at that level. The gentleman seeking tenure at the rank he held of full professor had made no effort at all at publication. He was denied tenure and offered a one year terminal contract. The case of the woman is more familiar to me as I served on the Rank and Tenure Committee the year her case came up for review. She had submitted as her second publication an article that she had published, but otherwise totally lacked merit. The body of the work was about two-thirds quotations taken from other sources, credit given, but not her own writing. There was no depth to the piece and no analytic effort. It looked dashed together. After a very contentious committee meeting we granted her tenure because she had literally met the publication requirement through publication in a law review of an ABA approved law school. But we refused to advance her from associate professor to full professor because of the weakness of her article. So she received her tenure but at the lesser level of associate professor.

In the fall of 1987 some of the senior student editors of the *Cumberland Law Review* asked me to be the *Review's* faculty advisor. Unlike the system that prevailed at Detroit College of Law, the *Cumberland Law Review* advisor received no additional remuneration or teaching unit credit. As discussed in chapter one, the student editors of the *Law Review* are the brightest minds of the school, and it is always a pleasure to work with them, and the lack of additional pay did not enter into my thinking when I immediately accepted their offer.

Unlike in Detroit, the *Cumberland Law Review* did not wish my attendance at their officer elections, so I stayed away from that. I was once or twice asked to comment on the status of proposed authors. Most of my time with the law review, and I served far beyond the 1987-1990 period, was quite tranquil. In general, most of my contact with the *Law Review* editors was to enjoy their sparkling conversation at *Law Review* parties. Samford University being a Baptist institution, discretion and some element of deception was always needed regarding parties at which liquor was served. The law school itself practiced this. For example, if the law school wanted to hold a banquet for (say) 30-40 members of the bar, the law school itself could never serve any liquor. But what it could do, and did, was to persuade some Birmingham law firm to sponsor a cocktail hour before the dinner and at the same location. Those invited by the law firm to its cocktail party would be exactly those whom Cumberland had invited to its dinner. The cocktail hour flowed seamlessly into the dinner. The *Law Review* maintained a shadow organization called the Cumberland Yacht Club, to which the student editors made modest contributions, and out of these funds occasional parties were held at local watering holes. In the spring and fall of 1990, I sponsored parties for the law review editors, spouses, and significant others held at my home. One Saturday evening in June 1990, some 30-35 students jammed into my house, the largest party I have ever held.

The big exception to this generality of tranquility as a *Law Review* advisor was the academic year 1988-1989 when all hell seemed to break loose and in two separate incidents I had to intervene as somewhat of a shield between the law review editors and an upset administration. The editor-in-chief for that year, Richard Davis, was very bright and a bit feisty, as was also his Board of Editors.

The autonomous student control of law reviews, a notable hallmark of American law reviews, necessarily means more than deciding what articles to publish and what to reject. Since so much of the work is done by students, as explained previously, there needs to be some control over and even power of expulsion of students who refuse to do their cite checks, or their preemption searches, or write their articles. The *Review* requires all student editors to write a specific number of articles, whether ultimately published or not, to provide a pool from which a good selection can be made. A student editor who just does not do the work requires other editors to do more, and furthermore receives the unearned cachet of listing oneself on an employment resume as a law review editor. A law review cannot permit such an unearned advantage and to prevent demoralization among those who are actually doing what is required a student who is not doing the work must be expelled from the law review.

I had occasion to talk with my predecessor *Law Review* advisor who served in the years 1976-1987. He advised that during these years the sanction of expulsion had been frequently applied by the student editors on delinquent students, but he did not recall any incident in that time where a student decision on an expulsion had been questioned by the Cumberland administration. I reviewed all the *Law Review* by-laws from 1971 through 1987 and until August 1987 there was no procedure for administrative review of student disciplinary decisions. However, in August 1987, the month before I became advisor, the by-laws were amended to provide for administrative review of the Board of Editors' disciplinary decisions by the Cumberland Dean for Academic Affairs.

A student on the review, whom I will call W, had a paper due in the fall of 1988. He did not turn it in. After various extensions and warnings and the paper still not presented, the Board of Editors expelled W from the review in the spring of 1989. W complained to Alex Bolla, the Associate Dean for Academic Affairs. At that point the matter became somewhat politicized as it turned out that W was not just a delinquent student but was also the stepson of a university trustee.

Bolla then proceeded to hold hearings in April 1989 on the propriety of the Board expulsion of W. Dean Bolla took the testimony of twelve witnesses, including all of the 9-person Board of Editors, W himself, and two other witnesses whose identities I do not recall. I spent twelve hours with the Academic Dean, reviewing documents and listening to the testimony of the twelve witnesses. I had the impression that Bolla tried to put words into the mouths of the Board members to find a reason to reverse the expulsion. Perhaps I am wrong, but that was my impression. The sum and substance of the Board's testimony was that they did nothing unusual or in any way different than with any other non-performing *Review* member. W testified for two hours and said he did not write his paper in the summer of 1988, when he was supposed to, in order to have it ready in the early fall, because his grandfather died and he had too many weddings to attend that summer.

Bolla decided to reinstate W but to put him in poor standing on the *Review*. Since graduation was coming in weeks, that meant that if W did not resign from the *Review* he would have a permanent notation on his transcript that when he graduated from Cumberland he was in poor standing on the *Law Review*. W did not resign, but petitioned the Board of Editors for reinstatement in good standing, which was denied.

The annual *Cumberland Law Review* banquet was held on April 14, 1989, right in the middle of all this. The Editor-in-Chief Richard Davis asked me to give the talk at the dinner, and I spoke on the topic of "Autonomy and the *Cumberland Law Review*." I warned my listeners that my remarks would be a sharp departure from the usual self-congratulatory banquet oratory. I did not refer to W by name, but did criticize the waste of time in the hearings, and the demoralization among the law reviewers that the administration had caused. I also said that student autonomy meant that the student Board ought to control discipline with the possible exception of allegations of individualized animus or disparate treatment of people similarly situated, neither of which was alleged by W. I urged the immediate repeal of the new by-law that permitted this review. I cautioned my listeners that the recent incident has "caused so much demoralization among the reviewers, as I perceive things, that it challenges us to take immediate remedial steps." Richard Davis was so taken by my remarks that he asked to reprint them in an upcoming issue of the *Review*. I agreed, provided I could, in good law review fashion, add a few footnotes. This Board made me an honorary editor and gave me a nice certificate that I had framed and which still hangs on the wall of my study.

As the W affair bubbled along, another incident was brewing and about to boil over. A student wrote a case note on a recent decision of the United States Supreme Court concerning "dirty words" and First Amendment freedoms. It involved a tee-shirt on which the words "SHIT HAPPENS" were printed. The Supreme Court considered and determined that this was speech protected by the First Amendment. The case note made liberal use of the capitalized phrase SHIT HAPPENS in its analysis of the case, perhaps a bit more use than really needed to be made, I thought in retrospect.

On May 9, 1989 I received a letter from the City Attorney of the City of Gadsden criticizing the *Law Review* for the SHIT HAPPENS article. I replied immediately. I pointed out that SHIT HAPPENS was capitalized both on the original tee-shirt and in the Supreme Court opinion, and that a case note had to consider the actual facts. The *Law Review* must necessarily write about unpleasant realities that face courts and legislatures. I assumed that the administration would also receive complaints, so the very next day I saw Dean Williams and showed him my letter to the City Attorney. As I handed him the letter he had a look on his face that seemed to connote: "What trouble have you guys gotten into now." Nevertheless he thought well of my response and thanked me for a copy for his use in the event he received any calls. A week later Parham told me that he had received not just some but many angry telephone calls about the SHIT HAPPENS article and that Tom Corts, the university president, had gotten at least one. Corts wanted to develop guidelines for the use of "dirty words" in the *Review*. Some guidelines were drafted for the university as a whole, put to a vote by schools, and four of eight schools disapproved in the form submitted. I do not believe the guidelines were ever put in place.

I never asked for an advanced look at anything to be published in the *Review*. That would be a form of prior restraint, and really inconsistent with the notion of student control over content. If the editor had asked me about this particular article, I probably would have said, "Run it if you think the legal analysis is good," but I would have encouraged cutting down the number of times the author used the SHIT HAPPENS phrase.

In 1988 I began a tradition of holding an annual wine tasting party, the Beaujolais Bash, in the week before Thanksgiving. This is the time when the new Beaujolais, just a year old, is introduced into the market. I gathered up as many brands of the Nouveau Beaujolais as I could find, invited all the law faculty, professional law librarians, spouses, and significant others to my home for a wine tasting of the young fresh Beaujolais, serving cheese and crackers, some years even more elaborate fare, along with the wine. The event never became wildly popular, and the usual attendance was about 20-25 persons. Yet those who came enjoyed themselves. Few opportunities existed for evening socializing among the faculty and their spouses. I continued the Beaujolais Bash for 25 years. In later years attendance began to drop, and I became tired of the work involved in going around to different wine shops to buy various brands, picking up the rental glasses, and straightening up the house. It was fun while it lasted.

Samford is a Baptist school, but its Christian commitment can show up in ways that are embarrassing to its academic goals. President Tom Corts had a vision of Samford as a Baptist Notre Dame. But others in the university had more radical views of its Christian component. At a university-wide faculty meeting in November 1989 a proposal was tendered by some faculty committee that the religious element of university mission statement be changed from "instilling respect and understanding of the Christian tradition" to a more forceful "instilling a personal commitment and allegiance to Christianity." I rose to object and argued that this would create a terrible public relations image for the school, and might lead people to think that we were running a Sunday school and not a university. The proposal was tabled. Shortly afterward, the University Provost called me and co-opted my opposition by inviting me to help draft a different statement.

1990 brought an even more insidious proposal that all full time faculty should be Christians. Again I spoke up, pointing out that Jews were disproportionately represented in legal education. For Samford to adopt a university-wide anti-Semitic hiring policy would have a significant adverse effect on Cumberland's reputation. I noted that the law school had spent years trying to enter into the mainstream of legal education, through its new faculty hiring, its tougher admissions requirements, and the publication requirement for tenure. I told the full faculty that a Christian-only hiring policy would undo our efforts in a flash and Cumberland would be once again in the backwaters of legal education. Several law faculty later congratulated me on my candor.

President Corts put out the word that as far as he was concerned the various schools ought to hire the most academically qualified candidates. That put an end to Christian-only hiring for decades. However, this bigoted Christian-only approach to hiring faculty may have returned due to increased trustee pressure and the recent appointment of a new Senior Associate Provost. He has promulgated a new faculty search process document, dated April 30, 2018, and approved by the university trustees. This new policy requires that prospective faculty "will excel in teaching, service, and scholarly output," but it *additionally* mandates that faculty candidates possess a "strong Christian commitment." To enforce this, each faculty candidate must submit a form, the "Faculty Applicant Christian Mission Statement," wherein they must give a "detailed response" to two specific questions: (1) "How do you envision your skills, experiences, and qualifications being a good fit with Samford University as it specifically relates to our Christian mission?" and (2) "Please describe your personal Christian faith journey and how your faith would inform your role as a faculty member." It is difficult to imagine that a talented faculty candidate from a religious tradition other than evangelical Christian could answer the second question.

Persons in many different faith traditions including many Christians would find it puzzling to describe a "faith journey."

According to the new faculty search process it is only in the case where no one is found with both "academic acumen and strong Christian commitment" that faculty may be hired "from among those persons who may not have strong Christian commitment – but who understand the special Christian mission of the University, and sympathize with it, even if their personal beliefs are not completely concomitant." Such a non-Christian hire is allowed only where the "best search efforts" have failed to find a suitable Christian. I cannot imagine any non-Christian, and a good many Christians, reacting with other than revulsion to these bigoted policies, although I understand that more recently they have been somewhat ameliorated.

A couple of other job possibilities came along during these five years. Sometime in early 1987 John Reid called me about New Mexico School of Law: it was looking for a legal historian and would I be interested. I said I might be but that I felt a little guilty at leaving Cumberland so quickly, and in any event I had tenure now and did not want to accept any job that did not have tenure with it. I think this was just John's feeler, and in any event the suggestion went nowhere.

In September 1989 Nick Revelos, my friend and former colleague at Detroit College of Law, called me to inquire whether I might be interested in visiting there for a semester, teaching one course and additionally writing a history of DCL for its centennial observance. I told Nick that I would be very interested in such a project, but that I was only two years away from a sabbatical and Cumberland required six years of *continuous* teaching to be eligible. Perhaps we could work something out for a summer. A few days later I made a specific offer to Nick: I would work 10 weeks in the summer of 1990, with some Detroit College of Law help in gathering materials prior to that, for $15,000 plus actual research expenses as needed up to $3,000. I pointed out that this $15,000 was less than half of a semester he had suggested I combine with teaching one course. A month later I talked with Nick again. The dean at DCL thought their history could be written in less time and with less money. That was too bad since I would have enjoyed spending some time in Detroit again.

In May 1990 I was approached with the possibility of a deanship at Northern Illinois School of Law in DeKalb. It paid $108,000. I said I might be interested, but would need more details about the school and the job. Time went by and while waiting for a shoe to drop, I began having doubts. Deaning is a 12 month job, and $108,000 over 12 months is not much better than $74,000 (my then current salary) over eight and a half months. A dean needs to be friendly with everyone, not an easy task for me. The amount of time involved in being a dean would mean the death of my scholarship.

In late October 1990, Malcolm Morris called me. He said he was the head of the decanal selection committee at Northern Illinois Law School and that I was one of the leading candidates. I did not mention my monetary concerns, but I did point out that I was only one year away from a sabbatical. He said that they would have to convince me of the worthiness of the school and the position.

I understood that he was going to suggest times for me to visit the school, see its facilities and visit faculty and students. But then nothing happened, and I never heard from Northern Illinois again. I do not know what went wrong, but in retrospect I am happy that this did not go any further. In the years to come Cumberland continued to be generous to me, both with travel money and salary. On my side I continued to enjoy scholarship and I am certain that I published many books that I would not have had the time to write had I been a dean.

My second book, *Thomas O. Larkin: A Life of Patriotism and Profit in Old California* (Oklahoma, 1990), at least on my part, had a very reluctant beginning. At the 1985 meeting of the Western History Association in Sacramento, California, Harlan Hague, a California historian with whom I had a passing acquaintance, earnestly approached me. Would I be interested in collaborating on a biography of Thomas Larkin, a notable merchant in early California and the first and only American consul to Mexican California? I told

Harlan that frankly I was not terribly interested because I was primarily focused on legal history, and, in any event, Larkin seemed a fairly minor figure. Harlan pointed out that plenty of more minor, even obscure, figures in nineteenth century California history had biographies, yet Larkin lacked one, excepting one inadequate book based only on Larkin's letters without much analysis.

Harlan began a campaign to induce me to change my mind, and he eventually wore me down and I agreed. Part of our agreement provided that I would do nothing whatsoever until the *Law and Community* book went into production and all I had left with it was going over the copyeditor's suggestions. That eventuality came in mid-1986, and I became fully focused on Larkin. I took the first part of Larkin's life from childhood through his role as a merchant in California, and Harlan would focus on Larkin's role in the American conquest, his land speculation and later life. There were some chapters or partial chapters that overlapped these boundaries, yet internally for the two of us there were no blurred boundaries. We had a precise outline and then division of responsibility for who would write which parts. Then we left each other alone. Even so we consulted often, because there were many topics that began in my period but ended in his, and then the question arose who would write it up, since it would be awkward to divide into two discussions. And we often talked on the telephone about perplexities we had concerning some particular aspect of Larkin's life.

Although I had been importuned by Harlan into co-writing the Larkin biography, once started I warmed to the task. Since Larkin was a leading merchant in Mexican California I could use his experiences to more generally describe mercantile practices and how the American and British merchants interacted socially and professionally with their major customers. Larkin also proved to be an interesting individual, searching for wealth from his youth and ultimately becoming one of the first of many Americans to set out for California in search of fortune.

George P. Hammond had published a ten volume set of Larkin's correspondence and papers, and although not complete by any means, it was a good place for me to start. I fully read and made notes on the first five of the volumes and dipped into the last five as required. I also read a few master's dissertations on Larkin which gave me leads for other sources: Larkin's own youthful autobiography; additional Larkin materials not included in Hammond's compilation; and many merchants' papers held at the Bancroft Library, some of which I had seen before but for a different purpose when writing the *Law and Community* book. Within a few months I had a huge mass of notes, quotations, and short memos to myself reminding me of connections between events or incidents. What to do with this mass? How to organize it?

What I did next, and what I did with every book hereafter, is so simple that I am a little embarrassed to describe it. The technique is not exactly a paragon of sophistication, but then I developed it before computer data programs. Recall that we had a precise outline that included the contents of each chapter. I read through or at least analyzed every letter, document or note I had accumulated and marked it on the top with a I, II, III, IV, or V, etc., depending on the chapter to which it related. Next, I put the papers into large expanding files also marked I, II, III, etc. This is not very elaborate, but it does the trick. It also gave me an opportunity for the second time to read every document, quotation, or note I had taken.

During this sorting I often had insights, or what I fancied as such, regarding phenomena I had not observed before. I made notes of the connection or observation and filed them away in the appropriate, burgeoning file folders. Occasionally, a document, note, or observation would be related to two chapters, not just one, and in that case I marked the document with two file numbers, say "III" and "V," and carefully filed it in the lower-numbered file.

Next, I further refined the chapter outlines with numbered sections. Starting with the first chapter folder I re-read every piece of paper, some now for the third time. I opened a small manila folder for each section of my chapter outline. Then I marked each document, quotation, or note with the number on my chapter outline to which the paper related, and placed the papers in the manila folders to which they belonged. I went on to the second chapter and subsequent chapters and did the same thing. Now each document would have two

162

numbers, for example II-7, meaning that the note pertained to the seventh section of the second chapter. If a note or document related to two or three sections of a chapter, I marked it for every section, and then filed it under the lowest section number. The next step was to write, always working in order from the earliest chapter to the last, and within the chapters from the lowest section to the highest. That gave me an opportunity to physically move a document marked with two or three sections for the particular chapter upward to the next manila folder, which assured me that I would consider every note for each relevant section of the chapter.

Obviously, one cannot write a book successfully as an extended string of quotations. However, I freely admit that I use quotations from and notes on primary sources to guide my thoughts while composing. When, for example, a particular section of a chapter described some event or condition, I might have three or four contemporary, first-hand descriptions of the event. I might not quote any of these primary sources but instead describe the event entirely in my own voice. That depended on how much quotation had already been used nearby and how piquant the available contemporary observations read. But the quotations within a section folder reminded me that I was to describe this event next, and gave me many of the details that I would mention even if I put them entirely in my own words.

I finished my half of the manuscript by early December 1988, and Harlan did the same by late January 1989. John Drayton, Editor-in-Chief at University of Oklahoma Press, called on April 3, 1989. He said he was pleased with our work, and he would send it to the original outside readers who had preliminarily approved the manuscript, for their suggestions. He thought we could be on the 1990 publication list. I began to work on collecting photographs and other graphics. We dealt with the few outside readers' thoughts by June, but then a bombshell arrived in July. The university's editorial committee wanted 85 pages cut from Harlan's half and 26 from mine. I called Drayton to protest. I pointed out that this biography was not like one on a well-known person, for example George Custer or John Frémont, where if one book does not cover some topic the next one will. There will probably be no other Larkin biography, and we had an obligation to be thorough. John warmed to my position, and said that perhaps a foundation could subsidize the paper and printing costs. He did find one, the Hayes Foundation, which granted a subvention of $5,000. Drayton allowed me $500 of this for the graphics, usually an author expense.

On the first of December 1989 I sent in the title page, table of contents, and the list of illustrations to the copyeditor. The copyeditor finished in early February, and I very promptly went over the proposed changes that were mostly style changes I often changed back to my original. The first page proofs arrived in May 1990, and I read them over and made corrections within a few days. As the last step I received the page proofs with final pagination and used them to prepare the index. That is somewhat of a painful process and best to prepare it carefully yet quickly. Some authors hire professional indexers to do this task. However, author-prepared indices are better as they include more concepts and subject areas beyond nouns and names. I put in all the accent marks and sent the index back. We were done! I had the feeling that it was not by any means a brilliant book, but that Harlan and I had done a solid job.

Oklahoma released the Larkin book on September 24, 1990, and the first two copies arrived in my office the next day. I learned that the California State Parks was sending out 1,500 invitations to a signing at the Larkin House State Park in Monterey, set for October 13, 1990. They estimated, too optimistically, that 400 people might show up. Naturally, I specifically invited all my friends. October 13 was overcast and cool and that may have depressed attendance. The Park folks estimated 100-125 came to the event. But everyone at the reception held in the garden outside the house had a good time, talking about books, Larkin specifically, and drinking wine. I was touched by the number of friends who came: Bruce and Carol Christenson, my former law partner and wife; Barbara Jeskalian, friend from San Jose days; Bernadette, my former wife, and a lady friend of hers; Dean and Liza Puccini, my stepson and his wife; Ann Glashagel Schumacher, long-term friend from my Elgin years, and her husband John; Stanley Siddle, friend from San Francisco, and his wife Joan.

Harlan and I signed about 40 books for purchasers and another 40 for sale at the nearby Cooper House Park. After the reception, my girlfriend Grace and I, with all my friends, went to a bar now called La Vida in the Sanchez Adobe on Alvarado Street. Steinbeck mentioned this bar in *Travels with Charlie*. We had a wonderful conversation. I felt really honored and really happy that so many friends had gathered together to celebrate my book.

Grace and I had dinner with Bruce and Carol in San Jose at a gourmet Greek restaurant, an unusual place, and then we went to the West Valley Opera in Palo Alto by ourselves. It was a busy, fun-filled day. A couple days later we went to Stockton to a bookstore where Harlan had arranged a signing. We did not sell more than a dozen books, but the owner of the store had us sign a couple dozen more for future sales. Then, on October 18th, we attended the Western History Association convention and sold 15 books and signed many more. This is as close to a book tour as I have ever experienced.

Thomas O. Larkin received some generous reviews. Jackson K. Putnam, reviewing in the *American Historical Review*, deemed it "a fascinating book," and the noted Jesuit scholar Robert M. Senkewicz wrote in *The Journal of American History* that Harlan and I had told the story of Larkin's mercantile activities "clearly and crisply," and that the book was "prodigiously researched, well-written, and nicely illustrated." Yet there were some darker reactions to the work that to me reflect what I regard as an "anti-biography" bias in American scholarship. Generally, we no longer believe in the great man theory of history, but rather that our destinies are controlled by various collective consciences or economic and social forces. The individual person, it is now widely thought in historical circles, can hardly matter, except perhaps to illustrate some of the collectivities or forces. For example, John P. Reid, a senior legal scholar and a man who highly praised my *Law and Community* book, was almost angry with me for writing the Larkin biography. It was, he thought, a waste of my analytical skills.

I happen to think that human beings are interesting in their own right, and do not need to be tied to vast historical forces to be worthy of study for their own sakes. The interpretive reconstruction of a life, my working definition of biography, does not need to be bogged down with historiographical and theoretical analysis. Of course, a life must be bottomed on the events and currents of the time in which the subject lived, and contextualized in that sense. Though background is needed, the life itself can stand on its own. An example of this sort of critique came in Roger Nichols's review in the *Pacific Historical Quarterly* where he wrote of our book that "those seeking general patterns in early California history or in mid-19th-century American expansion will have to search elsewhere. With their view of Larkin's actions, it seems a shame that the authors chose to avoid using William H. Goetzmann's ideas about entrepreneurs during the Jackson era." In other words it was a shame that we did not force Larkin's life into a conceptual framework that would support or detract from some abstract theory about entrepreneurs. I reject that idea as contrary to the true office of biography, the interpretive reconstruction of a specific life.

I received word in the fall of 1991 that the *Larkin* book won the Caroline Bancroft History for the best book of the year on western American history. The prize, administered by the Denver Public Library, entailed a cash payment and certificate given at a public conference in Denver. Harlan and I were expected to give two brief talks apiece on the writing of the book. The Library would pay all our travel and accommodation expenses. The conference took place in May 1992 and was well attended, especially the evening session. My father joined me there, the experience was quite festive, and I collected my third book prize.

I was engaged in an array of other scholarly matters in the closing years of the 1980s. I attended many academic conferences, those of the Association of American Law Schools, Western Historical Association, and the American Society for Legal History, for example, and gave papers at many of them. In December 1989 the University of Alabama asked me to serve as a referee, a first reader, to critique a book manuscript and give the press guidance as to publication. I had been asked to serve a similar role for many journal articles, but this was my first job as a referee for a book manuscript. I took it as an honor to be asked and a part of my professional "dues" to serve university presses in this regard, and more such opportunities soon presented themselves.

During the late 1980s a colleague, William G. Ross, often consulted with me, asking advice about issues ranging from the use of research assistants, various university presses, and other matters concerning academic writing. I enjoyed the role of being old enough and published enough to be somewhat of a mentor. We had many dinners together and discussed each other's research projects. Our collegiality became even closer and more helpful for both of us in the following decade.

In 1990 I applied for fellowships for my 1991-1992 sabbatical year with the National Endowment for the Humanities, the National Humanities Center, and several other institutions. I felt humbled that the only place that wanted to take me on was New York University Law School as a Golieb Fellow, but that only on a non-stipendiary basis – no money. I had other benefits and did participate in this program in fall 1991, as explained in more detail in the next chapter.

By 1990 I was becoming more and more concerned with the new historical abstractions such as deconstructionism and the loss of the goal of neutrality and objectivity in scholarly writing. Particularly, I had the feeling that several Chicano scholars had a political agenda in their scholarship that weakened their work. This practice evolved from the notion that there could be no real objectivity; it was simply impossible. Since that was the case, a minority scholar might just as well tell his people's side of the story of any controversy, making little attempt to ferret out any objective truth. I had a conversation about this with Michael and Jean Sherrill, publishers of *California History*. They said that when they ran factual, objective, and thoroughly vetted articles, they inevitably received complaints that Indians, Chicanos, or whoever, were not put in an affirmatively favorable light. We talked about deconstructionism, the loss of any faith in objectivity, and with it the abandonment by some historians at any attempt at neutrality. We agreed that there was no reason scholars should not attempt to be neutral, and that authors demeaned the profession by just telling "stories" of one group's perspective.

As a result of these considerations I thought I would spread my scholarly net, as it were, a bit more widely. I would finish the present article projects I had planned in the area of Hispanic California's history, but then move on to other topics in other historical fields that also interested me.

By late 1988 I knew that my next book would be a history of the origins and varying interpretations over time of a federal statute known as the White Slave Traffic Act, or more popularly the Mann Act, so labelled after Congressman James R. Mann, the author of the law. Because the statute is centered on sexuality in American society, I knew that I had a considerable amount of background reading to do before I could even begin an examination of the legal materials. I began by reading various social histories of the United States, two excellent books on American sexual history in the late 1800s, *The Response to Prostitution in the Progressive* Era, by Mark Thomas Connelly, and *Purity Crusade: Sexual Morality and Social Control. 1868-1900*, by David J. Pivar, as well as other books and articles dealing with sexual history.

The Mann Act criminalized men who were in any way involved in the interstate transportation of women for "prostitution, debauchery, or any other immoral purpose." In an early case following its 1910 enactment, the United States Supreme Court ruled that the Act applied to ordinary boyfriend-girlfriend travel that crossed a state line, without any monetary consideration whatsoever. If an ordinary unmarried couple shared a vacation, driving for example from Chicago to the Rocky Mountains, and sex occurred during the trip, the boyfriend was guilty of a federal felony that carried significant prison time. The girlfriends were regarded as mere victims. Worse, sex did not actually have to happen; it was sufficient if the boyfriend had that hope at the time they crossed a state line. So, like Orwell's *1984*, the Mann Act sometimes punished mere "bad thought."

I was somewhat neutral regarding the transportation of prostitutes, but my Libertarian beliefs were outraged by the federal government's aggression against harmless, consensual, non-commercial sexual activities of ordinary men and women. I was curious to learn of the role of evangelical churches and other moral pressure groups in the passage of the statute and the extension of a law clearly intended by Congress to curb prostitution into private non-commercial sex. I was curious to learn if the courts had re-interpreted the Act over time, particularly when faced with the social fact of the sexual revolution of the 1960s. I also hoped, here and there, to make an acerbic comment about the federal government for its outrageous intrusion into the mores of its citizens. When I say "hoped" it is because I am a scholar before I am a Libertarian, and in my research I had to find solid evidence before I could reach such strong conclusions.

In those years I also had the thought that a history of the Cumberland School of Law would be a fine thing for our upcoming sesquicentennial in 1997. I mentioned the Cumberland history to our dean, Parham Williams, and while he agreed that would be a good project, I also insisted that the Mann Act book had to come first as I had so much time already invested in it.

By January 1989 I had two paid research assistants, one more than generally allowed. Earl Reuther was working on the Mann Act, while Monte Horton was cite checking the Larkin book until March, when he too began to work on the Mann Act project. We started with indexes, the Index to Periodical Literature and the Index to Legal Periodicals, and I highlighted all the articles I thought possibly pertinent. Earl Reuther photocopied them all, while I was still engaged in background reading. Monte Horton printed up all the published Mann Act judicial opinions. Then I photocopied the indexes to the *New York Times*, and marked all the articles I needed to be copied. I was building up a good horde of papers. Fortunately, Becky Clapp, Cumberland's Librarian, allowed me the exclusive use of a large conference room with a book case, so I had plenty of room to store materials.

By June 1989 I was disheartened that I was still mostly occupied in gathering materials and reading background books and articles. However, the Mann Act was a completely new area for me, and I needed to acquire considerable context. For the Larkin book I had a much deeper preexisting background on Mexican California, but this sexual social history was all new. Student research assistants do not stay on indefinitely. They graduate and move on to better things. In 1990 I had a new research assistant, Mary Godofsky, drawn from the

Law Review board as my research assistants have always been. She checked my huge pile of Mann Act cases to make sure we had them all, but her major task was to read them enough to separate out the prostitution trafficking cases from the non-commercial boyfriend-girlfriend interstate travel, also a crime under the Mann Act. My book would concentrate on the non-commercial cases, because my Libertarian beliefs were most offended by the federal government's aggression regarding private, consensual sexual relations. This is what fascinated me most about the Mann Act. By spring 1990 I was finished with my background reading and I turned to reading the articles expressly about the Mann Act, followed by a massive reading of the opinions, mostly appellate, generated by Mann Act prosecutions.

I was spending a bit of time, not too much, on the Cumberland book as well. I had concluded that, especially for the period 1940 onward, the book needed the help of someone who knew the Southern context in far more detail than I, a Californian cum Chicagoan, could ever learn. I asked Howard Walthall, native Alabamian and also a Harvard history graduate, to join me, and he agreed. We also agreed on 1919 as an appropriate boundary. I took the earlier period, 1847-1919, and he took the later. We also agreed that the only worthwhile history would be a solid analytical work, not the usual "puff piece" that passes for institutional history. Most importantly, Howard agreed that the project would be deferred until after I finished the Mann Act book.

We wanted to do one thing right away. Arthur Weeks, the first dean of Cumberland in Birmingham, the dean who had obtained accreditation for Cumberland while the school was still in Lebanon, Tennessee, and the man who was most influential in moving the school from Tennessee to Birmingham, was obviously an extremely important figure in the school's history. He was elderly and, although in seemingly good health, Howard and I thought it prudent to interview him quickly. We did so, engaging him in fascinating conversation as he had a nearly perfect recollection of events, in a three-hour interview on April 10, 1990, and then finished up with three and a half more hours on May 29th. On June 12, 1990 Howard and I had a conference with Dean Williams. We resolved three things. First, we were pleased to learn that Williams also was disposed toward a serious, analytical history of Cumberland and not an anecdotal, promotional sort. Second, he would give Howard and me two summer research stipends apiece to do the work. Third, he would commit the school to buy a substantial number of copies for its own promotional use. I thought that such a major commitment would help attract the attention of a university press.

That much having been done by June 1990, the Cumberland history then went on the back burner. Howard worked on his own projects, and I finished the research and writing of the Mann Act book, *Crossing over the Line: Legislating Morality and the Mann Act.*

Birmingham had a very vibrant cultural scene in the late 1980s, more lively than exists today. The Alabama Symphony Orchestra performed symphonic music, as it still does. It is now a better orchestra than it was in 1985-1990 so there has been progress here. In addition to the Alabama Symphony, in 1985-1990 the Birmingham Music Club also brought outside orchestras to town. That organization now has diminished interest in classical music. There were then four or five jazz clubs, with a steady rotation of well-known musicians, the best club being Grundy's on Fourth Avenue South. We still have lots of raucous rock clubs, but there is only one left that concentrates on jazz, although here Birmingham's decline reflects an increased national disinterest in jazz.

Birmingham had a steady flow of foreign films at a local theatre. That is gone. We were on the annual tour of the New York City Opera, and that tour has been long defunct. In 1985-1990 Birmingham had three or four small theatres that put on plays, occasionally musicals, with local actors. Here is another area where Birmingham is just as vibrant today, in 2020, as the city has almost half a dozen small theatres scattered throughout the downtown area. There was a small amount of chamber music available in the late 1980s, three or four concerts a year, and that is about what is still available. In 1985-1990 the city's Opera Birmingham put on two or sometimes three performances a year. We still have Opera Birmingham, but it has gone into decline. Now it offers only one full scale opera each year, and a second opera in cabaret form, often a modern opera and often significantly shortened. Opera Birmingham performed a shortened cabaret-style version of *Carmen* a few years ago for which it altered the plot. Instead of the frustrated Don Jose stabbing Carmen at the end, Opera Birmingham's version had Carmen, angry at being stalked, kill Don Jose. I asked later why they had done that, and a company executive told me that it was a gesture to the modern-day empowerment of women. I stopped attending Opera Birmingham's performances totally as a quiet protest against altering a dead librettist's work to make a political point.

The cultural feature of Birmingham that most impressed me during this period, 1985-1990, was what appeared to be a friendly competition among the city's many church choirs, and their eagerness to perform classical choral music. Hardly a month went by without a Bach cantata or mass, a Schubert or Mozart mass, or a requiem by Verdi or Brahms. I looked through my diary to refresh my memory, and in 1989 I attended eight different classical choral works in eight different churches. I am sure that I missed a few. These church choirs were no substitute for the Robert Shaw Chorale, yet their performances were all well-rehearsed, well-performed, well-attended, and a delight for those of us who love classical choral music. For the most part these are gone, replaced by a few choral evensong services and two or three *Messiah* performances before Christmas. In 1985, Birmingham had at least four used bookstores, quirky in nature and a delight to browse. In 2020, it has one used bookstore that primarily sells remainders rather than used books.

In sum, Birmingham still has a thriving symphony and small theatre scene, but the rest of the cultural vibrancy that existed in 1985-1990 has atrophied. It is a shame, but it perhaps simply reflects this generation's disinterest in choral music and books, and that is an even bigger shame.

I read when I could in 1985-1990, but frankly not as much as in earlier years. My friend and colleague Bill Ross once commented to me on the irony that those who write books, and therefore most enjoy reading them, actually have less time to do that than those who are not writers. I still read 20-25 books a year, but that is less than previously. I was reading more biography as I worked on the Larkin book, and became intrigued by the process of reconstructing a life on paper and offering context and interpretation with it. I became interested in Henry Dwight Sedgwick, an amateur biographer, knowledgeable if not learned, who in the first half of the 20th century wrote essays and biographies about world leaders of the past. He came from an old and distinguished Massachusetts family, and the books of his that I was able to find were quite good.

In October 1989 I was in Boston and spent quite a few hours prowling used bookstores looking for the Sedgwick books I lacked. Sadly, the Internet has since destroyed much of the pleasure of a physical search for obscure books. Earlier in 1989 Boston, I reflected on my failure to find a single one of Sedgwick's books. Henry Dwight Sedgwick was a man who had left the practice of law to write books, much the same as I had done, excepting I had my teaching income for support. Sedgwick produced some 12-15 well-written books. Yet some 30-40 years after his death, even the used book dealers in his own patch of the world had never heard of him. How transient his work and life seemed, even at this short remove.

How pointless it seemed to strive to build an intellectual monument. Better, perhaps, to simply do work that one enjoys and hope for the best as to ultimate recognition. I felt sorry for Sedgwick, who seemed an excellent writer and deserving of more recognition. But he was primarily a biographer, and as we no longer believe in great men, biography as a literary genre has declined. Yet I myself felt increasingly drawn toward biography, even if that would mean doing the work I enjoyed without much hope of recognition.

Chapter 7

Life, Teaching, and Scholarship in Birmingham:
Fall 1990-Summer 2000,
Part One

By the spring of 1991 I felt I was at the end of finding Mann Act materials, although I had hardly read all of the many hundred articles and judicial opinions that had been unearthed. My goals for the remainder of the spring and the summer were to read the few dissertations touching on the Mann Act; research the Mobile, Alabama court dockets, 1910-1944, for Mann Act prosecutions; prepare a master outline of the book; read the judicial opinions in those Mann Act prosecutions involving non-commercial sexual activities; and finally, organize and box up all my materials for shipment to New York for my fall 1991 Golieb Fellowship. I did everything except reading the opinions, and that I had to defer until I was in New York.

I decided to read whatever records were extant, usually just the clerk's dockets, of the prosecutions in Mobile, Alabama and Providence, Rhode Island. Because the dockets in the period 1910-1944 generally indicated "colored," or equivalent, for black defendants, I thought examining the records in two fairly similar cities, one in the North and the other in the South, might yield a clue as to whether the Mann Act was employed in the South as one tool among many others for the social control of blacks. The Mobile court dockets are held at the East Point, Georgia regional branch of the National Archives. In April 1991 I spent five days there, looked at hundreds of Mobile Mann Act prosecutions, and worked out the percentages that were non-commercial rather than involving prostitutes, the average sentences, and whether there was any indication that sentences were higher for black defendants. I looked at the equivalent Providence records the following year.

On August 5, 1991, my girlfriend Grace and I took Amtrak from Birmingham to New York, with four transfer cases, a small box, and a suitcase, loaded with opinions, notes, articles, and other data, in addition to our own hand luggage. We stored all this in a condo that Grace's sister owned, while we looked at apartments. Grace was a big help to me in finding a place. I settled into a one bedroom sub-let in Waterside Plaza at 23rd and the East River. It was good sized, with a fabulous view all the way from the World Trade Center (still standing) to the Chrysler Building. More to the point, the large living room had a counter running the width of the room that I could use both as a desk and storage space. One weekend that fall, several Cumberland administrators were in New York and I had a cocktail party in their honor. The large living room was able to comfortably accommodate about eight of us.

Most of my time in New York, aside from the Metropolitan Opera, New York's many art museums, and countless other cultural activities, was spent reading opinions and placing them and other materials into the folders that corresponded to my detailed outline. I spent a half day at the Museum of Broadcasting, which had plot summaries for thousands of movies, but nothing on the Mann Act. I did research in the NYU libraries. I also made a quick trip to Washington, D.C., where I took the shuttle the National Archives runs from the side of its building to its Suitland, Maryland facility where I found eight boxes tightly packed with correspondence to the FBI regarding the Mann Act. This first trip to Suitland was exploratory, and I knew I would have to return.

The Golieb Colloquium, about twenty scholars in total, met every Wednesday in a conference room inside the NYU law school. Over the course of the fall, we each submitted a paper of a project we individually were working on, usually a chapter of a projected book. We had the papers about a week in advance, and when we came together we discussed and critiqued the paper of the week. I decided I would write the *Caminetti* case as my first full chapter and submit it as my offering for the colloquium. *Caminetti v. United States* (1917) is interesting, in part because of the politics behind it, but more importantly because it was the case where the United States Supreme Court definitively ruled that the Mann Act applied to consensual boyfriend-girlfriend interstate travel and was not limited to commerce in prostitutes.

In general my paper was well received. In fact, several thought highly of my effort to present a full discussion of a legal historical topic to a general audience, and wished me well. However, some people in the colloquium urged me to write more about how the *Caminetti* case fit into evolving concepts of federalism, especially the growth of federal power through increasing the scope of the Constitution's interstate commerce clause. I suppose one could try to write a book on the role of the Mann Act in expanding the reach of the federal government through the commerce clause, but that was not the book I wanted to write. First, although I think the Mann Act was an important vehicle for the expansion of the FBI, I do not believe it was an important milestone at all for the expansion of the interstate commerce clause. Second, I was uninterested in using the Mann Act to make global claims about the American legal system.

My idea about legal history was that the law powerfully affects the most vital of human activities: jobs, housing, sexuality, and religion. I hoped to find a way to make the history of the regulation of these activities interesting to a mass audience. The Mann Act is interesting in itself, and although I wanted to provide a reader with plenty of background information on the law, and historical information about the social history of sexuality before and after the passage of the statute, I did not think arcane discussion of the impact of *Caminetti* on the legal system as a whole had any role in presenting the underlying story.

After my fellowship ended in New York, I returned to Birmingham. I had taken a full year's sabbatical at half-pay, so I had quite a bit of time to work in the winter and spring of 1992. I continued the sorting of notes into appropriate categories and the reading of a few remaining articles in my library command post, and did some writing there as well. However, most of the actual writing was accomplished typing on my computer at the long wooden tables of the heavily wooded main reading room of the Lynn-Henley Research Library within the Birmingham Public Library. I often worked there entire days, walking over to the Birmingham Art Museum for lunch. Frequently I had that wonderful feeling of being lost in work, the losing track of time and any consciousness of its passage that is a sure sign of high productivity. Bit by bit I finished chapter after chapter.

I took two major research trips that spring. In early March 1992 I read the Providence, Rhode Island federal court records contained in the regional National Archives in Waltham, Massachusetts. This was the companion to the research in the Mobile cases that I had finished previously. I had to take a day trip to Providence itself, since the federal judges there had refused to release to the National Archives their indexes for the dockets more recent than 1931, and I was going as far as 1944, as I had with the Mobile records. I spent five days at Waltham and Providence, the same amount of time I had been in East Point, Georgia. I uncovered no significant difference between the rate of non-commercial cases in the North (Providence) and South (Mobile). There was also no evidence that Mann Act prosecutions were an instrument of race control, nor that the self-righteous religiosity of the South led to greater sentences. I dug out little previous information from these ten days of research. But it was a form of due diligence, and I probably would have felt guilty later, and worried whether I had missed something important, if I had not done the digging.

Later that same month I returned for six days to the National Archives at Suitland to sample the thousands of letters, 1910-1944, from citizens to the FBI or Department of Justice, concerning the Mann Act. I enjoyed the routine of work there. I usually took the 8:15AM van that left from the side of the main National Archives building and went directly to the Washington National Records Center at Suitland, Maryland. The complimentary vans operated throughout the day, but the final return was at 4:00PM. They held about 12 persons and were filled with good-natured historians out for their research. A particular degree of camaraderie accompanied the late afternoon returning van, with many jokes, gossip about colleagues, even an occasional song. The day's work was done, and a drink and dinner would soon be at hand.

That fall I had enough chapters completed that I could begin to send them out to the friends, Laura Redoutey and Ann Schumacher, who had volunteered to read them critically. I also provided friend and colleague William Ross with copies, so he could make his incisive comments and begin his excellent fine editing. I polished off two more chapters in draft in the summer of 1992, returning to New York and sub-letting a wonderful pre-war apartment on Central Park West, to which I was referred by a friend I had made the previous fall. Both my daughter, Virginia, and my father visited me in New York that summer; I had plenty of room to put them up, and we had a great time together eating out, going to film festivals, museums, and historic buildings. By December 1992 I had only two chapters left to write in draft, and I knew it was time to think about a publisher.

Because I wanted to reach the general reader, I wanted to publish the manuscript as a trade book, with its ample publisher promotion and trade royalties, higher than the 10% of net income to publisher for university press books. I sent a formal proposal and two sample chapters to four literary agents, but that went nowhere. I sent proposals on my own to such "higher-toned" trade presses as Norton, Basic Books, Morrow, and Free Press, all to no avail. Then I turned to the more prestigious university presses such as Harvard, Oxford, Cambridge, Chicago, and Johns Hopkins. I also contacted Oklahoma and the Legal History Series of the American Society for Legal History. I heard from several. Oxford told me that while my "writing style does make the material appropriate for the general reader," their press did not think there was enough readership for the book for them to take it on. Tom Green, my former dissertation advisor and the editor of the American Society for Legal History's series, called me. He thought that my manuscript stood in between a trade book and a scholarly monograph, and that books in that position often slip through the cracks since they are too scholarly for the public but lack the over-arching analytics desired by scholars. He said I could turn my work into a true monograph by using the Mann Act to make more general claims about the nature of the legal process as, for example, a case study in crime becoming more national in scope and requiring federal intervention and tying it in with Prohibition and the beginnings of the War on Drugs.

That was good advice, but I just did not want to write a case study coupled with a highly generalized thesis about the nature of American law. I think these generalized theses ought to be derived from many case studies, and not concocted from one example. Beyond that I just wanted to tell the fascinating story of this harmful federal statute to the general reader, to give that reader plenty enough law for a thorough understanding of the background and development of the Mann Act, but not go outside the scope of the Mann Act by proposing theories about the nature of the legal system in general and outside of the immediate scope of what I was discussing (although I did make some speculation in the book about the Mann Act being an example of how much easier it is to pass a statute than repeal it).

I had a serious flirtation with Oklahoma, whom I approached with a proposal that it publish the manuscript as a trade book. From the beginnings of our exploration of the publication possibilities, George Bauer, Oklahoma's director, was enthusiastic while his executive staff was not. Oklahoma sent the manuscript out to readers. The second reader reported that "the manuscript is very well written, easily understood and easy to follow. Additionally, a reader not affiliated with the field of law and especially federal litigation can readily understand the reasoning and the concept of the text." The first reader was a constitutional law professor who thought my style "engaging and interesting. My only criticism is that at times he sacrifices depth of legal analysis in the interest of keeping the narrative moving. It is more of a choice than a deficit." Both recommended in favor of publication. I wrote back to John Drayton, the Editor-in-Chief, and the editor who had guided my previous *Law and Community* and *Larkin* books:

> One could write an essentially different book, say "The Role of the Mann Act in Expanding Federal Powers and Constitutional Interpretation." It would be a very legalistic approach that might fascinate the 250 constitutional law professors in America, but would turn off everyone else. It would be a history of constitutional law and not the Mann Act, and I would be as disinterested (and unqualified) to write that as I would a book about colonization on Mars.

The Oklahoma executives pondered all this, and eventually concluded that they would deny publication of the manuscript as a trade book. The director, George Bauer, wrote me on September 24, 1992:

A leader without followers is in a precarious position, and I am afraid that is the situation in which I find myself with regard to your manuscript on the Mann Act. From the beginning I have been enthusiastic about the prospect of publishing it here at Oklahoma. Unhappily, I have not been able to generate similar enthusiasm among other key members of the Press staff. No one doubts the quality of your work. Rather, they lack confidence in the Press's ability to reach the broad trade audience you visualize.

Editor-in-Chief John Drayton was presumably one of the key staff members lacking Bauer's enthusiasm. Drayton told me privately that Oklahoma would be pleased to publish my Mann Act book as a university press book, but not as a trade book. So it was the publicity and promotion that soured the deal that I had proposed to Oklahoma.

Two university presses did express interest, Chicago and Johns Hopkins. Chicago had caught me first and sent the manuscript to its outside readers before I heard from Johns Hopkins. Academic authors often send out multiple proposals, but once a university press expresses an interest and then goes to the trouble of sending the manuscript to paid outside readers for comment and recommendation, then the general ethics are that the author should follow through with the press that has taken those initial steps.

On February 11, 1993 John Tryneski, an editor at the University of Chicago Press, called me and said "I like it." He sent the manuscript to outside readers. The first editor was the editor of the series, "Sexuality, History, and Society," in which the Mann Act book would appear. He liked it, and wanted it in his series. The second reader was Judge Richard Posner, who looked over the manuscript but lacked the time to read it fully. He liked the writing and scholarship but had expected a more analytical approach. Since Posner sat on the Publications Board that makes the final determination, Tryneski sent it out to a new second reader. Meanwhile Tryneski was calling around about me. He called Albert Alschuler and Richard Helmholz, both professors at Chicago's law school and both of whom knew me, Al from being a debate opponent during high school days, and Dick from his position as the President of the American Society for Legal History, under whom I served as a member of the Board's executive committee. Both affirmed my good reputation as a scholar.

The new second reader looked at my manuscript as a case study and complained that the book did not seem to have a central question or thesis. I told Tryneski that I would add more analytical context, especially around the interstate commerce clause, but insisted that I did not want to get into an extended discussion about constitutional issues since "this is a book about the Mann Act and its role in the social life of the United States. It is not a book on 'The Role of the Mann Act in Expanding Visions of Federal Power' or similar."

I submitted some revisions, particularly more discussion of the interstate commerce clause. The second reader thought my revisions were on the right track, and Tyrneski did tell me that the current trend in scholarship was to make a case study support some huge thesis. That might explain why there seemed to be a persistent critique of my lack of a grand thesis, although it did not detract from the quality of the study when viewed as the book it was intended to be. Judge Posner looked at my revisions and liked the book now. Since everyone was now on board, John said it was a "lock," and indeed the Publications Board formally approved the publication on July 28, 1993. In bringing all these different people together, Tryneski was acting in a role I have often noticed in university press book editors. After becoming convinced in his or her own mind of the value of the manuscript, the editor then becomes an advocate by unifying all the different viewpoints of readers, other editors, publication boards, and so forth. In addition, editors during this early point of the publication process try to involve as many readers and others with information as possible, such as Alschuler and Helmholz, to create a wide consensus. I think this is a highly bureaucratic mechanism to defuse responsibility, as insurance that blame is not narrowly focused in the event of an absolute debacle.

I signed the formal contract with the University of Chicago Press on September 1, 1993 in Grace's company at Birmingham's Ruth Chris Steak House, continuing a practice of signing book contracts over a nice meal. At some point during our negotiations I requested that the

Press publish the book as a trade book, and Tryneski responded that they would have been pleased to publish the book as a trade book 25 years earlier, but that the market for intelligent and serious books aimed at general readers had almost vanished. John did promise that Chicago would give the book "trade treatment," although not trade royalties. Indeed, he arranged with distributors to stock many bookstores and he tried, but failed, to entice the History Book Club into printing its own edition. He did not hire a publicist for the book. We still had a little way to go – the press's copy editing, my corrections to the copy edits, and proofing – but that was all downhill, and *Crossing over the Line: Legislating Morality and the Mann Act* appeared in the fall of 1994.

The book received a good number of reviews, 20 that I know of, and I'm sure there are a few more. This is more than the usual scholarly book receives. Most of the reviews were mixed, generally with praise for the scholarship and writing, but deploring that I had not covered areas the particular reviewer would have emphasized had he or she gone to the trouble of writing the book themselves. Some of the critiques were inconsistent. A few of the mixed reviews complained that I did not take women's complaints seriously enough, whereas other reviews noted my use of feminist sources. One reviewer groused that my book was "analytical, not theoretical." A reviewer ought to consider what the author intended his book to be before criticizing it for what it was never intended to be.

The 2-3 reviews that were seriously critical were pieces whose authors were offended by my Libertarian and anti-government tone. I made no secret of my position. In fact, I dedicated the book to the "Victims of the Department of Justice." The writing of a scholarly book is a long and arduous process, and the author's personal and political passions often provide the driving force to move forward. For my part, my libertarianism and outrage that the federal government would criminalize boyfriend-girlfriend travel, provided real incentive for me to begin this book and then to carry it, over several years of hard work, to completion. Of course, the scholar must add depth of research and objectivity to the passion or the work becomes mere polemic.

Obviously, I liked the reviews most favorable to my work. The review in the *American Historical Review* concluded "this thought-provoking book should be read by everyone." Stanley Katz of the American Council of Learned Societies wrote in *Choice* that I had written a "model of good narrative history, sound legal and political analysis, and straightforward exposition." One reviewer, Bernard A. Weisberger, clearly saw my effort to demonstrate how the federal government had changed its interpretation of the Mann Act over time in accord with the changing mores of the American people. He wrote that "what Langum has done is to study the changing application of a law, in its social context, a procedure that dissolves boundaries between legal history and social history and other disciplines to the benefit of them all. His story cuts across women's, urban, family, and religious history, public opinion formation and its media enhancement, and the legislative impact of ideological lobbies."

Chicago asked Lawrence M. Friedman to look at the manuscript and provide a letter from which the press could extract some blurbs. Friedman, a law professor at Stanford, is one of the leading lights in the law and society movement, a group that sees legal history as a response to the evolving impact of social and economic factors playing on the law. It is the opposite of those who study legal opinions in an effort to see a sort of autonomous change in legal doctrine arising out of the cases themselves. Friedman sent Chicago a glowing report, with a copy to me in which he said he meant every word. Friedman wrote that the book

> is beautifully written—fresh, lucid, at times witty, at times intense and passionate. It will certainly be the definitive study of the rise and fall of this ignoble experiment in behavior control. ... I came away impressed with the breadth of Langum's scholarship, his wisdom, his erudition, his ability to apply technical mastery, broad understanding, and keen insight to this rather sordid chapter in our social history.

Several of the reviews referred to my writing as both witty and passionate, and seeing that appraisal pleased me very much. That was clearly my intent. The witty in my writing was something I had to work on. The passionate came more naturally because of my strong libertarian beliefs and hatred of the federal government.

Two reviews particularly pleased me for where they were published. A long, favorable review appeared only a few weeks after publication in the *Los Angeles Times.* I hoped that this would be the first breakthrough into reaching a general audience. Later two or three additional reviews appeared in smaller daily newspapers, but it certainly was not the breakthrough I hoped. Although John Tryneski had promised me the book would receive "trade treatment," Chicago did not hire a publicist for the book. Without a publicist, radio and television interviews and appearances would be almost impossible, and there were none. The second review that pleased me because of its location was a full page review on March 31, 1995 in the (London) *Times Literary Supplement.* As with its American equivalent, the *New York Review of Books*, it is a signal honor to be reviewed in either.

The sales of *Crossing over the Line* were not significant, around 1,600 in hardback and 500 more in paperback. A fellow legal historian told me that for a university press book this constituted a "best seller." His own books had never sold as well. A few college teachers adopted it for classroom use.   At a book signing at Books-a-Million in Birmingham, one buyer told me he had heard about the book from a radio talk show. I wish I knew more about any radio publicity. Various local groups invited me to talk over lunch or dinner about the book.

Immediately after publication, I held an informal gathering at my house of all the research assistants who had worked on the book, together with their spouses or girlfriends. We drank some wine, told some stories, and I gave each of them an inscribed copy in which I specifically mentioned what they had done for the book, their individual projects. Over the years I've received a lot of fan letters for this book, and inquiries from criminal lawyers thinking to hire me as an expert witness. Also I've received congratulatory notes from my own Cumberland colleagues. The nicest was from Tom Berg who wrote that my book was "a total pleasure to read. You do a wonderful job of moving from the stories of the individuals caught in the Act's web, to the broader social background, to the legal questions. ... It is really an honor to be the colleague of a historian as good as you." Those are nice words from a former Rhodes Scholar.

During this decade I did a fair amount of traveling to Europe. At the end of 1989 and first few days of 1990 I travelled with a group on an art tour of The Netherlands and Belgium. Then in March 1991 Grace and I travelled by ourselves to Britain, where I introduced her to many friends there, followed by Paris and Luxembourg in February and March 1992 and Dublin in March 1994. I took my oldest daughter Virginia to England in July 1994 and to Dublin in July 1995. In the early 1990s I took a few trips to England on my own, on one occasion in December 1992 to visit my good friend Stanley Siddle, while he and his wife were living in Wiltshire. Of course Grace and I travelled domestically as well and in the early 1990s visited Boston, San Francisco and the Bay Area (to visit my stepchildren and good friends Stanley Siddle, Ann Schumacher, and Barbara Jeskalian), Reno (to visit good friends Gene and Adele Malott), Los Angeles, New York, Cherokee, North Carolina (for a blue grass festival), Asheville, Mobile (to visit Grace's relatives), Memphis, Chicago (to visit my parents), New Orleans, Natchez, and Tucson (to visit my parents at their winter home). I'm sure I've overlooked many places.

The beginnings of new school terms, especially the opening fall term, was generally an exciting time at Cumberland. Not only would new freshmen enter the school, but there were sometimes new colleagues, and often new courses, although for me new classes were limited to the spring terms, because I taught required courses, Evidence and Property, in the fall. Throughout this decade we held freshmen dialogues, in which 12-15 new students would discuss studying in law school, along with a faculty member who taught freshman courses, in his or her home. The Student Bar Association supplied pizza and cokes, and I always supplied the beer. We had a good time talking about study techniques, exams, and why the faculty always pretended to be so gruff and foreboding in class (to prepare them to face judges who were often much worse). I also enjoyed teaching mock classes as part of the freshman orientation.

But as the decade wore on, I came to enjoy these weeks of beginnings less and less. I saw them as a significant end to research. To be sure, there was still time available during the term. I usually taught six hours in the week, and I prepared for an hour or sometimes two, amounting to about 15 hours a week spent directly on teaching. I might spend half an hour per day (on average) talking with students and about 2-3 hours per week on faculty committee work, but at the end of adding all this up, my hours per week on faculty work other than teaching amounted to only about 20. So there was plenty of time available during the term for writing, editing, or reading books or articles. What could not be done conveniently during a term was archival research where I would have to travel to a distant manuscript collection or archives. On top of this, I was feeling a bit burned out, and in the late 1990s during the beginnings of new terms I often remarked in my diary how I looked forward to retirement.

Meanwhile I was still teaching at my full pace. I was somewhat traditional in my approach to teaching, probably more Socratic in style than my younger colleagues. Even though as a student I had not liked the Socratic method, this was the traditional method of teaching law. I knew that my students were not prepared to engage in the heavy solitary reading that I needed to compensate for my lack of class attendance. If I were somewhat abrasive in asking questions, I thought of it as a game, and told the students that at the beginning of every course. In terms of grades I thought I was reasonable, and I did use a modified curve. It was very hard to earn an A from me, although I did give some in every course, but it was also almost impossible to flunk. B's and C's predominated, although I had no problem giving D's to bad students, some of whom really deserved an F. I reflected, and I believe accurately, on my career in my diary for February 24, 2000:

> I've done reasonably well at my second career (i.e., after leaving the practice of law), although I know I have not kept my nose to the "law grindstone." I have certainly kept abreast of developments in Evidence and Property (my principal courses, aside from Legal History) to conduct good

introductory survey courses, but I certainly have not kept abreast of these developments to qualify as a scholar of Evidence or a scholar of Property and have never claimed to be either. My journal articles in history (and law) are largely descriptive and are not keenly analytical. My true claim to scholarship lies in my books.

I still received a lot of negative student comments on their evaluation forms. Apparently I was abrasive and disrespectful toward students, although even my harshest critics praised my knowledge of the material and organization of the course. However, these evaluations must be taken with a grain of salt. Many, many former students at post-graduation parties came up to me or even wrote me by letter to say how much they had enjoyed a particular course, how much they had learned from it, and if reviewing for the bar examination, how much better prepared they felt than other bar candidates.

Four tributes to my teaching are particularly noteworthy. Sharon Donaldson, the daughter of Frank Donaldson, former Deputy Attorney General for Alabama, was in my Property class. She was an excellent student and graduated near the top of her class. Three or four years after she graduated Frank told me that Sharon had remarked to him that I was the best professor she had had at Cumberland. About ten years after his graduation Jack Caldwell gave two small denomination gold coins to a colleague, Tom Stone, and myself. He had had a case involving rent payable in gold coins, and he said our courses, in Contracts (Stone) and Property (me) had been very helpful.

The most spectacular gesture of thanks came in July 1994 in London. My daughter and I had just left the Tube and were headed toward a theatre when a man rushed up and asked "You're David Langum, aren't you?" I admitted as much, and he went on to say that he had just won a multi-million-dollar verdict, and what I had taught him in Evidence several years back gave him a real advantage over his opposition and helped him win his case. He shook my hand and thanked me. My 13-year-old daughter was very impressed that her dad could be plucked out of the streets of London to be given praise and thanks. I was a bit impressed myself. Probably the thanks that made me happiest was from a recent graduate who came by my office to say that before my course in legal history he had never been particularly interested in history. Now he regularly included history among his reading.

In 1990-1991, I served on the Faculty Recruitment Committee. In the next academic year, I was on the Self-Study Committee, charged with drafting the document that would be of much importance for our fall 1992 ABA inspection. I spent many hours in January 1991 analyzing the accomplishments of the faculty over the previous seven years, then sent it out to the faculty for comments, and finished it up in April 1991. In 1993-1994, I was on the Admissions Committee. We were in a difficult position since Cumberland's endowment did not permit her to ride out any shortfalls in admissions, and we simply had to have a class of 235 to pay our bills. So we as a committee had to hold our noses and take people who probably should not have been in law school. Although there was some administrative pressure to meet admissions quotas, to Cumberland's credit there was never any hint of pressure to grade easier to facilitate retention in the second and third years.

The most important committee I served on was the Policy Committee, the one committee elected by the faculty and not appointed by the dean. It gives guidance to the dean on important and sometimes urgent matters, often before full disclosure to the faculty. When the school is not in session it acts on behalf of the entire faculty. Several colleagues had asked me to run for this office in the late 1980s, and then importuned me to run again for the next two years. The last time I ran, in spring 1990, for the 1991-1992, year I made it clear that I was not going to re-run for a few years. However, I was back on this critical committee for academic years 1994-1995 and again in 1999-2000. By then there was an abundance of bright younger academics at Cumberland who could take over these responsibilities.

The joint inspection by the American Bar Association (ABA) and the Association of American Law Schools (AALS) arrived in the fall of 1992. The ABA portion went reasonably well except its concern over our much crowded and outdated law library. The Dean promised prompt action. The AALS was very concerned with our "diversity," meaning that we did not have enough black faculty or students. These good liberals were not at all concerned with quality, merely numbers, and insisted on a re-inspection in the following year. One AALS inspector in 1993 was a legal historian, and he and I hit it off very well. I emphasized that our affirmative action program for minorities was conservative. We did not accept black students just for the sake of having more black students, but really considered the likelihood of their success in law school. As a result, we had a high retention rate among minorities. One of the inspectors said he had talked with several black students and reported that they felt good about Cumberland and not at all alienated.

Their principal concern was with the low number of black faculty at Cumberland, and the AALS put tremendous pressure on the Dean. He committed to budget for one new position to be filled by a black female for that year, a second new black female hire for the year afterward, and a third black hire, male or female, the year after that. The dean reported to the faculty that Cumberland *must* hire a black female faculty member, regardless of whether we could find one who met our normal standards of scholarship. The problem with affirmative action for minority faculty is that there is a relatively low pool of available candidates, and the truly outstanding black prospects are snatched up by the Harvards, Yales, and Stanfords. Lesser quality schools, such as Cumberland, have to dig deeper into the pool. Cumberland has been relatively fortunate in minority faculty hiring. Most of our affirmative action hires, but not all of them, have become good teachers and scholars. However, if affirmative action had never been a consideration, I am certain that the Cumberland faculty would be more distinguished.

During the 1990s I was involved in a number of academic or at least Samford-related controversies. I became strongly opposed to the Gulf War in 1991, perhaps out of a feeling of guilt that I had done so little to protest Vietnam. I participated in a protest rally in front of the Old Federal Building after which a reporter came up to me, said that I did not look like the typical protestor, and wanted to interview me. I replied that I thought the federal government had just dreamed up the war because it did not want any other bully in the Mideast except for its satrap, Israel. She asked me my profession, I replied law professor, but I refused to say at which institution I taught. She reported all of that accurately in an article that appeared the next day in the local newspaper.

Jim Sullivan, an Assistant U.S. Attorney, complained to Tom Corts, Samford's president and to my dean, that I was picketing the U.S. Courthouse. I told Dean Williams that I had been there, but had declined to tell the reporter what university I worked for. Parham said that I was well within the university guidelines and within my rights, and that he would tell Sullivan. I asked him to tell Tom Corts as well. President Corts wrote me back and said that he appreciated "your consideration for the law school and the university. I understand that your expression of opinion was totally proper and certainly within bounds. Your sensitivity is appreciated, though it is my intent to assure you the widest possible freedom to express your own personal views."

During the buildup to the Gulf War, a gathering was held at the Divinity School questioning U.S. Iraqi policy. After some brief talks by a panel the meeting opened to questions. One student asked what they as students could really do to oppose the imminent war. A Christian activist on the panel replied that students could write letters and attend church vigils. I stood up to a packed audience and asserted that there was a whole lot more students could do. The bully-like nature of the federal government was backed by its huge military, just as during the time in Vietnam. I questioned whether it was appropriate to socialize young people into the culture of militarism by encouraging "hired killers" on an educational campus. Something quite specific they could do was to struggle and pressure the administration to rid Samford of the ROTC and in the meantime to ostracize students who were a part of it, and therefore in training to become killers for hire. Dead silence prevailed in the crowded room, and very shortly thereafter the student moderator adjourned the meeting. Timothy George, Dean of the Beeson Divinity School at Samford, came up to me, shook my hand, and told me he appreciated my remarks.

I travelled on an overnight bus with fellow Birmingham protestors, almost all in their 20s, to participate in a protest march in

Washington, D.C. denouncing the war. Unlike my fellow protestors, however, I did not return to Birmingham on a second overnight bus ride. Instead, I had a nice dinner with a friend, Steve Burns, and then flew back. Paradoxically, Steve was an employee of the government in the Internal Revenue Service. That was not the only paradox of the weekend. I noticed that the parking lot of choice for buses carrying protestors from all over the country was the Pentagon parking lot. The military graciously allowed those marching against the military to park at the military's parking lot while they did their marching. That was a quintessential exercise of confidence and power, and at the same time a wonderful demonstration of the government's respect for the right of its citizens to assemble and protest. Even if I hate the federal government, I have to give the devil its due.

Samford employed and still uses a net nanny to censor the internet that comes into the campus. I made several appeals to various committees to urge the administration to permit free speech on campus, to no avail. On August 22, 1998 Samford's net nanny censored the entire *Washington Post,* probably because that edition carried too many naughty words arising from the Clinton/Lewinski scandal. I immediately wrote the entire university faculty that "nothing could be a better example of the folly and intellectual immorality of Samford's censorship. How can a place that dares call itself a university wield such a clumsy fist over the free flow of information?" I sent a copy of the email to the Provost and within 45 minutes the *Washington Post* was unblocked. I received several thank-you emails, ranging all the way from a secretary in the Business School, to the chairman of the Religion Department, and to Rod Davis, the Chairman of the School of Arts & Sciences. However, one stubborn critique came from a professor in the Pharmacy School, who opined that it was better some "good information" be blocked than smut and spam enter the campus, and therefore censorship was the "morally correct choice."

The year 2000 brought the incident which I called the faculty gag order. In April of that year a mentally-disturbed man named Richard Baumhammers went on a shooting rage in Pittsburgh, killing five persons. Cumberland promptly admitted that this mass murderer was a graduate, Class of 1992. Dean Currier emailed the entire law faculty and requested that they not talk with the media. I sent an email to the law faculty protesting even this request. But then the *Birmingham News* carried an article on the local connection of this man and quoted Virginia Loftin, Director of Communications for Cumberland, as saying "the faculty have been instructed not to comment on this." I sent a second email to the law school faculty that "no remark by any faculty member can possibly do as much damage to Cumberland's (and Samford's) reputation as did Virginia Loftin's remark. It gives the impression of a closed up, secretive, defensive (right wing religious) school that probably has a lot to hide. It is the opposite of the free and open air that ought to be the hallmark of a university." The Dean sent the law faculty an email saying that Virginia Loftin had been misquoted.

The most academically important controversy of this decade was the university library's (not law library) policy of throwing away older but still useful materials, specifically 19th and early 20th century journals, including the *Survey* that both Bill Ross and I had used quite a bit in our research. I tracked down the fellow, Tom Skinner, who had conducted the actual trashing ("deaccessioning" is the librarian euphemism), and he admitted it. Moreover the library kept no records of what they had trashed or given to another institution. I asked him about a modification whereby they give the campus advance notice in the monthly newsletter of what they propose to throw out, rather than do it secretly. He took umbrage in my characterization of secrecy, on the incredible reasoning that any faculty member could have walked into the library and seen workmen removing the periodicals, as though faculty need to post a constant watch at the library to make sure it did not trash its collection.

Skinner refused to even consider any other approach than what he currently did: ask two librarians for their consent before he threw things out. I pointed out that this was inadequate as librarians might not know what periodicals were of use to researchers, as they are used entirely in the library and there are no records generated of their use. So I wrote a formal complaint, sending an email to Jean Thomason, the acting director of the university library, with copies to the university library committee, the entire faculty of the history department, and of course to Tom Skinner. I repeated my complaint made previously to Skinner about the secrecy of throwing out library material and suggested ways of giving notice, and closed with what I thought was a stirring call to action:

> Librarians are trustees of the written essence of our civilization, as books and journals are the distillation of the thought processes of the past. Librarians have duties that run not only to the present patrons but to future generations of users. By throwing away books without a thorough deliberation librarians are breaching their fiduciary duties. A future generation that needs vanished books will hardly care whether they were lost through book-burnings conducted by raving fanatics or, instead, by the silent, secret work of librarians. A book "weeded" or "deaccessioned" is lost just as much as a book burnt.

> And the irony is in your failure to even maintain records of what you throw out. Future generations will never be able to tell how great a library Samford might have had, but for your policies.

I had thought that I would have natural allies in the geography and history faculty to whom I sent copies of my letter. But I misjudged the parochialism of the undergraduate faculty. Professor Greg Jeanne (geography) wrote me that I had made a "personal attack" against Jean Thomason and that he was offended by my tone and arrogance. "You owe an apology to Jean for the unfounded accusations of acting in secret with implied malice, and for the slurs against her character." I showed my letter to the law librarian, Becky Clapp, and several other law librarians, and they did not see anything personal in my letter. Professor Clapp suggested that maybe the feel good culture outside of the law school had gotten to the point where any criticism was taken as a personal attack.

Professor Jim Brown in the History Department then weighed in, attacking me, not the throw-away policy. He called my memo "hot and heavy" and claimed I had made a "vindictive personal attack" but against Tom Skinner, a different victim than Greg Jeanne thought. Brown sent a copy of his memo to Dean Parham Williams and said that the Dean ought to "encourage" me to make a public apology. The university librarians and the faculty angry at my criticism of Tom Skinner seemed oblivious to a university's role in promoting scholarship, and that there were scholars on the Samford campus who might have a use for obscure and rarely-used journals.

Bill Ross and Tom Berg met with Williams on behalf of the law school library committee to inquire what, if anything, it should do about the controversy. According to Tom Berg, Parham was not at all concerned and felt my original memo was more or less appropriate. Meanwhile, Becky Clapp wrote Jean Thomason to assure her that I had definitely not meant anything personal in my original complaint, and that I just had "a strong manner of endeavoring to stimulate intellectual discussions on subjects." I genuinely believe there was a cultural overlay at work here. Most southerners expect someone to sidle up to them personally, inquire about their health, sweet talk them about their kids and houses, and only later make a subtle and indirect criticism. Straightforward criticism and in writing completely unnerves them.

In the fall of 1993, Gerald Bray of the Divinity School and I organized a biography reading group to read and discuss biographies. It was not truly a Samford club, as it was open to anyone interested and we always met off campus for dinner and discussion, usually at a local bookstore that was connected with a restaurant. We tried to meet monthly, although these intentions were frequently interrupted by other concerns. Still, it had a remarkable staying power, and we met a minimum of three to four times a year for the rest of the decade. At first we tried to read multiple biographies of the same subject, to compare biographical styles. Our first subject was Czar Nicholas II, and we found four current biographies that we read over a period of nine months. A bit too much in retrospect. I think the only other multi-book subjects were Georgia O'Keefe and John Steinbeck, and they were only two books apiece. Gradually we drifted apart. Grace dropped out after we split up as a couple. My later wife, Frances, left the group in the fall of 2000 as she had our toddler to care for, and just did not have the time to read. Gerald moved back to England in the early 2000s. However, for the eight years or so it lasted, we had a cohort of five to seven people who regularly attended, and we learned a lot about interesting people and biographical styles.

In February 1994 a colleague, Tom Berg, and I spoke with Dean Williams about our idea of organizing a Cumberland Colloquium on Law, Religion, and Culture, in which an in-house or an outside academic would present a work in progress for critique and discussion with interested attendees. Parham thought that a good idea and agreed to fund $1500 per academic year to bring in outside academics to read papers. Through 1997 we held several colloquia per academic year and generated interest and attendance among theologians as well as law faculty. Usually we attracted only seven to eight people, but we had some meetings that brought in 14-15 persons. After 1997 the number of meetings per year dropped to one or two, but our Colloquium on Law, Religion, and Culture carried on through the decade.

Bill Ross and I organized another Cumberland Colloquium, this one focused on American legal history. Our opening session was in February 1996 when I spoke on legal education in the antebellum South. We had an attendance of 15, including history professors from Birmingham-Southern College as well as Samford. The legal history colloquia often attracted 14-15 attendees and often from outside the law school, generally more people than the equivalent law, religion, and culture program. In both of the programs we sometimes brought in outside academics, and among the pleasures of this work were the nice dinners we had with the visiting faculty. Bill and I were the only ones generating topics and inviting speakers, and by the end of the decade we were just burned out.

In 1994, three of my colleagues, Trisha Olson, Tom Berg, and David Smolin, and I had the thought of developing a graduate program leading to the LL.M. and S.J.D. degrees, master and doctor of law, in the field of law, religion, and culture. It would be modeled after Michigan's LL.M./S.J.D. program, with which I was of course familiar, but would differ in that the year in residence would not consist of attending seminars but rather would be tutorial. The four of us would conduct tutorials during divided portions of the year. This way the graduate students would have exposure in American religious history, my area, and also the sociology of religion in America, theology, and contemporary American law and religion. Each of the candidates would read books we selected, write papers, and then meet with the appropriate faculty member to discuss the book in tutorial style. At the end of the first year, the candidate would be awarded the LL.M., and then have four years to complete a dissertation.

The LL.M./S.J.D. program turned out to be a disaster. First, it took so long to come to fruition. We needed only a month to write up a tentative proposal and gain our own law faculty's approval. Then it took almost two years to deal with the university administrators' objections and concerns. But ultimately they passed on it and we gained the approval of the university's trustees. The four faculty proposing the program all agreed to conduct tutorials for no additional compensation and no diminution of their course loads. I agreed to act as the Program Director, appropriate because I was the only one of us who actually had a doctorate in law. After everything was settled in the law school and university, we needed acquiescence from the ABA, which had its own concerns, mainly to make sure the new program had no impact on our regular J.D. program. By 2000 we were preparing our application forms when we faced yet another hurdle. I had mocked up a basic short application form similar to that used in the Business School, and turned it over to Virginia Loftin, the same woman involved with the faculty gag order. She prepared a new form, possibly under Dean Currier's direction, that contained all sorts of language about Samford being a Christian school, and required each candidate to initial their understanding of that and further that they would not engage in any improper conduct, that they had never committed a crime, and that they understood they could be expelled if they lied on the application. It went on and on, giving every sign that we were indeed a bigoted institution.

I asked for a meeting with Dean Barry Currier and Virginia Loftin and raised my concerns. Currier thought I had crossed the line from academic to administrative and I should not be concerned with it. I replied that I was called the Program Director, that most people would think that carried some administrative responsibilities, and I thought the proposed heavily religious and moral issues on the application verged on the bigoted. I could not be the Director of a program that sent that sort of message on its application form, and if they really insisted on its use I would have to resign as Program Director. They took a few days to think it over and acceded to the Business School form as adapted to our needs.

So we had a program now, it was advertised and ready for applications. However, although we had some inquiries, we had very few actual applications. We began that fall with two students in the program, one of whom dropped out after only a few weeks. The single remaining student was not an exemplar of diligence, and often did not show up for his tutorials, nor call to cancel. When asked why he did not come, he usually said he had been in court trying a case. Obviously this academic program was low on his priorities. However, he did do the work, even if not so brilliantly, so at the end of the year we awarded him the LL.M. degree, and he indicated that he did not intend to prepare a dissertation for the S.J.D. Our continued advertising for the next two years attracted no acceptable candidates. Then Trisha Olson and Tom Berg both left Samford. So the entire program just collapsed in 2002.

I had some small amount of side work during the years 1991-2000. I did no consulting for law firms during this period. In 1997 I led an Equal Employment Opportunities workshop for several dozen non-lawyer investigators. It was a day and a half affair in which I summarized most of the rules of evidence and then took questions on evidentiary issues that came up in their work, what sorts of troubles they experienced in obtaining admissible proof. The government paid me $950, and I thought that reasonable although other faculty were making far more in consulting.

In March 1995 a litigation lawyer with the major downtown firm of Balch and Bingham called me in to review proposed multi-state bar examination questions, in multiple choice form, for possible future use on the national portion of the bar examination. He and I took a mini-bar quiz of 30 evidentiary questions in examination format, and then compared our answers to those proposed by the national bar examiners. The litigator-lawyer had only 20 of the 30 correct, whereas I had 27. He told me that Cumberland quite clearly had me teaching the right course, Evidence, and that my score would be higher than ever attained in Alabama and in the 99+ percentile nationally. He offered me a job on the spot to come back to take model Evidence exams and also comment on whether any questions were misleading or poorly worded.

For the next year and a half I went down to Balch and Bingham for several two hour sessions of exam taking, paid $100 per hour by the Multistate Bar Exam. I made easy money, it was kind of fun, and it very much impressed my students. I could not remember the exact questions, and I had no way of knowing which of the hundreds of questions I answered would be on their own bar exams. So I thought it no ethical violation at all to disclose my bar exam work. Then in August 1996, my boss the trial litigator was promoted by the Multistate Bar people to its national board, and that was the end of my employment reading questions for future bar exams.

Chapter 8

Life, Teaching, and Scholarship in Birmingham:
Fall 1990-Summer 2000,
Part Two

By 1999 I was seriously interested in buying a summer home in the West. I noticed a summer teaching job in Property available at Seattle University, applied for it and got the position, classes beginning early in mid-May. I was by myself for a month or so, before Frances and little David, Jr. came out to live with me in Tacoma. Seattle University's law school had not yet moved to the main campus in Seattle, so I worked and lived in Tacoma. My schedule gave me a long weekend, and I made great use of that by driving through various towns around Puget Sound, looking for possible locations for a summer home. I ultimately fell in love with Port Townsend, and purchased the Victorian era house I call "Greystones" to use as a summer home. I raised the ceiling back to the original height, removed the carpet and polished the original wood floor, converted the garage into a beautiful study, and thereby fell in love with "Greystones" as well as Port Townsend.

In Tacoma I had an evening class of 73 students, most in their 30s and 40s. I began with future interests, which is a very difficult topic in Property. Probably I should have started with something else, and the beginning couple of weeks were very rough. The Seattle students were quite aggressive and demanding in their questioning, far more than at Cumberland or even in the days at Lincoln Law School. However, things smoothed out and thereafter went well. When I finished the course in mid-July there was considerable applause from the students, much more than I was used to at Cumberland. One student took my picture, and another expressed the hope that I would return next summer to teach Evidence.

Throughout the early 1990s I began to despair about John. None of the communication techniques that Children's Hospital recommended had been implemented. True, John's control of his body, every part, was so poor that access to a computer was very difficult and continued to be so even when his high school became serious about fitting him to a communication device in the later 1990s. Earlier he had a program that included only five or six pre-programmed messages from which he could select by using his eyes. Obviously that was simply an introductory step and not a communication system. The first time I saw John with that device, he made a few movements with his eyes, then looked at me while a mechanical voice came out of his machine saying "I love you." That was really the only time my son John ever told me anything at all, the one and only oral communication. I cried and hugged John, thanked him for telling me that, and said I loved him too.

John began to resist learning. I read to him often, but once I began showing him the actual words, or using a card to move down the page, he understood I was trying to teach him and turned his head away, looking up into the air. He had moved far beyond the happy little boy he once was. As wonderful and intelligent as Virginia was, I became determined that, if possible, I would have more children. My girlfriend Grace was ambivalent about having a child. In 1992 she turned forty, had never had any experience with babies, and worried about a baby's interference with her work at the custom picture framing shop she owned. She certainly was not enthusiastic about having a child. We drifted apart, and I looked around for another mate. I had a lot of regrets, as I really cared for Grace, and she was so kind, helpful, and personally generous to me.

I met my third wife, Frances, through a dating service for men and women who were seeking mates outside of their own age brackets. Frances was 23 years my junior and worked in Boston on the *Christian Science Monitor's* computer help desk, helping reporters around the world resolve their computer problems. She was (and is) fiercely intelligent, well-educated, Brandeis undergraduate and Harvard Divinity School masters, and urgently wanted children. In fact she virtually cross-examined me in our first telephone contact on whether I was truly certain I wanted more children. In the event, we married on June 22, 1996 in Concord, Massachusetts, and we ultimately had (and have) three wonderful children, David John, Jr. , born October 21, 1998; Audrey Leora Kari, born July 2, 2002; and Anna Louisa Kari, born February 26, 2004. To complete this family portrait, I should add that John died in July 2001, just a few weeks short of his 18th birthday. My first wife Bernadette died in August 1995. I flew out to San Jose before her passing, and after she died I felt honored that her children, my stepchildren, asked me to give the eulogy at her funeral. My second wife JoAnne died in August 2009. Virginia flew into Birmingham to be with her, but I had difficulty finding a flight from Seattle that could accommodate my three quite young children as well as myself. I arrived back in Birmingham just a day or two after JoAnne died but before her funeral.

By September 1993, I was ready to take up the Cumberland history project again. The Mann Act manuscript was in production with the University of Chicago Press, and I now had the time to research the next book. The history of Cumberland University had already generated two books. They had very little about the law school, but I read them carefully to get institutional background. I pestered Edward Craig, our law library's reference librarian, to borrow on inter-library loan hundreds of nineteenth and early twentieth century magazine articles and dozens of early books that touched on Cumberland University or her law school. An example is an 1858 article on the history of Cumberland University, the earliest such account. I read all relevant pages, photocopied them, and set them aside for the classification work I planned for the summer of 1994. I also began a detailed correspondence with G. Frank Burns, official historian of Cumberland University, to gather information about obscure sources and to establish my own credentials with him.

I used the pre-internet *National Union Catalog of Manuscript Collections* and learned that the University of North Carolina held an entire collection of the correspondence of Robert L. Caruthers, the first chairman of Cumberland University's board and in that position when the law school was founded. He was also the brother of the first law professor at Cumberland. I anticipated a week's trip to Chapel Hill and considerable digging through hundreds of letters to find an occasional nugget. But the collection had a guide, or finding aide, no doubt lovingly compiled by a librarian many decades ago. I wrote for a copy and miraculously it had a description of the date and correspondent for each of Caruthers's letters. The North Carolina library would supply copies for a modest fee, and I simply ordered copies of letters from each of Caruthers's correspondents that I knew to be associated with the law school. Dean Williams never knew that I had saved the school hundreds of dollars for a research trip that I did not have to take because I bought about thirty dollars' worth of copies by mail.

One trip I needed to make was to Lebanon, Tennessee, home of Cumberland University, the host of Cumberland School of Law until 1961. That university's archives contain most of the old records that would be pertinent: trustees' minutes, yearbooks, a very limited run of a student newspaper, a very limited amount of faculty minutes and reports. Actually, I made three short trips rather than one long one, because the first two were in February 1994 and had to be sandwiched between classes. It was important to my work schedule – all planned out – that I finish the research by summer 1994 so I could devote that summer to sorting out the data. I made the first trip to Lebanon on February 10, 1994. It was a terrible drive to get there. Freezing rain had iced the trees in northern Alabama and Tennessee. Traffic slowed to a crawl, many cars and trucks were in the ditch, and whatever traffic was still moving had to dodge trees that had fallen onto the freeway.

I met Frank Burns at 9:00 the next morning at the Cumberland University's Vise Library. He turned out to be a pleasant and intelligent man. I started working on the trustees' minutes he pulled for me from the archives. They began in 1842 with the founding of the university and were handwritten. I typed long extracts onto a disk in my notebook computer. Copying everything that could conceivably be useful, it was a slow process, and by the end of the afternoon I was only up to 1848. It was a very strange day. It was Friday, but the ice storm had closed the library. Burns let me in because we had arranged for that time, and he was working there himself. The heat was off, and the lights did not work, except in a few of the rooms including the one in which I worked. I wore a sweater, Burns furnished me with a flashlight, and whenever I wanted to use the water fountain or bathroom I had to pick my way through a building foreign to me.

Howard Walthall, my co-author, arrived the next morning, and we worked together at the library. He started with more recent minutes, and I continued with the nineteenth century books. The library was operational by then, and we did a lot of work. We took Frank to lunch, and then he showed us around town and guided us to the earlier antebellum location of the school. Lebanon is now a distant suburb of Nashville, although earlier it was a distinct area and a more important place. That night I had dinner in Nashville with two of our recent graduates, Jeff Foster and his girlfriend Liz, later wife. They had bought an older house in Nashville and were proudly fixing it up.

The next morning I drove back to Birmingham for a few days of classes, and then returned on Wednesday, February 16, after my Evidence class. I checked into my motel and was at work on the trustees' minutes by 3:00PM and stayed at them until the library closed at 10:00. Then I discovered that it is difficult to find something to eat that late in small town Lebanon. After a number of false starts, I had a bowl of excellent chili in a bar. I could have gone out for dinner earlier, but when I visit an out-of-town archives or manuscript collection, I often work straight through until closing. I am usually intense, have limited time, and simply want to sit there and do the work.

I spent the next day, Thursday, entirely on reading trustees' minutes, excepting lunch and a brief stroll around the Cumberland campus. I thought that Lebanon was a crummy town, but the Cumberland campus grew on me. It was so quiet, and the faculty and staff were very nice. The following day, Friday, was the same. I reached the turn of the century in the trustees' minutes and turned my attention to the yearbooks. I ate lunch in the campus cafeteria, and that evening I took Frank Burns to dinner at Meecham's, a nice Italian place with good food and nice décor, Lebanon's only first-class restaurant.

I worked until 4:30 on Saturday. Frank and I visited a local photographer he recommended. Our agreement was that the photographer would make negatives of images that Cumberland University had of law school buildings and personnel, Walthall and I would then use them in our book, and when the project was over we would give the negatives back to the Cumberland archives.

I did not return to Lebanon until early May 1994, after my classes were over for the spring. I worked there May 2-4. Frank Burns was not there, but the librarians let me roam freely in the archives, and I found many new things: 1850s correspondence of a law professor packed with information on the school, lecture notes from 1919, and early student newspaper articles about law students. I finished the trustees' minutes through 1920, copied those law school catalogues that were missing in our Birmingham collection, and read the early alumni magazines. I took the rest of the photographs I wanted duplicated to the photographer.

Jeff and Liz Foster came over from Nashville on Monday, May 2. I felt like an "old hand" in Lebanon by then, and I gave them a tour of the sites associated with the law school. We drove through town and then wandered through Memorial Hall. In the original chapel, then basketball court, and now auditorium, we looked over the imposing portraits of the proud-looking, nineteenth century Cumberland luminaries whose papers I was researching. They are footnote fodder now, I thought. Over dinner at Meecham's, Jeff talked with excitement about his forthcoming M.A. program at Vanderbilt. He is the only law student I have taught who has then worked on an advanced degree in legal history. One drawback of teaching in a law school is the lack of graduate students interested in one's own field who then go forward themselves in equivalent fields. That must be a source of considerable satisfaction to history faculty, although I am not for a minute complaining about teaching in a law school. Measured against this single drawback, there are many great advantages law school faculty enjoy, including higher compensation and far more time for research and writing because of sharply lower class loads. These advantages were due to American Bar Association pressure on central administrations, and have diminished somewhat in recent years due to an antitrust suit brought against the ABA by the Clinton

Administration in 1995. No longer can the ABA consider faculty compensation as a factor in approving law schools, and it therefore no longer enjoys the threat of disapproval as a device to demand high salaries for law faculty.

I did not know it at the time, but apparently a Cumberland trustee observed me during my May 1994 trip working in the archives room and taking photographs to the studio, and became alarmed. There are still a number of local, Lebanon families represented on Cumberland University's Board, and many are descendants of the people we were writing about. Credible sources have since told me that my presence and particularly my questions about past university policies had caused some worry. Additionally, although I did not know this either, Cumberland University and Samford University were then engaged in litigation over the issue of whether Cumberland University could start up a new law school and call it Cumberland University Law School. To some, Howard and I might have seemed like a pair of marauding litigators seeking evidence to use against Cumberland University. After I had completely finished, but before Howard was through with the records, Cumberland University sharply curtailed our use of their records.

By the summer of 1994, I had accumulated hundreds and hundreds of pieces of relevant paper: photocopies of articles, extracts from trustees' minutes, typed or photocopied letters, notes based on primary and secondary sources, and simply my own thoughts and observations that I had typed onto a disk and printed out. Each fact and each of my observations was on letter-sized 8½ by 11 inch paper. Even relevant pages of books had been photocopied.

The next step was to prepare a master outline. Howard and I had already agreed on 1919 as the logical division between our two portions of the book. I planned an institutional theme for the opening chapter for the antebellum years, 1847-1861 followed by a curricular and student themed chapter for the same years. The long period from 1865 to 1919, a major year in the context of the law school's history, did not have a natural break equivalent to the closing of the school by the Civil War. Nonetheless, there was too much material for 1865-1919 to cover in just two chapters of reasonable length.

I picked the construction of Caruthers Hall in 1878 as a break in that long period. In the late nineteenth- and twentieth-century (to 1961), the public associated Cumberland School of Law with that building. I decided on a single, and third, chapter for 1865-1878 to cover all three themes, institutional, curricular, and students, with the period 1878-1919 divided into two chapters. I wanted to close my half of the book with a dramatic institutional moment shortly after the death of long-term professor Nathan Green in 1919. So I reversed the order of the themes covered from that I had used for the antebellum years. Chapter four would be curricular and student developments and chapter five, institutional.

I have previously described my technique of marking each single piece of paper with the number (or numbers) of the chapter in which it will be used, and then placing them in burgeoning file jackets for the separate chapters. By the end of the summer 1994 I had five large bulging file pockets, expanded to their limits. Each jacket was self-sufficient and contained the thoughts, observations, and most importantly the sources from which I could write a chapter. Each was portable, and I could take them to any part of the world to do the actual writing.

I had always wanted to spend a significant amount of time immediately adjacent to the ocean, so close I could go to sleep at night listening to the surf. I chose Gulf Shores, Alabama as a good place to write chapters one and two, and rented a house there for December 1994. Not only was the house right on the Gulf, but it had a wheelchair ramp. That meant that my son John could visit me, as I could push him in his wheelchair up the ramp and into the house.

I've described earlier how I create outlines for each chapter, then re-read all my paperwork and place it into manila folders within the expanding chapter folder, each piece of paper marked with the division number in the chapter outline. That meant I re-read each piece of paper, often for the third time. Then I was ready to write.

My own rules for writing are brief and essentially derived from Strunk and White's classic *The Elements of Style*. Search for scintillating verbs and precise adjectives. Keep sentences short. Avoid passive voice. Prefer the specific to the general. Re-read *The Elements of Style* before writing each book. However, some days only bland verbs and vague adjectives come to mind. Sentences tend toward length, passive is pervasive, and generalities abound. Other days it is difficult to get started and once started hard to keep going. Words sometimes do not flow, and when they do flow they do so poorly.

My solution to these common problems of writers is to force myself to put words down, no matter how badly written. I have a detailed outline, and I know what must be covered. If it is a bad day, I write what I must to explain the next point on my outline, even if in the worst syntax imaginable and with consistently poor word choice. I put it down on the computer pages, then figuratively put the pages up on the shelf, and edit those portions when I have a better day. I took a portable printer to Gulf Shores. After writing two or three sections of each chapter I printed the accumulated text and edited it. When the chapter was complete, I edited the entire text.

Gulf Shores was great fun. By December, the Alabama-based residents and visitors had left, but most of the snowbirds had not yet arrived. Still, enough people were around so that the restaurants and clubs were open. My house was far to the west of the downtown, and in the evenings I had to count down several houses in each direction to see another house with lights on. In the mornings, when I took my walks, the beach was deserted except for the flocks of several species of birds, which seemed to arrive in separate waves every 15 minutes. Alabamians tend to think of Gulf Shores as cold in December, but as someone who spent his youthful Decembers in Chicago, I thought the weather was invigorating, perhaps cool at worst, not cold at all.

I had a few distractions at the beach, but some were very pleasant. Grace came down from Birmingham to visit twice, and also my son and daughter, John and Virginia, spent the week between Christmas and New Year's with me. I had to make very brief returns to Birmingham a few times that month, taking at least two days because of the length of the drive. But most days, I was able to work from

9:00AM to 6:00PM. I accomplished a lot of writing that month, but to be honest the highlights of my Gulf Shores experience were flying a kite with the kids one afternoon on the beach and fireworks on New Year's Eve.

For years I have had a suppressed desire to shoot rockets as a part of a personal fireworks display. When I was eight years old, my family visited an aunt who lived in the country outside Bellingham, Washington. I fired off a rocket on the Fourth of July and either hit a neighbor's cow about a block's distance away, or came perilously close to doing so. We never launched rockets again. As an adult, I wanted badly to include rockets as a part of festive occasions. But I always lived in urban areas and worried that I might burn down somebody's house. However, on December 31, 1994, I bought the biggest rockets I could find, planted them in the sands of the beach, and shot them out into the Gulf of Mexico. What fun!

I thought I could not possibly find a more interesting place to write chapters three through five than I already had in my previous stay in Gulf Shores. I succeeded, however, and wrote the final three chapters during June and July 1995, in Dublin, Ireland. I rented a townhouse in the suburbs and followed the same procedures I used before.

It was a perfect location for serious work. If I needed food or mail service, both a grocery store and post office were within walking distance. However, I could not reach any distractions by foot, excepting my unit's television, and that has never interested me very much. I had to take a bus to get to a restaurant, pub, museum, theatre, or cinema. There could be no sliding into temptation in those circumstances. I had to consciously stop working and take a fifteen minute bus ride into the centre of Dublin.

As mentioned before, I had always marked on my detailed outlines the exact dates when I wanted to reach each specific point. But there was a stick and carrot feature to my situation in Dublin that gave added force to these self-imposed deadlines. My deadlines were 5:00PM on each and every day. If I had finished the sections or editing required by my detailed outline by that time, but only if I had, I then allowed myself the liberty to hop on a bus and visit a pub, take in some of

Dublin's wonderful theatre, or eat excellent lamb in a favorite grill down by the River Liffey. This gave me a powerful incentive to work hard and stay on track. A couple of nights I failed to meet my deadline and I stewed in my townhouse, furious with myself. Generally, I went out, most every night, although I did not stay out late since the last bus that ran to my neighborhood left central Dublin at 11:30PM.

I scheduled my time to permit distractions. I left time to travel around Ireland, and I also had visitors who could use my extra bedroom. My friend and colleague William Ross visited for a few days. Several Cumberland law students flew over to Dublin from the Cumberland program at Durham, England, and stayed with me. My fiancée Frances came over from Boston for almost a week early in the summer, as did my daughter Virginia at the end of my stay. I had a wonderful time in Dublin, but I also took care of business and wrote the final three chapters of the Cumberland book.

In my understanding with Howard Walthall, I agreed to take the laboring oar in finding a publisher. My first thought was to contact the University of Alabama Press, which I did in February 1994 when only an outline and precis were available. Alabama said that it was interested but thought a contract would be premature. That was undoubtedly correct, yet I detected a certain underlying discouragement, perhaps incorrectly, and I resolved to wait until we had more to show a publisher and also that I would try some other presses.

In March 1995, when I had two chapters, a formal book proposal, and a precis of each remaining chapter, I tried again. John Tryneski, my editor in Chicago, liked it but Chicago did not publish institutional histories except for institutions very close to the University or city of Chicago. Louisiana State University gave us a quick formulaic rejection that "the subject is not well-suited to the current needs of our editorial program," patter that it must use on a regular basis.

Howard Walthall suggested that we might investigate a Southern legal history series published by the University of Georgia Press. I sent a copy of the proposal and two chapters to Paul Finkelman and Kermit Hall, the general editors of that series, in early May 1995. They were immediately encouraging. Negotiations slowed down while I was in Ireland, but by October we had a contract. The manuscript still had to be completed, and then vetted by the editors and outside readers for their suggestions and approval, and then ultimately approved by the Press's editorial board.

Once a press regards a manuscript in a generally receptive light, the vetting process poses no real problem to the author. Editorial suggestions are an integral part of the publishing process, and almost always improve a manuscript. A writer may feel hemmed in and frustrated by a loss of some control over his project as more and more editors, designers, and then production managers begin to have input into materials the author was once able to control exclusively. But if one can set ego aside and look at the good of the project as primary, and particularly if the author can compromise creatively, the vetting process and later production process are never serious obstacles to the ultimate publication of a manuscript.

Two final stages in the manuscript production remained, cite-checking and fine editing. Donna K. Vandever, my research assistant in 1995-1996, did a wonderful job cite-checking both my chapters and also Howard's. Our colleague, William G. Ross, not only has a great gift for fine editing but even claims that he enjoys doing it, something almost everyone else hates. He and I regularly read and discuss each other's legal history drafts, although obviously we make each our own final decisions. He was again kind enough to look over my chapters for fine-tuning suggestions. I did some basic editing for Howard's chapters before Bill Ross read them over as well.

One editing decision I made for Howard's final chapter dealt with his mention of each and every current faculty member. The final chapter was intended and described in our preface as entirely celebratory and not the analytical critique that we intended the book as a whole to be. That was because this epilogue covered a period, 1984-1997, when Howard and I had been active at Cumberland. We thought nothing would be gained by rehashing our respective views of nearly contemporaneous controversies. In his first draft of this epilogue/chapter, Howard had worked in the name of every current Cumberland faculty member, and managed to say something congratulatory about each. When he handed me the draft for editing he cautioned me to be careful lest one or two names be cut and feelings hurt. What I did was to expunge *all* of our names and accomplishments. I thought that Howard's specificity and praise for all would lessen the value of the book. When Howard received back his edited copy, he sputtered to me "How can you do this? These are your colleagues. How can you just take them all out of the book?" I joked that my Yankee insensitivity enabled me, but I also explained to Howard that the removal would improve the book's staying power.

The first box of our books arrived on June 12, 1997. Its title incorporated our purpose to celebrate Cumberland's sesquicentennial: *From Maverick to Mainstream: Cumberland School of Law, 1847-1997.* We had a good number of sesquicentennial commemorations in 1997, at which the book was mentioned and praised. We did not expect a great deal of notice to be taken of the book outside the Cumberland community. Most institutional histories are so boosterish in tone and skimpy in analysis that many historical journals will not review them. Accordingly, only about a half dozen reviews of the book appeared, and most of those reviews come from southern regional or state journals. The two leading American legal history journals both favorably reviewed *From Maverick to Mainstream*, and both in their opening paragraphs emphasize the objective and critical posture of our book. The review in the *American Journal of Legal History* noted that faculty-written studies of their own institutions are rarely objective, but "to the contrary, though, Langum and Walthall present both the bright and the dark of Cumberland's history, and the authors neither shy away from objectivity nor do they neglect to include less than admirable aspects of Cumberland's history." Two of the reviews praised our inclusion of much detail about student life. But the major thrust of the reviews was praise for our objectivity. As the review in a national historical periodical, *The Journal of American History*, put it:

> David J. Langum and Howard P. Walthall have written one of the few critical scholarly examinations of the history of an American law school. Drawing on rich primary sources, they have created a detailed narrative of teachers, courses, and student activities and a thorough analysis of the

transformation of a stubbornly nineteenth-century school into a model of modern American legal education.

My greatest participation in scholarly conferences was during the decade of the 1990s, when I attended dozens. Cumberland School of Law paid for my travel, hotel, and dining expenses for almost all of these, and I presented a paper or made a commentary at most. Their venues were scattered all over the United States, Canada, and one in Europe. They gave me an opportunity to talk with other historians and legal historians, but also, depending on exactly where they were held, to visit with friends or my stepchildren. The sessions where papers were read were quite scholarly. However, the conversations amongst the attendees were generally not so intellectual but mostly gossip about other historians and vignettes of our current research and writing interests.

I attended three of the annual meetings of the Organization of American Historians during the 1990s, and four of the American Historical Association. I went to six annual conferences of the Western History Association during those ten years. The WHA meetings were immensely enjoyable as well as intellectually stimulating since they were usually held at attractive locales and with interesting side excursions. I attended the annual meetings of the Association of American Law Schools twice during these years, somewhat less than I had in the 1980s. The conferences described above were large and open to public participation, but I attended smaller meetings, more selective, as well.

In July 1991 I gave a paper on the Spanish legal system, as distinct from Mexican, in California at a small conference held at the University of California, Santa Barbara, and in 1992 I was invited to deliver a paper and attend a conference sponsored by the Huntington Library in honor of the Columbus Quincentenary. This was an elaborate affair attended by the Spanish consul. The Huntington put up all the conferees and spouses at the Ritz-Carlton and fed us royally. It seemed regrettable after all this honor that I was leaving the field of Hispanic history. I was invited to a conference to honor the 85th (I believe) birthday of John Reid at New York University in May 1995, and in 1999 was invited by Boston University to talk about the life and work of Bill Kunstler. Also in 1999, the Roosevelt Institute for American Studies in Middelburg, The Netherlands, invited me to present a paper on the history of the regulation of prostitution in the United States. I was to read this paper at a forthcoming conference comparing the regulation of morals and mores in the United States and The Netherlands. Fortunately, Cumberland paid for my round trip ticket to Amsterdam, and I was able to attend the conference in September 1999. Eventually the papers given at the conference, including my own, appeared as a book.

Since I write in the field of legal history, it is not surprising that the single conference I most steadfastly attended was that of the American Society for Legal History, with eight annual meetings in the 1990s. During his term as president of the society, Lawrence Friedman appointed me as the program director for the 1991 meeting. It proved to be a tremendous amount of work. I did have a committee, but after dropping off stimulating ideas during our single meeting, the implementation of these ideas, and the selection and invitation of speakers, was left largely to me as program director. I organized 66 different presenters, and was innovative. For years the program sessions had been characterized by junior scholars divesting themselves of 30-45 minutes of wisdom on truly arcane topics (e.g., conveyancing in 13th century Normandy). These specific sessions will always be important as sounding boards for vetting of doctoral dissertations, through which junior scholars can get valuable feedback from more seasoned scholars.

However, I wanted to see if we could develop more over-arching themes with sessions that would be of general interest to all legal historians. I crafted a plenary session with a panel of top people in the histories of Roman, American, English, and Canon law, devoted to the issue of whether legal historians, all off in their tiny corners, have anything to say to one another. In other words, is there a common denominator? And I diversified in terms of the presenters themselves. I induced people to give papers who had never been active in our society or programs before: faculty from political science and English departments and a school of education; two federal judges; an employee of the National Archives; and a San Francisco policeman who had studied law enforcement in early American California. At this same 1991 conference I was elected to a 3 year term as a member of the Board of Directors of the Society. The association's format calls for contested elections, with more nominations than slots available. I believe my success was due to both the influence of Lawrence Friedman and also as a token of respect with which my first book, *Law and Community on the Mexican-California Frontier*, was held by many in the Society.

My own school, Cumberland School of Law, held elaborate conferences, called the Rushton Distinguished Lecture Series, in the years 1995-1997. We had notable keynote speakers, including Akhil Reed Amar and Anthony T. Kronman, of Yale, and also Lawrence M. Friedman, of Stanford, who came at my behest. Additional auxiliary speakers included James Boyd White, of Michigan, Griffin Bell (President Carter's Attorney General), and several Cumberland faculty, including myself, who contributed papers. These were three day affairs and somewhat tiring. The primary lectures continued on, but were stand-alone, without other speakers.

Frances and I made some international travels in the late 1990s, including Tuscany, Italy in spring 1997 followed by Britain in the late fall of 1997. I took my daughter Virginia to Ireland in 1998, and we returned for a briefer, more business-like trip in late winter 2000 for her to look over Trinity College in Dublin as a place to spend her undergraduate years. She liked it, attended for four academic years, and received her A.B. there, in English Literature with first class honors.

William M. Kunstler, the famous radical lawyer, died on September 4, 1995, and I read his obituary in *The New York Times* the following day. I had met Kunstler in San Jose, California, when he gave a talk before a small group of radical lawyers that I crashed into, and tried to stir us into action. Before beginning the long obituary I was aware of many of Kunstler's long list of controversial cases, including only in part: his role in the Chicago 7 trial; the Pine Ridge Indian activists' trial; his defense of H. Rap Brown, the Berrigan brothers and the east coast Black Panthers; his representation of gangster John Gotti; and his promotion of the "black rage" defense on behalf of Colin Ferguson, the mass murderer on the Long Island Railroad. Reading the obituary I learned of even more notorious clients Kunstler had represented, but also how complex a man he seemed to be. He was a lover of opera, a reader of French poetry, and a writer of several books of his own. I admired Kunstler because of his willingness to fight the federal government at every opportunity.

I decided I wanted to write Kunstler's biography. That very evening, September 5th, I rushed to a bookstore and bought his recently published autobiography. I read it immediately and concluded it would not be competitive with a true biography, and that my book would be much more evaluative. There was hardly any introspection in Bill Kunstler's book, and I would treat it as simply a primary source. Over the next few days I checked out how much source material was available, and found that there were dozens of interviews of and articles about Kunstler, and several books that Bill Kunstler wrote himself, aside from the autobiography. Even though it came close to the beginning of our marriage, and obviously would drain much of my time, Frances was enthusiastic about this major project. So I decided to do it. I reasoned that research on such an interesting man, including the opportunities to interview his radical colleagues, would be great fun. Also, such a book might very well become a trade book with large sales to the public generally.

I dug into the research as I always have, by first gathering all the available written materials. Our law librarian, Becky Clapp, allowed me the exclusive use of a seminar room, complete with book shelves, for 18 months. It became my Kunstler Command Post, where I stored and read the 6,000+ newspaper and 100+ periodical articles and 50+ books with significant Kunstler references that my research assistants and I gathered. My daughter Virginia helped by going through all the *New York Times* articles that even mentioned Kunstler, and setting aside for my reading those with extensive discussion.

In January 1996 I worked up a thorough research strategy for my biography, and determined how I would classify data, and what categories I would establish for their keeping. It seemed endless, as it has for every major project, as though I were at the very bottom of a huge sand pile, a mountain of data, with so very much to scale. Yet as I read and assimilated more information, and climbed higher up the mountain of sand, all I did was slip backward. Every step seemed to dislodge more sand, more data. Every fact unearthed in historical or biographical research seems to raise more questions, call for more research. Yet gradually I seemed to get a more solid foothold on my mountain of data, and eventually I could see the project as a whole from on top of the hill.

For this Kunstler biography I did far more interviewing than I had needed in the earlier books, because there were so many living persons that had known Kunstler personally. I conducted some of my interviews by telephone, getting consent for recording, and then worked with a transcript. However, most of the important interviews with family, friends, and colleagues I conducted face to face, with a recording machine. I took two four- or five-day trips to New York City, and single day trips to Albany and Baltimore for these important sessions. I talked with four individuals who knew Kunstler in his younger years; with his family, including both wives, his four daughters, and his sister; two former clients; three judges before whom Bill Kunstler had practiced; three prosecutors with whom he had battled; three former colleagues; several close personal friends; and his partner at the time of his death, Ronald L. Kuby. All were kind and helpful. Ron Kuby especially was friendly and very helpful in his recollections, over many hours of talking together. I interviewed Kunstler's secretary, still employed by Kuby. I gathered the views toward Kunstler of twice that number of other judges, clients, and prosecutors through published interviews. Secretaries transcribed my interviews, and provided a written record I could work from.

I prepared a tentative outline, wrote an introductory chapter, a complete proposal, and sent it out to agents, with the hope that finally I would publish a trade book. Most of the agents I emailed never bothered to respond, an example of the New York style of courtesy. One agent who did contact me wrote that she would have liked a more critical biography, because an expose would sell more copies to the many New Yorkers who hated Kunstler. I eventually did sign with the Valcourt Agency in October 1996. Richard Valcourt sent my proposal and sample chapter to seven or eight mainstream trade publishers, all of whom rejected the manuscript. The Free Press, amusingly, rejected my manuscript because it was too even handed. I terminated the relationship with my agent in September 1997, and pitched it myself to various left-of-center publishers, all of whom turned it down. Then I turned to Columbia University Press and New York University Press. Columbia passed on the book, but I received a note expressing interest from Niko Pfund, the Director of the New York University Press, asking for whatever completed chapters I had available.

I did much of the writing in Birmingham, most in my Command Post, but some in the wonderful reading room of the Birmingham Public Library. I had a sabbatical in the spring term of 1998, and a great deal of the writing was done in that time. Ucross Foundation in Clearmont, Wyoming is an old ranch, northwest of Gillette, Wyoming, and situated amidst very calming and scenic countryside. The ranch's primary buildings have been converted into studios for the use of authors and artists during residencies, usually of a month duration. I applied for a residency and was lucky enough to be granted one for March 1998. Sadly, my father died on February 26, 1998, literally the day before I had intended to leave Birmingham and drive to Ucross. The funeral arrangements, services in Tucson with burial in Minneapolis, followed by the still-necessary drive to Wyoming, meant that I had only three weeks of my allotted month.

Ucross created an environment where there were absolutely no excuses not to work hard. A central building served as living room, dining room, and kitchen. Breakfasts were simple and on our own. Then everyone retreated to their own spaces, and the standing rule was that no one could visit another's space without express advance permission. Of course, the resident could individually take a walk along the creek or in the woods, but the idea was to create, as much as possible, a monastic-like atmosphere of silence and individual work. An employee came around to each room at lunchtime, knocked discreetly at the door, and dropped off a bag at the doorstep, usually containing a sandwich, fruit, dessert, and a drink. Dinner was at

7:00PM, and we ate gourmet food prepared by a professional chef and socialized as a group. After dinner some of us watched a video, some of us drove over to Sheridan, Wyoming to catch a movie, and most of us went back to work. It was a place for working, and I wrote just short of two chapters the three weeks I was there.

Niko Pfund, who now is the President and Academic Publisher of the Oxford University Press, was an excellent editor. Many issues come up in the course of writing a book that demand some communication between author and editor. Niko was the very best editor I have ever had in terms of rapid replies to my concerns or inquiries. It would usually take no more than 30 minutes from my email to his reply. In February 1998, I received the definitive word from NYU Press. Its editorial board had agreed that they would publish the biography of Kunstler, and furthermore publish it as a general interest book, with galley proofs sent out to reviewers in advance of publication and trade discounts. Niko confided in me that the two primary factors in the board's approval were that there was no other biography of Kunstler and that I had once won the Hurst Prize.

By September 4, 1998 I had completed the entire first draft of the book and by February I had revised the copy edited manuscript. Shortly thereafter I prepared the index from the proofs. *William M. Kunstler: The Most Hated Lawyer in America* appeared on September 1, 1999. True to his word to promote *Kunstler* as a trade book, Pfund hired a publicist who interviewed me over the telephone, and was enthusiastic about the prospects. I thought the east coast would be the natural marketplace for the book, as that was the venue for most of Kunstler's practice. Kunstler was a man whose provocative words were quoted constantly in the newspapers and who was interviewed extensively in New York newspapers and television, and I felt certain that there would be widespread media interest in the book.

However, the publicist was never able to line up any television or radio interviews for me to promote the book. Eventually, she did manage to have the book reviewed in the *New York Times* and *Washington Post*, a brief and neutral paragraph apiece, but the publicity campaign essentially fizzled. In late November 1999 the publicist expressed surprise to me that there had not been more play on the Kunstler book, and in early December she said that she sensed a great deal of hostility toward Kunstler among her contacts. The slow sales and lack of public interest in the book depressed me. It had become clear to me that the disinterest of trade presses, and in a very current topic, meant that I was destined to write only university press books. Then, even with a publicist, the sales were relatively low, around 2,500 copies, even though the book was about Kunstler, a relatively current and very controversial figure. This brought home an added implication that I would probably never write anything that would catch much attention, or bring me any sort of fame, or make me special in the public eye. I would have to be satisfied with being a scholar, and a fairly unknown one at that. In Joseph Conrad's words I would take my "place in the ranks and begin the journey towards the bottomless pit."

In the meantime, a fair number of reviews came in, around 23-24, or just a few more than for the Mann Act book. The majority of the reviews were in legal journals, bar association magazines, and the like, or political science reviews. In addition to *The New York Times* and *Washington Post*, the black operated *New York Amsterdam News* also reviewed the book. Its review was quite lengthy, but concerned Kunstler more than the biography. The book was also reviewed in a few mainstream scholarly journals. The flattering review in *The Journal of American History* called me "a widely respected legal historian who has produced a biography that, while sympathetic, is also critical and circumspect. In the hands of lesser talent, a biography of Kunstler would risk becoming either an exercise in hagiography or a polemic attack. What emerges in Langum's book is a far more nuanced and complex character." That felt good to read.

The review in *The American Journal of Legal History* labelled my book a "fair-minded, richly detailed and fiercely researched biography." I especially liked the fiercely researched bit. The prestigious *Library Journal* noted that "Langum's spectacular and thoughtful biography of radical lawyer William Kunstler is distinguished by an even-handed presentation and deep research." I was particularly pleased when the *Chronicle for Higher Education*, the weekly newspaper that covers all aspects of American higher education, carried my Kunstler book as its featured book of the week. However, as Niko Pfund once told me, aside from the major urban newspapers, good reviews do not sell books. The total sales are around 3,100.

Three important matters in my life occurred at the very end of the 1990s, but the bulk of my activities on them came in the following years that are just beyond this chapter. I will mention them very briefly here, and then discuss them more fully in the next chapter.

In 1999 the Illinois State Historical Library (now the mis-named Abraham Lincoln Presidential Library) agreed to access my family's papers, and I began the long task of organizing these papers into record groups and then transporting them, more than 120 archival boxes, to Springfield, Illinois. I delivered the first small portion of this massive collection in May 2000. In the spring of 1999 I was offered a seat on the Board of Directors of the American Civil Liberties Union of Alabama and shortly thereafter elected vice president of the Board. In the late fall of 2000, the president of the Board began a campaign to fire our executive director that precipitated acrimony and ultimately the president's resignation. As the vice president, I became the president of the ACLU of Alabama on November 18, 2000.

In November 1999 I became treasurer of the Friends of the Birmingham Public Library, a 501(c)(3) support group. In November 2001 I was elected as the president of the Friends group, a position I held for the next five years.

In addition to the board responsibilities, I took on several miscellaneous *pro bono* responsibilities during the 1990s. In the academic year 1993-1994, I was on the speakers bureau of the Alabama Humanities Foundation, and went all over the state giving talks on the Harrison Act and the opening shots in 1914 of America's so-called War on Drugs. That fall I spoke before the women residing at the Bread and Roses Shelter on the Alabama landlord-tenant law. I was invited by a woman in my Property class who was a volunteer there.

On May 23, 1998, I delivered the commencement address for the History Department graduation exercises at San Jose State University. It was so much fun to go back to where I had so long before studied and earned my master's degree. A very few of my former professors were still there, on active or retired status, and I had a wonderful opportunity to talk with them. Sue Miller, my former employer while I was in law school, then my client, and always a friend, flew up from Los Angeles to hear me speak. After the talk she had lunch with Frances and myself, and then flew back. In March 2000, I presented a few sessions, on a pro bono basis, no compensation, at a writers' conference held at the University of Miami.

Other writing opportunities besides my three books came to me during the decade 1991-2000. I vetted book manuscripts and wrote critiques for several university presses, including Chicago, Alabama, Nebraska, Kentucky, and several for Oklahoma. Each required several days of work. I also reviewed many article submissions for more than nine different journals. These required some four or five hours of work apiece, and unlike the book manuscripts, no payment came for reviewing article submissions. However, the work was important to the process of historical writing, and I was pleased to be asked. One curious incident arose when in very short order I received magazine submissions from both *Western Historical Quarterly* and *Law and History Review*. The names of the authors are generally removed by the journals before sending them out to referees. However I could see that they were obviously written by the same author as there were substantial verbatim overlaps in the two pieces. I disclosed the situation to each journal, yet recommended that both be published because they dealt with substantially different themes based on a single lawsuit. I also recommended that one of the journals require that the overlap portion be re-written. Of course, it was just the laziness of the author that caused the problem; doubtless he assumed the two publications would not send the article to the same person for review.

I continued to be asked to write short encyclopedia articles, as well as to write my own longer articles for journal or book-chapter publication. No multitude of articles appeared in the years 1991-

2000, since research and writing three separate books had consumed so much time. Nevertheless there were some, and the two I thought most important were "A Personal Voyage of Exploration Through the Literature of Abortion History," published by *Law and Social Inquiry* in spring 2000, and "A Short History of American Prostitution and Prostitution Policy," which was published in The Netherlands in 2000, as a collection of papers contributed to the 1999 conference at the Roosevelt Institute for American Studies, previously mentioned. This was my second foreign publication.

The most curious writing I did in these years came when I was hired by the Alabama State Attorney General to draft an opinion letter concerning a somewhat obscure problem involving future interests in property law and some land owned by the state. The Attorney General knew of me specifically, so I surmise that a student who had taken the Property course from me advised him of my interest in this quirky area of real property law. Ultimately the Attorney General used my approach to the issues presented by the facts and also some of my language verbatim.

Other miscellaneous scholarly opportunities in this decade included television. Quest Productions interviewed me for some commentary for a PBS documentary it was making. Lawrence Friedman, the principal commentator, had suggested me as a commentator on the Progressive Era and the Mann Act. The show aired as "Crime and Punishment in America" in January 1997. Then in summer 2000 a different production company interviewed me at my house, Greystones, in Port Townsend. They were putting together a documentary, "Sex in the 20th Century," for television's History Channel. The interview was set for July 5, 2000, and I alerted the local newspaper covering the Olympic Peninsula, *The Peninsula Daily News*. That a film crew and interviewers would fly up from Los Angeles to interview a local resident is real news in a quite small town, and on the day of the interview, the newspaper sent out a reporter to interview the interviewer. The result was an article on the interview and me in the front section of our daily newspaper, full page width and three inches deep. The interview itself went well, and I was hired as a consultant to check over their coverage of Anthony Comstock, the notorious anti-pornography and purity zealot.

I was interviewed by some local Birmingham weekly newspapers for articles on Alabama's sex laws and similar topics of breathless interest. I gave at least one "faculty shoptalk" during these ten years, talks on current research presented by faculty members in all the schools, and available to the entire university. These usually do not attract a large audience, but I recall giving a talk on William Kunstler when much to my surprise in came the President, Tom Corts, and the Provost. During the question and answer period, Corts asked a couple of excellent questions; he told me later that he had always had an interest in Kunstler.

By the 1990s I began to see some good effects of my work. Already in the 1990s, the Mexican legal system book, *Law and Community*, and the Mann Act *Crossing over the Line* book were cited in numerous other scholarly works. By the end of 2018, the California book gathered 73 separate references in other articles and books, and the Mann Act book had more – 254 citations. Two doctoral dissertations, one in History and the other in the History of Economics, expressly based their analyses in significant part upon the *Law and Community* and *Larkin* works. In 1995, Myra K. Saunders, UCLA's law librarian, published a detailed article, "California Legal History: A Review of Spanish and Mexican Legal Institutions," in the national *Law Library Journal*. In it she wrote that because my *Law and Community* book was "the most accessible and clearly written secondary source concerning the Mexican legal system, this text is essential reading for students of this period." David J. Weber, probably the most preeminent modern historian of the Hispanic Southwest, founded a center for southwest studies at his home institution, Southern Methodist University. He thought my use of cultural factors in the *Law and Community* book was a novel and useful analytical tool, and had praised the book in a review he wrote after publication. In 1995, Weber offered me a $30,000 post-doctoral fellowship at his center at SMU, presumably to be used during a sabbatical year when I had other income as well. The fellowship was for the completion of a book on southwestern history, but I was free to pick the specific subject. I felt a bit of regret that I was receiving such a solid reputation in California studies, just as I was leaving that field, but I had other topics I wanted to explore and could not take him up on his kind offer.

A folksier incident that made me feel good about the impact of my historical scholarship came from a telephone call I received in April 1996 from a fellow in Utah. Someone had told him about my 1974 article concerning trials on the overland trails. He then read the article and realized that one of his ancestors was involved in one of the incidents I had described, and had a few questions for me. I was flattered, and answered the questions as best as I could although my recollection had dulled in the many years and other projects since 1974 and the time of his call. The irony occurred to me that the shelf life of a dead lawyer, Kunstler, had proved to be so short, whereas an article published in an historical journal that was not obscure but hardly well-known generally, had enjoyed a shelf life of 22 years.

Chapter 9

Pro Bono Work and Donative Endeavors:
2000-2020

I mentioned before that in November 1999 the membership of the Friends of the Birmingham Public Library at its annual meeting elected me as its treasurer. Two years later the members elected me as president, a position I held for the next five years.

We had a five person board and met in the library director's office at the central branch generally four times per year but excepting from that summers when we did not meet at all. As an independent supporting charity, we had our own income and determined our own budget. Our income came from modest dues on our membership and the proceeds from a used bookstore, located within the central library and operated by our volunteers.

Although we did make financial grants to the library, I think our biggest help was to serve as a sounding board representing the library patrons. Often the director and associate directors asked our opinion or advice concerning sensitive library issues such as censorship of the Internet; acquisitions policies, especially regarding the neighborhood branches; acceptance of federal funds for internet filters (we voted that down); or dealing with patrons who were obnoxious yet fell short of the point where the library could legitimately evict them.

The library was primarily dependent on the City of Birmingham's annual budgeting process. Once the budget was set, it was difficult to obtain additional funds from the city, but that obstacle did not prevent sudden financial emergencies from arising. One of our roles was to make grants at relatively short notice to deal with these exigencies. In addition, we had by tradition covered two or three specific library expenses. The one I can recall is the speaker's fee for the annual employee luncheon.

I developed a few new policies and categories of expense that my board adopted. We began in 2002 to recognize a bookstore "volunteer of the year," who received a Bulow Award, named in honor of a highly regarded former library director. In February 2004 our Friends group began a program of holding, and paying for, semi-annual appreciation luncheons for all the library volunteers, who would be mostly unpaid workers in the bookstore. They were absolutely essential for most of our revenue, and it struck me as strange that nothing had been done to formally recognize them. In fact, toward the end of my tenure as president of the board I invited one or two bookstore volunteers to become board members.

Of all the projects and ideas I brought to the Birmingham Public Library in my period as president of the Friends, I am most proud of the "Beyond the Budget Award." The idea was that the Friends would make an annual grant, in the range of $1,500-$2,000, for books, other media, equipment, or furnishings for a specific department in a branch or the central library, that could not be purchased in the current budget or the next year's anticipated budget. We developed a short one-page form in which we asked for the need for the request, the use and benefit, the specific items desired and their cost. The submissions could be made by any library employee working in any department. I brought this idea to the board in early 2003, and it received it enthusiastically as did the library director.

In the years following we generally received ten or slightly more submissions each year. One of our rules was that the submissions had to be read over personally by either the director or associate director, as I envisioned this project as a method of circulating information from the bottom of the library ranks up to the very top. The library staff developed some very good and sometimes innovative ideas. After the director had reviewed the submissions and given us her thoughts, our board made the final decision. For meritorious projects, but not the very best, I always wrote the submitter a letter encouraging him or her to re-apply the next year. Through this correspondence I learned that in a few cases there was no resubmission because the directors of the library had somehow found the funds to finance their projects. That information pleased me greatly because it demonstrated the efficacy of my "Beyond the Budget Award," not only to make specific grants, but also to facilitate the upward flow of information.

I made one other suggestion, adopted by the board, that I feel was salutary. The Birmingham Public Library has some eighteen branches of various sizes. I gathered the feeling from talking with employees at the branches, usually at the annual employee appreciation lunches, that in fact the branches did not feel very appreciated. Some felt they were second or third cousins to the massive and well-equipped central library. While I had no way to really turn that around, I thought one thing we might do as the Friends' board would be to hold meetings twice a year in different branch locations. We started to do that in 2005, and I believe the branch librarians were happy to see us visit them.

I agreed with my vice-president that I would not stand for election at the November 2006 annual membership meeting and allow her to take over the presidency. I had served for five years, had made several accomplishments, and it was time for someone else to take over. Actually, there was a bit of sourness to my final departure. The library is governed and controlled by a Library Board, a city agency to which the city council has delegated substantial autonomy. An obscure part of the city ordinances made the president of the Friends of the Birmingham Public Library, ex-officio a member of the governing Library Board. The knowledge of this ex-officio role of the Friends' president was the sort of arcane knowledge, deeply buried in the city ordinances, that would be well known to library directors, but not known to others, including myself. In my sixty months as president of the Friends group, I served under two library directors, Jack Bulow for three months and Barbara Sirmans for fifty-seven. During those entire five years, neither advised me of my ex-officio membership on the Library Board, although the Library Board and its somewhat conservative nature, were frequent topics of conversation, particularly between Barbara Sirmans and myself. My successor to the presidency knew about this ordinance as soon as she became the Friends president, presumably because she was immediately advised of her right to sit on the Library Board by Barbara Sirmans.

I would have enjoyed participating on the Library Board, but I had absolutely no knowledge that I was so entitled and was not advised of my right to do so. Accordingly, at the end of my term of office I felt deceived, felt ill-used, and felt that I had been a far better friend to the Birmingham Public Library than it had been to me. I resigned from the board of the Friends, and although I was talked into staying on for a short while longer, my heart was never again really in the work.

My son David, Jr. attended a local Montessori school, Creative Montessori in Homewood, Alabama. Montessori schools are independent, each with its own budget and goals. In the fall of 2001 the director invited me to join the board of directors. It was a small but active board and we met once a month. I received an appointment to the finance committee in early 2002.

In the summer of 2002 we discovered that David, Jr. was a high-functioning autistic. My wife and I provided him with a barrage of outside therapists, from speech and physical therapy, to applied behavioral analysis. Nevertheless, he had to be placed in a public school, which would have far more resources for teachers' aides, special programs for learning disabilities, such as a special pre-kindergarten, and the like. This was hugely successful, and David is now about to graduate from college.

The director of Creative Montessori asked me to stay on the board even after David went off to public school. I did stay on briefly, but by the end of 2002 thought I could use my time more effectively and also felt that the Montessori school ought to benefit from directors whose own children attended there.

We had thoroughly researched autism treatment, and it became apparent that the program of choice, more expensive but more effective, was Applied Behavioral Analysis. We hired Ashley Simmons Faust, a young therapist just finishing her training in California, to work with David for several hours a week. David made fantastic progress under her administration of Applied Behavioral Analysis. , and has steadily improved over the years. My wife Frances and I thought very altruistically that we might take training to become therapists ourselves, obtain our licenses, and serve some of the wretchedly poor country regions of Alabama. We actually did enroll in a distance learning course conducted by Penn State University, and in July 2002 began working with their lectures on dvd tapes and taking their tests. Frances soon found that she just did not have the time to devote to a serious learning program. Ashley suggested to me that I could do more good in this area by working as a lawyer representing parents who were seeking therapy services for their children in school.

I attended a convention in Birmingham for teachers who wished to apply Applied Behavioral Analysis. techniques with special needs students in their classrooms. They were all in their 20s and very enthusiastic. I was then in my early 60s, and the comparison with them, and their easy ability to play on the floor with young charges, gave me some pause. Also I found the actual university-level study of Applied Behavioral Analysis. more difficult and certainly more time consuming that I had presupposed. Those factors led me to conclude that Ashley's suggestion was correct, and that I could probably be more helpful as a lawyer representing families than as a therapist.

In the fall of 2004 I wrote to the Alabama Disabilities Advocacy Program (ADAP), a part of the federally-funded protection and advocacy program for persons with disabilities. It serves children and adults with disabilities in Alabama. I offered my services as a volunteer in special education advocacy for children and their parents beginning in the fall of 2005, a time that would fall shortly after my scheduled retirement from teaching. I had my license to practice law in Alabama, but needed training in special education law. In the spring of 2005 I attended a multi-day "boot camp" on legal representation and advocacy for special education, presented by a leading expert in the field, Peter Wright, and held in Albuquerque, New Mexico. I paid for the entire cost of the meeting fees, accommodation, meals, and transportation out of my own pocket.

I began working for ADAP in their Tuscaloosa, Alabama offices in the fall of 2005. One disputed educational case was assigned to me, and I brought it into a space of relative tranquility. This type of case seldom is fully resolved in the sense of most lawsuits which have a definitive resolution. But everything seemed so uncertain at ADAP. I went to their offices in Tuscaloosa four or five times but I was not given any office space or even a desk that I could call my own. No specific person gave me training in their office procedures, and aside from the initial case no one gave me anything to work on. I may have been their first lawyer volunteer, as I certainly had the feeling that ADAP did not really know what to do with me. I told the woman I thought was my supervisor that I needed more direction, but I did not receive it. My last trip to their Tuscaloosa offices was very late in 2005. I had called my supervisor in advance and told her I wanted something to do, something to work on. I arrived at their offices and wandered aimlessly about because I had no office, no desk, no chair for me to use, and no work for me to do. My supervisor was not there. Clearly, ADAP was not accustomed to working with volunteers. It probably has since cleaned up its act as it now has a volunteer lawyer who has been with them since 2008.

In the fall of 2001 Robert L. McCurley, the director of the Alabama Law Institute, invited me to join its property committee. The Alabama legislature created the Alabama Law Institute in 1967 to serve the legislature as a vetting process to clarify and simplify existing statutes and to propose new laws. It operates through committees of volunteers drawn from Alabama lawyers, judges, law professors, and lawyer-members of the legislature. A draft of the national uniform landlord-tenant act was then before the committee, for it to make revisions in the uniform act to make it more suitable for Alabama conditions, and to recommend for or against its adoption by the state legislature.

The chief significance of the uniform landlord-tenant act would be to adopt as law a requirement that landlords have a primary responsibility that the residential property they rent be at least habitable. The traditional law was that a landlord gave his tenant only the legal right to possession of the apartment or house rented. If, for example, the refrigerator stopped working, the repair was the sole responsibility of the tenant since the landlord only guaranteed the legal right to possession. Even if a house roof began leaking, repairs were the sole responsibility of the tenant, because the tenant was still in full possession, and that was all the landlord had promised. The lease or rental agreement could impose these responsibilities on the landlord, but particularly with poorer housing the landlords had far more power than tenants, and expansive provisions for landlord liability seldom appeared.

By the turn of the twenty-first century forty-eight of the American states had adopted landlord-tenant laws under which landlords impliedly warranted that the property they leased for residential purposes was habitable, and fit to live in. If it fell below that standard during the term of the lease or month-to-month rental, the landlord had to make the necessary repairs. After notification and a failure to fix the problem, the tenant could make the repairs to bring the house or apartment to the level of fitness to inhabit and deduct those costs from the rent.

The national Uniform Law Commission had promulgated a model law, and we as a committee had to review it line by line, to recommend what changes should be made for Alabama and also whether the uniform act, or some variation, ought to be adopted or rejected. This was a hot potato for the legislature because of the general conservatism of the state, and the power of wealthy and substantial landlords. Nevertheless, there was a feeling that something ought to be done since Alabama was once again, as in many other matters, among the last to move into the modern world. From the legislature's viewpoint it was a perfect project to pass off to the Alabama Law Institute.

About twenty-five of us constituted the property committee of the Institute. Although the majority was composed of lawyers practicing in the property field, we also had two or three judges, two law faculty from different universities, and at least one attorney- member of the legislature. We began working in November 2001 and usually met monthly, making our way line-by-line through the uniform act. We

233

engaged in close analysis and focused discussion about the effects of each section of the proposed model law, modifying some, rejecting some, and adopting other sections. "Thinking like a lawyer" may truly be only close analytical thinking on legal topics, but the discussions charged me up, as I had not engaged in this exact form of close thinking for many years. We usually met in a conference room of a local law firm, and the host firm always provided lunch, often sumptuous.

Two of the committee members clearly represented landlords and opposed most of the provisions under review. By mid-summer 2002 I thought I had discovered the real basis for their opposition. Their clients were not so much concerned with whether they had to repair broken stoves, or whether a poor tenant could withhold a relatively minor amount from their rent check for repairs to a dysfunctional refrigerator that the landlord refused to repair. They were concerned that an implied warranty of fitness for habitation could set a standard of care in tort cases that could expose them to substantial liability. Suppose the roof leaked and someone slipped on water, fell, and sustained serious injuries. Could a tort plaintiff claim that this implied warranty of habitability set the standard for the landlord's duty of care, not just for repairs, but for personal injuries?

Thinking that we should not let perfection be the enemy of the good, I introduced a provision into our proposed law that decoupled the responsibility of the landlord to provide decent housing from tort liability, by adding a provision that this act did not itself set a standard of care for negligence cases, and whether or not a landlord was negligent and liable for injuries in tort would be decided on a separate basis not including the warranty of habitability. Director McCurley privately praised me for this contribution, said it was a key concept, and thanked me for my participation on the committee.

In fact, the committee's work did seem to move along more smoothly now that the tort implications were put to rest. We finished our work on the Alabama Landlord-Tenant Act in November 2002, about a year from when we began, and submitted it to the legislature. With some slight modifications, and after several years delay, it was enacted in a very modified form. Significantly, the legislature rejected our proposal for withholding rent for repairs made by the tenant. I participated in other projects with the property committee, including a major revision to Alabama's Rule Against Perpetuities, adopted nearly in total by the legislature, but the landlord tenant work was the most intellectually stimulating and rewarding.

I performed as a supernumerary for Opera Birmingham for my own personal enjoyment and another, if minor, act of public service. I have long been an opera fan. Although I cannot carry a tune, I had for a long time longed to participate in an opera as a non-singing super. I noticed that Opera Birmingham planned to perform Verdi's *Aida* in late February 2005, and wrote to the director of Opera Birmingham the preceding November offering my services. I knew that *Aida* required more supernumeraries than most operas because it is filled with sword carriers and soldiers, especially in its triumphal march. John Jones, the director, wrote back within a week welcoming me as a super.

We began rehearsals February 12, 2005, slowly at first, only on Saturdays. The opera's acts, and even specific scenes within acts, were worked on separately, and then expanded. The pace picked up when we were about ten days from our first performance, and we then rehearsed four days a week in addition to Saturday. I enjoyed being with the singers and other supers. I had not been with so many artsy people since I dated Grace, before my marriage to Frances. I was intrigued to explore the complicated cluster of rehearsal rooms of the Alabama Theatre, the passageway behind the stage, and the many-storied length of its metal backstage stairway, leading to the dressing, storage, and rehearsal rooms, with its flights of steps seemingly suspended in the air. Mostly, above all, I was thrilled to be in the middle of this glorious operatic music.

As usual, Opera Birmingham had two performances, Friday evening and Sunday afternoon. I played the pharaoh's guard in one scene and a sword-carrying warrior at the beginning of the second act's famous triumphal march. Backstage I swapped my sword for a spear and became a spear-carrying warrior later in the march. There was no pay for this enjoyable effort, but I did receive listing in the program and two free tickets in an excellent location that I gave to my wife Frances and colleague Bill Ross.

I also performed the following year, March 2006, in Puccini's *Madama Butterfly*. This time I played Butterfly's cook and had a slight piece of non-verbal acting. My daughter, Virginia, was visiting and she and Frances shared my tickets. I was listed in the program as playing the specific role of cook. Perhaps because I played a specific very minor role, Opera Birmingham gave me a check for $100, which I promptly endorsed back to the company.

It was well that I satisfied my desire to be in an opera when I did, because not too many years later I would have been physically unable to move about as deftly as I did then. *Aida* required considerable marching, and in *Madama Butterfly* I had to stand up quickly from a squatting position to scurry off to fetch food. Virginia was surprised by my agility, but now that would be impossible. I was asked to perform a third time, for *La Boheme*. That is my favorite opera, the favorite of millions of others too, and I would have loved to have been in the midst of that sublime music. However, I had a travel conflict and could not participate.

In March 1999 Martin McCaffrey, the president of the Alabama ACLU chapter, offered me a position on its board of directors. The board was a busy group that met about monthly. In July the board appointed me as vice-president and also as the liaison between the board and the lawyers' committee, the group that initiated and monitored civil rights litigation. In the fall of 2000 a crisis developed over the executive director, Olivia Turner. Several directors, including the president, thought that she had engaged in backbiting to the extent that it had caused some staff to resign and others to lose morale. Some wanted to fire her outright. I pushed back on this, pointing out the unfairness of firing an employee of thirteen years without any warnings of alleged "wrongdoings." After a month of furious emails and hassles, toward which I was essentially a passive party, an agreement was reached for interim guidelines for Ms. Turner to follow and a formal hearing before the executive committee, then a referral to the entire board.

The hearing came on October 28, 2000, seven of us on the executive committee meeting in a conference room I had arranged for at Cumberland. Two lawyers represented Olivia Turner, and they called five witnesses, and introduced twenty-three written statements. The four directors who were most adamant about firing Ms. Turner sat at the conference table like stones, asking no questions of the witnesses, and after the hearing closed engaged in no real deliberation. They simply voted 4-3 to recommend that the full board fire the executive director, Ms. Turner. I agreed to prepare a minority report.

I wrote what I thought was a well-argued dissent, and apparently it was as my position was adopted by the full board, 6-5, with one abstention. Olivia Turner stayed on, Martin McCaffrey resigned in a huff, and as vice-president I became the new president of the ACLU Alabama affiliate. In my initial time as the head of the organization I had two major goals, first to strengthen the board both institutionally and through the gradual elimination of a few weak members. The second goal was to move the ACLU toward greater acceptance by the Alabama middle class that regards the ACLU as responsible for the entire civil rights movement although the actual record of the ACLU in the struggles of the 1960s was weak. Specifically, toward the first goal I suggested a lot more reporting from the lawyers' committee as to the types of cases that they had under review, and also a referral process whereby either the executive committee or the entire board had to approve actual litigation. I had other ideas for reaching that goal, but these were the major thoughts. Toward the second goal, I proposed that each director become available to talking before civic groups, such as Rotary, Kiwanis, or Lions, and that the central office advertise the availability of speakers through the clubs' periodicals and also direct mail.

Because I had done so much for Olivia Turner, I thought that we would have a good working relationship and that she would at least give an open ear to my suggestions. To my shock, she was immediately defensive with me. She ignored almost every suggestion I made and did not communicate readily with me. In my judgment

Olivia Turner was not prepared to allow anyone other than herself the ability to "exercise general charge and supervision of the affairs of the corporation," the precise responsibilities that our by-laws imposed upon the president. Most suggestions I made as to new procedures were met by her with either total rejection or by such delays as would cause a person not unduly sensitive to believe that unsolicited suggestions were unwanted. Questions that I raised as to existing procedures evoked extremely defensive replies from Ms. Turner. My reading was that questions or suggestions were unwelcome if they had any overtones that things might be done differently. That does not mean I was without a lot of work and responsibilities. I met often with the lawyers' committee regarding potential litigation; Olivia Turner regarding financial and broader issues concerning the affiliate; and disgruntled directors as to their concerns.

The board re-elected me as president in February 2002 at a special election. The regular election came up on August 31, 2002. Because of my terrible relationship with the executive director (I had actually reached the point where I had stomach pains every time I drove down to our Montgomery office for a meeting with her), and also because my wife and I had discovered David, Jr.'s autism and were enrolled in Penn State's course in Applied Behavioral Analysis. , I had reached the point where I could not continue. I notified the board on August 1, 2002 that I would not be a candidate for election at the oncoming meeting, explaining my reasons, but that I would be willing to remain on the board.

My stint as president of the Alabama ACLU brought many things in its wake besides a lot of hard work. It brought in hate mail, both to me and to officials at Samford University. Thomas Corts, Samford's president, shared with me a letter that asked how could he have on his faculty the president of the godless ACLU. Corts kindly told me I did not have to worry about this, at least from his viewpoint. One letter to the newspaper editor also attacked me as necessarily irreligious because of my work for the ACLU. I responded to that one and pointed out that I was in fact a member of the Anglican Church, and that I saw no conflict between my religious belief and my work for the ACLU. My presidency also brought a great amount of publicity. In the just-under two years I was the ACLU president, two newspaper reporters interviewed me, two radio talk shows hosted me, and five television shows brought me in for interviews or debates.

I remained on the executive committee as the immediate past president for three or four years after 2002. I enjoyed my participation on the executive committee as we often constituted an inner group to which Olivia Turner turned for advice. At the same time it lacked the one-on-one relationship with her that I had found so distressing. I resigned from the ACLU board itself ten years after my 1999 appointment. I thought that ten years was enough, and that younger blood and fresher ideas ought to have their chance.

Many in the national ACLU thinks of their Alabama affiliate as fighting behind enemy lines. Whether that is true or not, there was a great challenge with this work. Especially during the period 1999-2002, there always seemed to be ACLU work to be done, issues to be resolved. I would not care to repeat it, but it was a rewarding experience.

For all of my adult life I have been an avid collector of books, especially history, biography, and other non-fiction. I have particularly concentrated on books relating to topics I have been writing about or was thinking of making a project. For example, in my early years at Cumberland I published the article described earlier on risk of loss in leases of slaves. When I was finishing up the *Law and Community* book and before Harlan Hague talked me into the Larkin biography, I thought I might write a book on other aspects of the law of slavery, and even began some initial research. While I was thinking about slave law, I was simultaneously collecting as many books as I could find on slave law for my own library. It is essential to read widely in a field before one's own research in primary materials, and it is helpful to have books in hand for quick reference when organizing and outlining research materials.

But I did not proceed with slave law as other topics diverted my attention. I had a collection of about forty books on the law of American slavery that just sat on my office shelves. Eventually I decided that I was never going to return to slave law, and I donated my collection to the Beeson Law Library of Cumberland School of Law in January 2003. I had been donating money for a fund dedicated to the acquisition of legal history books throughout my time at Cumberland and by 2003 that fund had reached a level slightly over $10,000, and by 2020 approximated $20,000. It was re-purposed so that the library could add several books a year to my slave law collection out of the fund's income.

The slave law books were small potatoes compared with the books I collected on Spanish and especially Mexican California. I had been writing in this field from my master's thesis in the early 1970s at San Jose State, all the way to 2012 when I published my final scholarly work dealing with Mexican California with Texas Tech University Press. I accumulated primarily books, new and used, that were primary sources, e.g., collections of letters, speeches, or diaries written by Americans or Mexicans concerning California, 1776-1846. Most of the books were in English translation, but I also had Spanish, Mexican, and even Russian works. Russia, of course, had a brief colonial period of its own in California. These were not rare books, but were hard to come by. I had the ten volume collection of Thomas O. Larkin's correspondence, the seven volume set of the early California history of Herbert Howe Bancroft, collections of the diaries of the participants of the first overland journey to California, many recollections of the Mexican rancheros, and so forth. They totaled over 850 volumes, a collection large enough so that I created a catalogue. The collection represented years of concentrated and focused collecting, and having them at my immediate use was of very great help in writing the many articles and three books dealing with themes from Spanish and Mexican California.

Although the publication of *Quite Contrary: The Litigious Life of Mary Bennett Love* did not come until 2014, I knew I had finished the research several years earlier. With that work I was finished with Hispanic California. I had written about every topic that interested me personally, and the field of Spanish and Mexican California was filling up rapidly, mostly with Hispanic scholars. What to do with these books? My own children had no particular interest in Hispanic California, but I was proud of my collection and wanted an orderly disposition to obviate any possibility of their being simply pitched out or sold as used books in the event of my demise. My conditions were that the collection remain intact, carry my name, and be used for research, not circulation.

In 2008-2010 I queried many fine Western libraries to inquire as their interest. I contacted the McCracken Research Library of the Buffalo Bill Historical Center, the Thomas C. Donnelly Library of New Mexican Highlands University (that focuses on Hispanic history of the southwest), the Western History and Genealogy Department of the Denver Public Library, the Colorado College Special Collections, and the Delaney Southwest Research Library of Fort Lewis College. They all admired my collection, but could not meet my conditions. Some had policies mandating the placement of all donations within their general collections and could not keep my books intact as a special collection; McCracken Research Library thought it was too focused on California and not the West generally; and the largest of these libraries, the Denver Public Library, said it would love to acquire a small percentage of my volumes which would be of great use and which they did not have, but they already had about 90% of my collected books, and they would need to dispose of those as duplicates.

I am not sure why I did not think of the Monterey County Historical Society during my first two years of trying to locate a good home for my California collection. Perhaps I thought Salinas, California too remote. However, Salinas is certainly no more remote than Cody, Wyoming or Las Vegas, New Mexico (not Nevada's Las Vegas). Although the Society operates a museum and an adobe, it also has a formidable collection of primary materials that are used by many scholars. Not only does it contain most of the county's governmental records from the nineteenth century, but it also holds the Mexican judicial records that I had worked over for so many long hours while researching the *Law and Community* manuscript. When I used these Mexican records they were located at the Recorder's Office, but they since had been moved to the local historical library, the Monterey County Historical Society. What the Society lacked, however, was a collection of printed primary and secondary materials for the Spanish and Mexican periods. If a scholar were working within the Mexican records and that research raised a broader issue needed to put a particular record in context, the scholar had to stop research and go elsewhere to research that broader issue.

My collection was therefore an ideal acquisition for the Society, as a real aid to the use of their primary material. The placement of my collection with this Society was also ideal for me, since the Society did not want its materials circulated, and had no problem in keeping the materials together and associated with my name. I was also pleased by the fact that my collection would be in the same library as the same Mexican judicial records that had once been so important for my own work. We quickly reached an agreement at the very end of 2010, and I boxed up the books, and the Society paid for their shipping. We have had a very cordial relationship. For my part, I noticed one or two new books on Mexican California published in the years since my gift, and I have purchased those and presented them to be added to my existing collection. When I came out to Salinas a few years after the donation, the staff there was extremely gracious, showed me around their facilities, and took my wife and me to lunch at John Steinbeck's childhood home near downtown Salinas.

When my father died in 1998, I inherited all his papers, personal and professional. He had been first an academic, teaching at the University of California and the University of Indiana. In 1943 he became the vice president of the Federal Reserve Bank of Chicago, in charge of its research department, and then in 1951 he formed his own economic consulting firm. John K. Langum also played a very active role in civic affairs and served on the boards of a dozen or so charitable organizations as well as many corporate boards. He was a world class packrat and at his death had accumulated an enormous amount of business documents and personal records. He saved everything: all incoming letters, copies of many outgoing letters, both business and personal, handwritten notes on telephone calls, business documents he had prepared, and even earlier records from his childhood such as school records, childhood writings, and so forth.

In addition to his own papers, my dad had saved the papers of his own father, Henry Langum. Henry lacked the same proclivity toward document accumulation as his son John developed, but Henry had accumulated more than most people. For many years he taught high school biology, but he also had acquired and sometimes practiced his other professions of ordained Lutheran minister and licensed chiropractor. He had some documents from this activity. I too had papers. The acorn does not fall far from the tree, and I think most people would consider me a packrat. I had correspondence going back to my college years and going further back, school records of tests, teaching papers, and notes, going back further, a huge volume of my business and investment papers from the 1960s forward. Many of those ventures from the 1960s and 1970s I have discussed in earlier chapters.

I began to think that a research library with strong interests in the Midwest or Norwegians in the Midwest might be interested in a permanent accession of my materials. I began first with the Norwegian-American Historical Association, located at St. Olaf College. It was interested in Henry Langum's papers since he was of the immediate post-immigration generation as his father, Johan, migrated from Norway. It was interested in some of my father's childhood papers, since they illustrated the next generation of Norwegian-Americans. But the Historical Association was not interested in the bulk of my father's papers, and wanted none of mine. So it was out. The Illinois State Historical Library welcomed me, however, and thought, as I did, that our papers collectively represented a good example of a multi-generational Midwestern professional family.

Then I began the tremendous task of organizing this mass of papers. My own papers were in relatively decent shape. I had my correspondence arranged in annual folders, school papers were all together, my investment papers decently organized, and all the other matters of significant personal importance, such as divorces or graduate studies, in order. However, my father's papers and my grandfather's papers, that my father had taken in hand after Henry's death in 1967, decidedly were irregularly arranged. My dad may have been a world class packrat, but he was certainly no archivist. To be fair, he had moved the early papers, about many times. Nevertheless, any particular box might have business papers of the 1970s mixed with those of the 1980s; correspondence of the 1950s might be mixed with correspondence of the 1970s, and so forth.

Before I even began the three-generation Langum papers, I decided to first tackle the de Mattos materials, a much smaller collection. António and his sons Frederic and James, were the g-grandfather, grandfather, and g-uncle, respectively, of my mother Virginia de Mattos Langum. António was the pastor of a Protestant Portuguese settlement in antebellum Illinois, and I thought I might want someday to write up their histories, as I later did. I transcribed these papers into a typescript that I could use after handing them over to the Illinois State Historical Library (ISHL). So I began with these, and delivered this small part of an ultimately massive collection in May 2000.

About the time as I was finishing up the de Mattos materials, I began the much more massive task of dealing with my father's and then my papers. I first began by categorizing each page of my dad's papers: business or personal. If business, then from which era, which client; if personal then from which correspondent, what civic organization, dealing with what family member, and so forth. Then they needed to be organized into folders describing each cluster of documents, "itinerary of speeches, 1947-1949," or "published articles, 1939," and then the folders placed within large bankers' boxes that carried broader themes, such as "Speaking Engagements, Correspondence & Programs, 1950-1994," "Rate of Return Consultation and Testimony, 1923-1994," or "JKL's Travels, 1948-1998."

I organized my own papers with greater ease, both because they were better organized to begin with and also because I was more familiar with them and did not have to read, re-read, and ponder what a particular document was about, as I did sometimes with my dad's papers. The process consumed many hundreds of hours of my time, working on these papers mostly in the basement of my Alabama home but some in my office at my summer home in Port Townsend, Washington. In addition I made at least a dozen, probably more, drives to Springfield, Illinois with my car loaded with large archival boxes filled with our family papers to deliver. I took our old photographs, some from my grandmother's album, and worked for several days at a table in the Audio/Visual department of ISHL identifying the place and persons in the photograph as best I could. I was able, using other family records, to identify some going back to the late 19th century. I should add that on most of my trips to Springfield I had enjoyable lunches with John Paul, owner of the Prairie Archives, a wonderful used bookstore that faces the old state capitol building, and Gary Stockton, the acquisitions archivist who had first caused the ISHL to acquire the de Mattos and Langum Papers. From 2008 onward I also took a trip to Springfield as an opportunity to visit with my children. Sometimes when I could be there for a month or so, working on photos or writing a book or article, I would rent an apartment in Springfield. Each of my younger children, David, Jr., Audrey, and Anna would live with me in my apartment for a week, we would have breakfast and dinner together, and I would have the opportunity to take them to school and pick them up afterwards.

The process of taking my papers to Springfield took about fourteen years, 2000-2014, and the collection grew to about 102 boxes, including 22 for my father and 64 of my own. The balance were the smaller collections of my grandfather, Henry Langum, my mother, Virginia A. de Mattos Langum, and the de Mattos father and sons. I personally handled and classified each of the thousands of documents in those large bankers' boxes. The Library's structure and policies changed a great deal during that period, 2000-2014. First, it changed its name from Illinois State Historical Library to Abraham Lincoln Presidential Library (ALPL). The word "Lincoln" sells in Springfield, Illinois, and I suppose the powers that be thought that more publicity, grants, other good things could be acquired through the new name. It is a poor name, as ALPL is nothing at all like the presidential libraries run by the National Archives. The ALPL holds about 3,000 Lincoln documents, most pre-presidential, and some 12,000,000 non-Lincoln documents. Second, almost everyone I had known there during the most active time of organizing the papers and bringing them to Springfield -- the museum director, library director, acquisitions archivist, manuscripts curator, audio-visual curator, the individual curator who worked on our papers, Debbie Hamm, a very nice woman -- all retired.

Third, with replacements for those who have left, new policies have arrived. No longer does the ALPL have the nice separate rooms, one devoted to audio-visual, another to microfilm-microfiche, one to work with manuscripts, and a fourth larger room for printed materials. Now all materials from whichever former department has to be ordered from and then used within the larger reading room. Its previous system facilitated greater contact between curator and patron, allowing for ease in asking questions about specific collections that curators can often answer and thereby speed up research. At least in my judgment the former system of a separate room for manuscripts and another separate room for audio-visual was a better layout.

A fourth new policy that affected me directly was a change in the status of my own children's papers. I had been told by the Manuscript Curator that they would welcome my children's school papers, as there were few collections of children's papers. Accordingly, their mother, my former wife, and I worked assiduously to gather up every piece of paper that the kids themselves generated, drawings and early letters, and also every piece of paper that came from their schools: policies, grades, notes from the teachers, assignments, everything. I organized this mass of materials by child into their respective school years, and generated about twenty-five boxes of materials. I took it all to the ALPL, and Debbie Hamm actually began processing a small portion of my children's papers. Then with the shift of the powers that be at the ALPL, they refused to accept the children's papers beyond what Debbie Hamm had already processed, a very small portion of their papers.

A special class of papers also resided among my boxes and boxes of files. Those were my legal papers, case files from my practice in California 1968-1978. I had lugged those around with me, kept sometimes in storage, sometimes in a basement, for almost twenty-five years, thinking an inquiry or issue might arise for which these documents might be useful. No such inquiry occurred, and I turned my thinking toward whether these papers might be of historical

246

interest as a reflection of life in San Jose or the nature of its legal practice in those years.

Many lawyers have considered the possible historical use of their papers, but have been deterred from giving their papers to manuscript collections or other repositories for fear of breaching attorney-client confidences. When I went through my thirty or so boxes of legal files, I found enough files for which I was sure there would be no issue of confidentiality to fill three archival boxes. To be certain I went through them and removed the very few pages of notes on direct conversations with the clients. From the remaining boxes I culled out copies of depositions, interrogatories, and other fact-rich materials and organized them according to the type of case in which they originated, for example, domestic relations, personal injury, business and real property, and so forth. Since depositions and interrogatories are filed in the public court files, there is no issue of confidentiality at all. The total material extracted from the original thirty boxes was reduced to six boxes, three of complete files and three of partial files, interrogatories, and depositions. I shredded the remaining legal materials.

Gary Stockton, the acquisitions archivist of The Illinois State Historical Library, indicated that they would not be interested in acquiring these legal files. He was concerned not only with confidentiality issues, but also that these particular papers had little or nothing to do with my life in Illinois, the Midwest generally, or my larger career as an academic. I knew that the San Jose City Museum had a considerable manuscript collection, so I queried them, and they did not even bother to respond to my two letters. Then I thought of the Special Collections and Archives of San Jose State University. It might have a double interest in these papers, both for the history of San Jose and also because I was once a student there, earning my M.A. in history in 1976, a date covered by these legal papers.

I did not know it at the time I wrote to the Special Collections at San Jose State, but its director, Danelle Moon, had been a student at Fullerton State of Gordon Morris Bakken, a friend and fellow legal historian. Bakken died in 2014 at age 71, all too young. His scholarship and teaching was based on law in action, by which he meant how law was actually applied in society, not an abstract study of legal cases influencing later cases. This meant that legal history ought to be based on its effect on human lives. That led Ms. Moon to value the raw materials of actual cases and the fact-rich depositions that I was offering. In short, it became an easy negotiation, and I transferred my abridged legal papers, six archival boxes, to the San Jose State University on May 8, 2008.

On July 25, 2001 an idea floated into my head while I was on an airplane. The thought was to begin a foundation that might in some measure ameliorate the dismal general understanding of American history. I reasoned that too many historians today write only for each other's reading and not for the general public. In addition, many secondary schools and even colleges have dropped history from their curricula. As a result the American public is left uninformed of the richness of their nation's past, to the great detriment of both individual Americans and also the American body politic. I founded the Langum Initiative for Historical Literature in 2001, which quickly became The Langum Charitable Trust, and more recently The Langum Foundation. We try to at least partially remedy the dire state of general historical knowledge by offering annual book prizes in the areas of American historical fiction and American legal history. Our first awards were made in March 2002, for books published in 2001, and we have continued awarding these book prizes every year since then. The Internal Revenue Service issued our 501(c)(3) determination letter in June 2003. It is the most ambitious academic project I have begun.

To further our objective of making history accessible to the general public, we have always required that the American historical fiction winner be not only excellent history but also excellent literature. The American legal history winner must not only be rooted in sound scholarship, but also be accessible to the educated general public and with a theme that touches on matters of general concern to the American public, past or present. We began a new prize for recording community activism in 2008, made possible by the generous bequest of Adele R. Malott, although we had to defend a massive lawsuit

248

brought by Northwestern University to receive it. About the same time we began a travel to collections program for scholars wishing to research in the de Mattos or Langum Papers. We actually have had four researchers whose expenses we paid for lodging and travel to Springfield, Illinois to use the papers I laboriously compiled and delivered to the Abraham Lincoln Presidential Library.

Over the past twenty years we made a number of changes in the Foundation's operations. University presses have always dominated the legal history submissions, but in our early years we required that the winning historical fiction book be from a university press. When that did not produce a satisfactory number of submissions, we opened the prize up to independent press books. Still dissatisfied by the volume of American historical fiction submissions, we threw it open to all publishers. Initially we awarded our prizes at a convocation held in the auditorium of the Birmingham Public Library. We invited the two winning authors and also their spouses to come to Birmingham at our expense for a weekend, lodged them, and fed them. After I handed them their handsomely framed awards, the winners made some remarks and answered questions. Then we held a public reception in the library's board room, followed by a gala dinner at an outstanding white tablecloth restaurant for the winners, spouses, librarian and associate librarian, and all the trustees of the foundation who were in town. These gatherings were a lot of fun, and were always the occasion of scintillating conversation. However, they were also very expensive. If the library's auditorium had been consistently packed, perhaps I could have justified its continuance, but the audience was usually around thirty people, in addition to the authors, librarians, trustees, and spouses. It just wasn't enough bang for the buck, and I discontinued the programs in 2009, although we continued to honor books and writers, and to award the author of each winning book a $1,000.00 cash prize and the same handsomely framed certificate.

We generated a lot of favorable publicity for our efforts, especially when we began. The American Historical Association ran a long article about us in its newsletter *Perspectives* that specifically discussed my contention that historians too often wrote only for each other. *First Draft*, a periodical of The Alabama State Council on the

Arts ran an almost glowing account of our work. Probably the highest single generator of publicity was our boycott of Random House for its cowardly refusal to publish Sherry Jones's *The Jewel of Medina*, out of fear of Muslim attacks on the firm and its staff. We vowed not to consider Random House books until the book was published in English in the United States. Our stance triggered off hundreds of blogs, mostly favorable, from all over the world: the United States, Britain, France, Scandinavia, China, Germany, Canada, and Australia. Two others came from unspecified Arabic countries; I could not read the Arabic script to determine their exact origin. Probably the most satisfying piece was a generous article in the London *Guardian*.

Members of the three selection committees have changed from time to time. Even trustees have come and gone. One thing that has not changed over the years is the collegial debate within the selection committees as to the merits of the submissions. It involves a lot of reading and then writing of critiques for circulation. If I may say, I have had it the worst since until very recently I have been on all three committees. That touches on the problem of continuity the foundation faces. I cannot last forever, as I am pushing eighty years of age. While we can easily fund the prizes and all our other expenses, about $12,000.00 per year, from our endowment's income, we do not have an endowment sufficient to fund a salary for a paid director, the services of which I have provided gratis. My daughter Virginia does not want the directorship, although I had previously thought she did. So we have a task to face.

Chapter 10

Life, Teaching, and Scholarship in Birmingham: 2000-2020

From the late 1990s onward I had been thinking about retirement, how good it would be to concentrate only on research and writing, and also how good it would be to rid myself of faculty committee responsibilities, occasional confrontations with students, and above all to be rid of bluebooks to grade. I began making some initial moves toward the goal of retirement in the late 1990s. I was a member of the curriculum committee in the late 1990s when we cut the property course from six units to four and added four units to the evidence class, both being needed changes. We also placed both property and evidence in the spring term. I favored that greatly since these were both required classes that I taught repeatedly, and this would leave my fall term with only electives. This would greatly facilitate a step-retirement, which I was already beginning to contemplate. I knew that in retirement I would want to continue to work and write in my Cumberland office. I also knew that my cozy second floor corner office, that overlooked the college quad, would be much in demand from the full-time teaching faculty once I retired. However, there was a vacant third floor office that I had noticed was not a very popular draw over the years. It lacked an outside window except a small high window with no view except for clouds. On the other hand, the office had attractive hardwood floors and considerably more bookcase space than most Cumberland offices. In late fall 2002 I moved into the third floor office, which I still have today, knowing that it would not be coveted after I left the full time teaching faculty.

In the early 2000s I had again been appointed as the law review advisor. I regarded it as an honor, although it was not as much fun as the earlier years when the review board was always getting into trouble with firing the step-son of a trustee and publishing an article loaded with "dirty words." I also taught a new course in real estate transactions, the time made available because of my own suggestion on the curriculum committee that property be made real property only and cut to four hours. The real estate transactions course was very practical in approach, and I taught it that way. There were a series of excellent, non-theoretical questions after each narrative section of our casebook, and I asked the entire class to think of their responses, and then delegated the role of moderator to a different student each week. Of course, I jumped in with comments and suggestions when the back-and-forth seemed to be moving astray.

In March 2003 the university president, Tom Corts, sent an email to the entire faculty nicely demanding that we take an online course on sexual harassment, complete an exam, and send in the results. I regarded this as highly insulting, and never took the course. Corts announced his retirement in April 2005, effective at the end of the next academic year. I certainly did not agree with some of his Baptist-driven decisions, but he did a wonderful job of keeping the more radical Baptists at bay and in promoting academic excellence, concerns that are much less in evidence since he stepped down. He died after a few years from a heart condition. Corts was a very dignified man, but even so a lot of Midwestern friendliness (he was from Indiana) showed through that reserve. I know that if I had been in Corts's job and had to deal with the folks he had to work with, I would probably have lasted three or four days before being asked to leave.

In February 2003, when I had my first conversation with our dean John Carroll about early retirement, I raised the possibility of a research faculty position. He said he would find out the central administration's policy. The dean advised me in April that the research professorship was not a problem at all with the university, with library access, office, and research assistant, but that the university had no early retirement program. I talked again with Dean Carroll that fall and suggested a non-monetary way he could compensate me for retiring early. The incentive for the school would be the ability to hire a younger replacement for me at a lower salary. The incentive for me would be a full salary for my last two years with my assignment for the fall terms being only research, and during the last two years, 2003-04 and 2004-05, I would continue to teach the heavy enrollment property and evidence courses. He seemed interested and asked that I put this in a letter he would share with the central administration.

Without delay both the dean and the provost agreed to the plan of a step-retirement, giving me mini-sabbaticals for the 2003 and 2004 fall terms. Dean Carroll told me that mine was the first step-retirement that Samford has ever had, and some of the university bureaucrats were resisting, but it would work out. He said he had told his assistant dean to schedule me only for my own research for this fall.

The final agreement was that after I became a research professor I would have the use of the library, a research assistant as needed, and I would have continued faculty status, but with no committee assignments, and with voice but not vote at faculty meetings. He also promised that Cumberland would pay my expenses to attend the annual meetings of the American Society for Legal History. However, a few years later, financial exigencies caused the university administration to limit meeting reimbursements only to those who were presenting papers. At that point I did not request any expense reimbursements for travel and meeting expenses, even for the meeting John Carroll had agreed to cover.

Seattle University again invited me to teach a summer course, this time evidence for the summer of 2002. It agreed to pay $10,000 plus a $2,000 travel allowance (that I really did not need), and to provide a low cost dormitory room for the two nights a week it would be convenient to stay in Seattle. Actually, the school put me up in very nice hotels for my first two stays in Seattle, and then found me an almost complimentary pied-a-terre on Mercer Island, a ten minute drive from Seattle University. I thought the class went well; in fact a large round of applause accompanied the conclusion of my final class that summer, and two students came up to me while I was still in the classroom to tell me it had been a great class. However, when I saw the student evaluations I was shocked at the number of students who reported that they found me to be condescending, harsh to students, lacking respect, ill-tempered, contemptuous, and so forth. It was not my conception of what had gone on in the classroom.

Ten evaluations attacked me, thirteen were very positive, and the balance were unspecific. The favorable ones included "well done," "good work," "good class," and "hope to see you next year." One or two were thoughtful: "teaching style is archaic." One wrote "some peers may shy away from his Socratic method . . . [but still] an excellent professor," and another noted that "I'm sure that some will claim this prof was mean. I disagree," and still another "thank you for your time."

It probably was true by the 2000s, and in an age of computer-assisted learning such as smart boards, chat rooms, and synchronized computers, that my teaching style had become archaic. An irony here is that when I first began teaching, I thought that I was not Socratic enough, that I lectured far more than I recalled my own professors doing in the early 1960s. Students have always wanted straightforward expositions of the law, nothing that we had to work out by ourselves. Yet in the 1960s we were content to take what we were given, and believed that confrontational faculty might possibly sharpen us for courtroom repartee. In the 1970s consumerism entered the law school world and with it came the first student evaluations. Of course, I did not personally hold that much stock in classroom Socratic grilling. I had come to believe that my own law school delinquencies of attendance were a matter of leaving undone that which I ought to have done. In any event few of my students would put in the grueling solitary work I needed to make up for my class absences. I had to teach them, and the most efficient and most traditional way of teaching law is through asking students questions about actual cases found in their casebooks.

My final classes at Cumberland were in late April 2005. My evidence class ended quietly, but the students in property went all out. They gave me a cake and a card signed by many. Some asked about my plans, and some even asked about my papers at the Illinois State Historical Library. Since I had not mentioned that in class, it was a sure sign some students had actually looked at my foundation's website, and that pleased me immensely. For one of the two questions on my last Cumberland property exam I used one of my own 1963 property exam questions from Stanford, with some date modifications and one sub-part removed. After the Cumberland exam was over, I posted that I had borrowed this 1963 Stanford question in order to prove a point I had often told my students: that property law moves with the speed of a glacier. I doubt that any other area of the law has changed so little that one could use literally the same examination question forty-two years later.

That fall I had a slight bit more Cumberland teaching as I supervised a directed research paper involving American legal history. I did that without any compensation. The 2005 evidence and property students graduated in May 2007, and once again I joined the processional march and sat on the stage so I could see the last of "my students" receive their degrees. Most of these students remembered me, and several of them introduced me to their parents or spouse, and some even wanted a photo with me. However, it was over, and by 2007 I had already taken my teaching notes to the historical library in Springfield, Illinois for its collection of my papers.

Then suddenly it was not over. Georgia State University Law School, Atlanta, asked me to teach evidence in the fall term 2008. We negotiated a bit and agreed on a stipend of $25,000 that I thought was quite generous, although this was a regular term's course and not a summer session. I had to return to Springfield to take my evidence teaching notes out of "dry-dock," as it were, to the slight displeasure of Debbie Hamm, our curator, who had to photocopy about 200 pages of papers that neither of us had anticipated would be needed again so quickly. My last class was November 1, 2008, and with it my teaching career, 1965-2008, 1978-2005 full time, finally ended. It was a good run.

The years 2001-2005 were before retirement, and of course I continued to be busy with faculty committee work. For 2001-2002 the dean appointed me to serve on the rank and tenure committee. I was a bit reluctant because the principal work for the committee that year was a sharply disputed tenure decision over a female professor who had deeply divided the faculty. After considerable disputation within the committee, falling just short of rancor, the committee denied the woman tenure by a vote of 3-2, I being in the minority. In

2002-2003 I served on the faculty recruitment committee and helped to select the candidates that we later interviewed at the faculty appointments conference in Washington, D.C. In 2004 the law faculty once again elected me to the policy committee.

From 2001 to 2008 I published nine short articles in encyclopedias, the two most significant in my view being the entry on "William Kunstler" in the *Yale Biographical Dictionary of American Law* (2008) and the article on "Prostitution and Antiprostitution" in the *Oxford Companion to United States History* (2001). In this entire period I published no articles excepting the three de Mattos pieces, described later, that were intended to be a part of a book that I was forced to reduce in size to its core element.

In the 2010s, I pulled away from and ultimately dropped a book topic I had spent quite a bit of time researching: the legal history of American prostitution, a cat-and-mouse story of various ways authorities have tried to control prostitution over the years, and the reactions of the prostitution industry to evade those restrictions. I even wrote a one hundred page manuscript on the colonial period up until 1800. Perhaps someday I will publish that as an article. I lost interest in the topic for two reasons. First, my intellectual interests turned increasingly toward biography, albeit often with subjects who had some connection with the law. Second, the primary source material in the nineteenth century and thereafter tended to be concentrated in the larger cities, such as Boston, Chicago, and especially New York City. The stories of prostitution laws in those larger cities have been adequately written, and the materials for legal regulation of prostitution in the hinterlands are pretty slight. I sometimes regret that I did not complete this project, on which I spent a lot of time, reading court records from the colonial and early national periods, as well as many fascinating diaries.

I gave several talks, 2001-2010. In 2001 I spoke about free speech during wartime before the University of Alabama branch of the ACLU, and later that year I spoke to a dinner of the Alabama Libertarian Party on the history of the war on drugs. In 2003 I addressed the Mensa Southeast Regional gathering on the history of American prostitution. In 2008 I spoke on the Mann Act to a breakfast meeting of professional women active in various fields. This particular talk was arranged by William Nunnelley, the Samford director of public relations. He had been astonished that I had been recently quoted in more than one thousand articles. It was the time of the scandal of Governor Eliot Spitzer, when his conduct probably was a violation of the Mann Act. Some reporter reached me and must have gotten a good quote since thereafter it went viral.

In the fall of 2009, in Funchal, Madeira, I spoke about the writing of my de Mattos book at the same Presbyterian Church where he had preached in the nineteenth century, and then a few days later spoke to a large group of undergraduates on "The American Federal System," at the University of Madeira. The students fielded some excellent questions.

I talked about "The Protestant Portuguese Community in Antebellum Illinois" at the invitation of the Ferreira-Mendes Portuguese-American Archives" at the University of Massachusetts-Dartmouth, which paid my expenses. The audience consisted of Portuguese-Americans who said they had always heard that there were some Protestant Portuguese, but had no real information. The Portuguese consul attended the talk. My son, David, Jr. , accompanied me on this trip, and it gave me the opportunity to show him Boston, in particular the Boston Athenaeum of which I was one of the 1,049 proprietors. In 2012 I lectured to graduate students and faculty at the University of Umeå, in Umeå, Sweden on the "History of Prostitution in the United States: A Game of Cat and Mouse." My daughter Virginia, a professor at Umeå University, arranged for this to take place during a time I was visiting with her. I was actually given a modest compensation for the well-attended talk.

Probably the most interesting talk was before John Reid's New York University Law School's colloquium on American legal history. Not only did NYU pay for my travel expenses but it also furnished me with a handsome apartment in the heart of Greenwich Village, large enough for my wife, myself, and infant son. It was mine to use, not just the night before the talk, but for almost a week, thus making for a mini-vacation for my wife Frances and myself. The colloquium itself was fascinating. The students had all read my book on William Kunstler and asked me probing questions about the book, Kunstler himself, and my writing of the book. I had become accustomed to people critical of Kunstler's radicalism, but these law students at NYU attacked Kunstler from the left, arguing that Kunstler had made far too many compromises with the existing establishment.

Immediately after the colloquium ended I expressed surprise to John Reid about the attacks on Kunstler coming from a leftist position, and he said it did not surprise him as the NYU students, many of them anyway, were extremely leftwing in their views. An hour or two later, Frances and I had an early supper with Ron Kuby, Kunstler's former partner whom I had interviewed for many hours in researching the book. I explained to both Ron and Frances the attacks on Kunstler at the colloquium, that they did not come from the usual suspects, liberals and conservatives, but instead from those further to the left than Kunstler, whom most people regarded as a radical. Ron was not surprised either. I guess I was the only one surprised.

In the 2000s and shortly thereafter I continued to attend conferences, speaking at many of them, with almost all of my expenses still paid by Cumberland. In January 2001 I spoke about working with university presses at a conference, Words on the Waterfront, held in Port Townsend, Washington. I did not even ask for reimbursement of these costs, since Port Townsend is my summer home, and I was curious about what it was like in the winter. In October 2006 Cardozo School of Law in New York sponsored a conference on Jews and the Legal Profession. It invited me to speak on "Jewish Lawyering on the Left: The Comparative Jewishness of Arthur Kinoy and William Kunstler," and paid my transportation and lodging. It was a stimulating conference with a wonderful gala dinner. Even though I think I was the only *goy* present, everyone was extremely friendly and outgoing. In the summer of 2008, the Southeastern Association of Law Schools held its annual conference in Palm Beach, of all places, for that time of year. I was invited to participate on a panel and talk on writing law school histories. As usual for law conferences, it relied on individual law schools to cover the expenses of their faculty. Cumberland did so for me even though I was retired and this was not the conference it had agreed to cover for me.

While I was still on the teaching faculty I attended almost every conference of the American Society for Legal History. In the 2004 conference in Austin, Texas I was a commentator, now known for some reason as discussant, for one of the program's sessions. I remember that at the 2005 conference I had the conscious wish that I had a better capacity for remembering names. It has always been a problem for me, and I believe it has held me back from being more widely known in the Society.

This conference was the one for which Cumberland had agreed to reimburse my expenses as a research professor, and I attended them in 2006 (Baltimore), 2008 (Ottawa), and 2011 (Atlanta). Following this, if I attended I paid my own way, as the Samford funds for travel became tighter and tighter. I did attend the 2015 (Washington, D.C.) and 2019 (Boston) meetings.

At these conferences, especially the receptions, there is always a great amount of chit-chat for scholars, usually presenting itself in the question, "What are you working on now?" For many years I usually answered that I was still working on the legal history of prostitution. By 2008, however, that had become a little worn because I had said it for so long but no work had been actually produced. So at the 2008 conference I decided to talk about what I really in fact was working on: (1) preparing my father's and my own papers for the Abraham Lincoln Presidential Library, and (2) writing my mother's family into a book and three articles, all by then published except for the final article. I encountered great interest in these projects and absolute acceptance of them as perfectly legitimate. There was no innuendo whatsoever that this actual work I was doing was not worthy of a scholar. I should have been this forthright earlier.

In 2006 I published my next book, *António de Mattos and the Protestant Portuguese Community in Antebellum Illinois.* In the 1840s a group of Portuguese living on Madeira Island converted from Roman Catholicism to Presbyterianism. António de Mattos was one of these, and, because highly regarded by the Presbyterian ministers working on Madeira, he went to Scotland for training to become a minister. While he was studying in Scotland, the converted Madeirans were forced to flee the island, first to Trinidad, and then to central Illinois. António de Mattos became their minister in Jacksonville and Springfield, Illinois, although twenty years thereafter he returned to Portugal and was instrumental in establishing the Evangelical Presbyterian Church of Portugal. He is also my great-great-grandfather.

My personal involvement with the de Mattos story began around 1950 when I was 10 years old. My mother, father, and I drove from Elgin, Illinois, where we lived, to Jacksonville, Illinois, a distance of about 250 miles. My mother, whose maiden name was de Mattos, wanted to know more about her great-grandfather, António de Mattos. Looking back as an adult, I know it was a badly planned trip. They had not made arrangements ahead of time and could not find anyone in Jacksonville who knew much about de Mattos. We did accomplish two things. First, we found someone to let us into Northminster Presbyterian Church, the Portuguese-American Church, although I learned much later that this particular structure was built long after de Mattos's tenure as minister in Jacksonville. I suppose it comes from decades of burnishing the woodwork and pews, but Northminster has a pleasant and very distinctive aroma. When I next returned to Northminster in 1999 while working on this book, aged 58, I knew immediately that this was the same place I had been 48 years earlier.

The second accomplishment of that trip was that we learned António de Mattos was Portuguese, not Spanish. António's grandson, Dunbar W. de Mattos, and my grandfather, thought of genealogy on a vast scale, centered on origins, the middle ages, and whether he was entitled to use a crest of heraldry. Dunbar told everyone that his family was from the Basque region of Spain. That may actually be true if one wishes to go back to the 15th century, but it is very misleading. His daughter, my mother, grew up thinking her great-grandfather António was Spanish, and it was not until she was thirty-two years old and visited Jacksonville that she learned differently.

This became the shortest book I have ever written, and yet the most difficult to write. The brevity of the work, only 141 pages, comes from two factors. First, it was conceived by me as a family history including António's two sons, James P. de Mattos and Frederic Sandeman de Mattos, both of which had extensive professional careers, the first as a lawyer and politician, and the second as an Episcopalian priest. However, the publishing process forced me to cut out everything except the core, and that was António. As I explain later, I made a series of articles out of the material I could not incorporate into the book. So much of what I intended to be in the book never made it in that format. The second reason for the book's brevity is the paucity of materials with which I began my research. Here I refer to materials about António; materials for the sons will be taken up later.

António's son James collected and saved about a dozen letters to and from his father, together with three or four newspaper clippings, a calling card or two, mostly gathered up from his mother's relatives in New Brunswick, Canada. James died without issue in 1929 and his heir was Dunbar de Mattos, his nephew and my grandfather. Dunbar took possession of this very modest collection and stored them in a paper bag in his basement in Minneapolis, Minnesota. When Dunbar died in 1961, his daughter, my mother, told me about these letters and that they came from her uncle James, and then proceeded to store them in her basement in Elgin, Illinois. My mother died in 1967, but the papers stayed in Elgin until the late 1980s, when my father wanted to sell the house and summoned me to collect my remaining things. So the paper bag with its letters then moved to my basement in Birmingham, Alabama, and sat until 1999.

Meanwhile I had become an historian and had written several books, including biographies, and the thought was growing in my mind that I ought to at least take a look at these papers. They had not been opened since sometime in the 1920s; if I did not read them then probably no one ever would. I also thought that these papers might be suitable companions to the Langum family papers that I was in the process of preparing for the then Illinois State Historical Library, later to change its name to the Abraham Lincoln Presidential Library. To facilitate this, I made typed transcripts of the letters and in reading them for the first time, in 1999, I discovered that here was the nucleus of an interesting story.

This was very different from the two biographies I had previously written. I began with about a dozen letters from António and his wife, Isabella, and a few newspaper articles, a few calling cards, my knowledge that my great-great-grandfather was Portuguese, not Spanish, and had been a minister somewhere in Jacksonville, Illinois— that was about all I had. Biographers usually face a plethora, a superabundance of material. My task with my other two biographies, as is the usual job of biographers, was to read into and analyze a massive amount of material, try to find major themes to their subjects' lives, and then prune out excess so the reader will not become bogged down and can see the forest and not just the trees of one thing after another.

With António de Mattos I had to begin at the other end and ferret out materials about my subject. To that end I engaged in a massive letter writing campaign to gather information. Of course, as one piece of evidence after another came to hand, that raised additional questions and set off additional rounds of correspondence. This only made the research more exciting. The number of appreciations and thanks in the preface, more than customary, shows the large number of people I bothered for kernels of information. In the course of this search I obtained important documents for the story of the Protestant Portuguese in Illinois. For example, Robert Kalley, the nineteenth century evangelist who first converted many Madeirans, later spent an entire year, 1853-1854, in Springfield, Illinois. He kept a letter copybook, and also a daily diary, no longer extant but transcribed into a daily summary of events by his adopted son. I learned that the originals are in the library of the Fulminense Church in Rio de Janeiro, Brazil. Through the courtesy of Esther Marques Monteiro I was able to obtain good copies of these important papers that have now been added to the de Mattos Papers at the Abraham Lincoln Presidential Library in Springfield.

So many people helped in my research, but I must single out three. Deb Kleber was particularly helpful in the early stages of my work in 1999 in providing copies of the records of several Portuguese churches and putting me in touch with knowledgeable persons in Jacksonville, Illinois. I had an extended and very helpful correspondence with the Rev. William B. Forsyth, author of *The Wolf from Scotland*, a biography of the evangelist Robert Kalley. He put me in touch with Esther Marques Monteiro in Rio de Janeiro. Most importantly Geoffrey L. Gomes gave me sustained and significant help. Jeff Jewell of the Whatcom Museum of History and Art first put us in contact because Geoffrey had also made inquiries about James P. de Mattos.

When I explained my project Geoffrey was most enthusiastic and helpful, sending me photographs, articles, photocopies of relevant pages of obscure books, improving my pitiful attempts to translate Portuguese, and offering suggestion after suggestion for other leads to track down. The research went on for so long and had so many dead ends, that inevitably I suffered periods of frustration or even discouragement. Whenever Geoff sensed that I might be suffering from these moods, invariably he would offer a few words of encouragement and still more research leads and suggestions.

Many dramatic moments occurred during the research. Three specific issues were uncovering de Mattos's birth date, finding his death date, and most interesting, the question of an illegitimate child and who the father might be. Along with death, the date and location of a person's birth is a basic biographic fact. Yet well into the writing of the book I did not know the circumstances of António's birth. I did have his son James's application for an insurance policy. As part of the medical information, the application asked the age of his father. The answer to that question subtracted from the date of the insurance application gave 1820 as a probable birth date.

However, I needed better than that. I wanted an exact date and also the names and addresses of his parents so I could gauge his social and economic standing at birth, another important piece of biographic data. Funchal, Madeira has an extensive archives and manuscript collection and a computerized index of births, so I thought this would be no problem at all. The archives informed me that I needed to know the names of the *parents*, including their *first names*, in order to use its index. I thought that was strange. I knew I had to have the services of someone local, but that itself was easier said than done. I made five or six inquiries for someone, perhaps a history student, perhaps a genealogist, who could help. About all I received at first was confirmation that yes indeed I did need the full names of the parents to use that index, a fact that I found astonishing since in the United States most genealogical interest in birth certificates is to *discover* first names of a subject's parents and the maiden name of the mother. I consoled myself with the thought that in all probability the Portuguese might find the way we do things in the United States just as strange as I thought that index to be. I kept up the search to find someone to do a manual search through church records, page by page, and ultimately found Claudia Nobrega, a graduate student in history at the University of Madeira.

I had previously discovered an editorial in a Funchal newspaper denouncing de Mattos for causing riots during his 1875-1876 evangelization effort following his return from the United States. It was quoted by the American consul, and I had his reports available on microfilm. That editorial mentioned that de Mattos had been baptized in the cathedral in Funchal. So I asked Ms. Nobrega to begin with the cathedral records. She diligently searched, but no, they were not there. But we were not ready to give up.

A great deal of evidence suggested that the de Mattos family was wealthy. For one thing António was able to travel around quite a bit, even for personal purposes. Also, when he went to Scotland for ministerial study he did not need any training in the English language as he already knew it well enough to go straight into theological classes conducted in English. That meant António had to have enjoyed excellent private education in Funchal, and in turn that meant his family had the money to provide that education. All of this was confirmed in detail much later, and I just had these inferences at this juncture in time. So I asked Ms. Nobrega to check the church registers of one or two of the wealthier churches in the Funchal area. After several months of work she reported that António de Mattos had been christened at Santa Luzia Parish. I learned for the first time that his full name was António Joaquin de Mattos, Jr., although he almost never used his middle name or the junior, and that he had been born on August 20, 1822.

That then raised the question as to why his son James would say that his father was born in 1820. Surely James knew his father's birthdate as it must have been annually celebrated in some manner. This is somewhat of a mystery, but I have a suspicion, although this is *not* in the book because I have no real evidence. I think that António with the connivance of his wife Isabella practiced a minor deception and deliberately fabricated a false year for António's birth two years earlier than the actual. I suspect that António and Isabella probably told their children of the correct birthday, August 20, but an incorrect birth year of 1820. Why this? I know Isabella was born in 1821, and in the nineteenth century it was somewhat untoward, a bit improper, for a man to marry a woman older than he, even if only a year in difference. I wish I had found just a bit more evidence so that I could have put this in the book, but I did not have it and did not include it, although I made it clear what their actual ages were. One moral of this story for genealogical researchers is that if you think you know the year of a birth and cannot find what you are looking for, do not give up but always check a few years on either side.

Because I had to dig out so much information I spent several years writing this book. Until almost the end, I did not know the date or circumstances of de Mattos's death. The American consul in Funchal was good at including de Mattos evangelism, the resulting riots, and his arrest in his reports, 1875-1876. Then the State Department replaced him, and the new consul's reports said nothing about him. My initial thought was that de Mattos, who had tuberculosis for several years, might have died. I found the names of the superintendents of the British cemeteries in Funchal and Porto, and asked for their search of burial records. There was nothing there. I found the tombstone records of the Lisbon British Cemetery among the records of the Mormon Church and read them myself. In fact, it later turned out that this was where de Mattos was buried, but I was misled because these were tombstone records and not burial records, and his son James failed to provide the funds for a tombstone even though he was asked several times by the American consul in Lisbon to do so. It is easy to talk about this searching, but just this small part of the research took about two months, and the result was that there was no record of his death.

I was on the outlook for some articles written in an obscure publication of the Free Church of Scotland called the *Monthly Record*.

The Free Church's annual reports had said that some articles appeared in this monthly magazine about the re-evangelization of Madeira, and I thought that perhaps they could tell me what happened to de Mattos since he was a part of that re-evangelization. I contacted the Free Church of Scotland and learned to my delight that its archives held copies of the *Monthly Record*. After quite a bit of delay when their first shipment went astray in the post, I finally opened up a packet of articles from this journal for 1877. The news reports from Funchal stated that de Mattos left Madeira in August 1877, very suddenly and without explanation. The mystery remained.

I am summarizing in brief form a very long process. Every step along this path taken to discover de Mattos's activities after 1877 itself had a few twists and turns and each step required a month or more of time. Then a thick package of papers arrived from the Fulminense Church in Rio de Janeiro. There was a lot to read, but included was correspondence between Kalley and a colleague that said de Mattos had left Lisbon in late 1878 for the United States and did not intend to return to Portugal.

That was a low point. I had previously assumed that de Mattos had died in Madeira, or perhaps in mainland Portugal. Because of the unavailability of cemeteries to Protestants, other than the British cemeteries, I further surmised that he might be buried in a secret Protestant cemetery in the countryside, the location of which had probably long since been covered up by luxuriant growth. But now with evidence that he had been seen in Lisbon and either intended to or actually had returned to the United States, this solution to the mystery was invalid. Because of the highly decentralized nature of all nineteenth century vital records in the United States, including death records kept county by county, it was not likely that I would ever find information on a subsequent career and ultimate death.

Then I remembered my father's notes on a discussion he had with my grandfather Dunbar de Mattos, shortly after my mother and father were married. My father's notes said that Dunbar told him that his grandfather, António, had been the American consul in Paris. That made no sense to me. António lacked any political pull for that appointment, and I had no evidence that he knew French. However, even far-fetched family traditions can hold a kernel of truth, and I thought that perhaps, just perhaps, António de Mattos had moved to Paris and become a translator of the American consulate there. The consulate records are easily procured on microfilm from the National Archives in Washington, so our library ordered the rolls for the period 1878 through 1880 and I began reading. It took five or six days, shared with teaching responsibilities, to determine that this was a dead end. There was nothing.

Then it occurred to me that perhaps the true kernel of my grandfather's far-fetched tale was that his grandfather António had worked for an American consulate, and not the Paris part of the story. I knew that he had become a naturalized American citizen back in 1866 when he was still in Illinois, so it could have happened that he later worked for an American consulate. It was not likely to be in Funchal. I had looked at their consular records through 1880, hoping for reports, never made, of his trial for heretical preaching, and I certainly would have noticed any indication that he had been employed.

Then I thought that if de Mattos had in fact worked for a consulate the most likely one would be that in Lisbon. That consulate would require the most extensive translation service, and it seemed very likely that translation would be the work de Mattos would do. By the time I was trying to determine his post-1877 career and death, I already knew about most of his American career, including his translation work for both the Episcopal Church and the American Bible Society.

I turned to the ever-patient librarians at Cumberland School of Law and asked them to order still more consular records. The rolls it had already purchased for Funchal and Paris would not be enough. I needed the consular records for Lisbon as well, 1877 through 1886. Surely, I thought, the very ailing de Mattos would be deceased by then. The new rolls arrived and I began to read; nothing in 1877 or 1878. More reading; nothing for 1879 or 1880. More work, and yet nothing for 1881. The reading of the Lisbon consular records, document by document, had taken almost two tedious weeks, with no mention of de Mattos or even any suggestion of a translator. I decided to read one more year. I decided that if nothing appeared in 1882, I would stop and conclude that de Mattos had returned to the United States, and I would probably never locate him.

Then in the middle of the 1882 records something new appeared, never seen before in my reading of these documents: a register of American citizens residing in the Lisbon consular district. The list was not alphabetized, but it was not long either. I went through it name by name, when suddenly appeared "Anthony De Mattos," born in Madeira, a naturalized American citizen who had last resided within the United States in Springfield, Illinois. This was clearly my man. He was not dead; he had not returned to the United States. I would keep reading this series of records, and would ultimately learn he did work as a translator for the consulate and numerous other details of his later life and eventual death. By the time I read up through 1886 I knew I had to order still more rolls covering additional years, but that was a happy task as by then I knew I was on the true path.

From the time when I had traced de Mattos back to his return to Portugal in 1875 until I followed him to his death, my research required eighteen months. This lengthy process and the massive amount of correspondence is why I call it my most difficult book. The research, just on this narrow aspect of de Mattos's life, had consumed an enormous amount of time, spawned many false leads, and led to one dramatic breakthrough.

Another element of the research brought drama. In early 2002 I discovered baptismal records on a Mormon website that named António Joaquim de Mattos as the father of an illegitimate daughter born in 1844, and named the parish in which she was christened. The year 1844 was before my António's conversion to Presbyterianism and while he was still in Funchal. If this were the doing of the same man as the later pastor, the high relevance would be obvious, not just as to character, but even the appeal of conversion. The pastor de Mattos was what was termed then a "hard-shell" Calvinist, meaning among other things that he put great faith in predestination, essentially the idea that every human is predetermined as to heaven or hell regardless of one's sins. The attraction of that thought for a person weighed down with a consciousness of a particular sin seems obvious.

The evidence pointed in two directions. Toward this child being my António's was the fact that the record fully named "António Joaquim de Mattos." My understanding is that de Mattos is not a common surname, although not unique. António and Joaquim are common, but here they were also in the exact order. On the other hand I found this record in the Mormon Family Records, and it had been entered recently, since 1990, and there was no further information available. It did give the name of the parish but not its location. I asked another researcher to physically check the baptism records of every church with that name in the Funchal region, and he could not find it. I stopped my search because that parish could have been anywhere in Madeira, mainland Portugal, or even the Azores, and I certainly did not have the resources available to make that sort of universal search.

In late 2002 and early 2003 I really agonized over whether to use this information in the book. I am a professional historian/biographer and I thought I had an ethical obligation to present the reader with all documented elements that had relevance, even if negative. I genuinely wanted this to be an objective biography. On the other hand I did not want to make a gratuitous slash at a man's character, especially a dead man who was helpless to defend his reputation. I worried about this considerably, and with many misgivings decided not to use the information. It later developed that I had made the correct decision.

My research extended throughout 1999-2002, and it was not until August 2002 that I worked up my first proposal. My thinking was still a vast family history that would include not only António de Mattos and his two sons, but also my paternal grandfather and his immigrant family, who also settled in the Midwest and had a preacher, my grandfather, who was a Lutheran minister. I sent these proposals out broadly, to the university presses of Illinois, Northern Illinois, Southern Illinois, Nevada, Iowa, Iowa State, Missouri, and also to a couple of Canadian presses since much of Frederic Sandeman de

Mattos's ministerial work was in Manitoba. Throughout 2003 I received rejection letters from these presses. During 2003 I decided to drop great-grandfather Johan Langum from the book, since the amount of information I had collected about António de Mattos and his sons far exceeded what I knew about Johan Langum. The book would be very unbalanced. Also in 2003 I began playing with the idea of turning the material on James P. de Mattos into an article.

Forward progress was halted for a year from early spring 2004 to spring 2005 by the Gavea-Brown Press that had my manuscript under consideration for this entire time. They said they wanted to publish the core of the book on António de Mattos, perhaps with an epilogue on his sons. Gavea-Brown did nothing but delay and delay. I asked for a timeline, but it responded only that there were several books ahead of mine. Ultimately it turned out that they wanted a subsidy from someone or some organization on Madeira for them to publish the book, a fact it did not disclose to me for almost the entire time we were working together. By February 2005 I thought enough was enough, asked for the return of the manuscript, and terminated my relationship with Gavea-Brown.

During this long delay I did make an important decision. One of the editors of the university presses that had turned me down telephoned me and advised that, even though her press still would not take it, I could improve the manuscript if I cut everything to the core, meaning António de Mattos. Even though it would mean a very short book, I decided to trim the manuscript to António, with mention of his sons, but not extended discussion and analysis. I would re-write the James P. and Frederic S. chapters and try to place them as articles.

On October 29, 2004 at the reception of the annual conference of the American Society for Legal History, Bradley Williams, the editor of *Western Legal History*, asked me if I had anything I would like to publish in his journal. Indeed I did, and I described James P. de Mattos's career as a western lawyer, judge, and multi-term mayor of Bellingham, Washington. Brad thought it would be fine for the *Western Legal History*. For me it meant that at least a portion of my project would be published, although only about 1/8th of the entire manuscript. This journal is a fine one, I had published in it before, and Brad Williams was a nice fellow and easy to work with as an editor. I also thought it was only fair to James P. de Mattos to make the details of his fascinating life available to the public, even if, at that point, I could not publish his father António's material, nor that of his brother Frederic Sandeman.

That article appeared in the summer of 2005, and a columnist for the local Bellingham newspaper picked up on the story and wrote a column about James P. de Mattos and my article. Very quickly four or five de Mattos relatives living in the United States contacted me. They were descendants of my António's siblings, who had later themselves immigrated to the United States. It was a lot of fun working out our exact relationships with each other, and one, Richard de Mattos, even stopped by in Birmingham, Alabama en route to his home in North Carolina and had lunch with me. Around 1900 someone in that separate line of descent had written a family history, and they provided me with a copy.

I learned a great deal from that family history. It confirmed everything I had thought about the de Mattos family being wealthy wine merchants. Even more importantly, this new information confirmed that yes, *there was an illegitimate child born in 1844*. However, it was my António's *father* who had done the deed. My António Joaquim de Mattos, the Calvinist and Illinois pastor about whom I had just finished my manuscript, was a *junior*, although he never used that suffix. It was his father who was responsible for the illegitimate child. I was relieved that I had left the entire matter out of the book.

The James P. de Mattos article appeared in the *Western Legal History*, Winter/Summer 2003, although actually published in summer 2005, as "James P. de Mattos: Feisty Frontier Lawyer and Politician Extraordinaire." I eventually placed a much stripped-down version of the material on Frederic in the *Anglican and Episcopal History* through two biographical sketches titled "Frederic Sandeman de Mattos: Gentle Rogue and Talented Priest," Part One, "Ritualistic

Controversy" in June 2008 and Part Two, "Parish Work in Neepawa and Beyond," in December 2009. I must say the research for the James and Frederic pieces was almost as complicated as for their father António. This was particularly true for Frederic, who had served in more than a dozen Episcopal churches, requiring me to write for Vestry (governing board) minutes for each, and to several diocesan archives and the national Episcopal archive.

After I had stripped it down to the António core, I sent the book manuscript back to Southern Illinois University Press, the most appropriate one geographically. It again turned down the manuscript, but the editor called me, called the work a "worthwhile project," and recommended I send it to the Morgan County Historical Society, who had expressed to him an interest in seeing it. I had some hesitation at first and wanted to verify that the historical society published real books, not the spiral-bound sort of mishmash. Their prior books seemed fine, and I sent the António portion of the manuscript to the society. In June 2005 their director Rand Burnette called. He had read the manuscript and liked it, needed more approvals, and gave me a few helpful editorial suggestions, e.g., more on Northminster Church. Board approval came the following month. They wanted to publish the book that very year, but their printer pushed it back and it actually appeared late spring 2006.

The official launch was the society's annual dinner meeting on May 25, 2006. I was the primary speaker, and signed books at a reception table. For royalties I asked for 200 copies of the book. The additional press run would not be costly, and this arrangement gave the society all of the revenues from their book sales.

My daughter Virginia accompanied me, and afterwards told me that of all the books I had written this one would likely have the greatest impact on actual people. That might be true because while I was signing books several people mentioned to me that they had been waiting for a book to be written about their community.

It is a shame that the James P. and Frederic S. stories could not have been coupled with that of António since it would have made a book of conventional size and therefore more satisfying. The market dictated breaking up the book. The Morgan County Historical Society wanted to subsidize a short book focused on António and that also told the story of the Portuguese immigrants in Morgan County. The *Western Legal History* wanted the James P. article because he was a westerner and a lawyer. *Anglican and Episcopal History* accepted the Frederic piece because he was an Episcopal clergyman, was involved in many ecclesiastical controversies, and worked in the American West, an under-researched area of Episcopalian history. So the three stories ended up in their individually appropriate niches.

I worked on these de Mattos materials for almost nine years and to the exclusion of almost all other scholarship. I spent too much time on this project, but I fulfilled all my filial duties respecting my mother's family and then some. It is strange that I know more about my mother's family, at least on her father's side, than she did. It seems weird that even my grandfather did not know as much about his own grandfather as I do.

Since the book was essentially local history, I could not expect too much in the way of reviews. The local newspapers in Springfield and Jacksonville gave it favorable notices. Both the *Journal of the Illinois State Historical Society* and *Illinois Heritage* mentioned that my rigorous research began with very few sources. The Portuguese publications were the most enthusiastic. The *Luso-Americano* called the book a welcome contribution to Portuguese-American history and "given the paucity of materials available to the author when he began his research the result is quite remarkable." The *Portuguese Times* called the de Mattos book "simple, concise and accurate." The reader, it said, "follows the author through all the steps ... to find the tread in the exciting life of António de Mattos. Reading the book is simply fascinating."

In March 2007 I was asked to attend the lodge at the beautiful Pere Marquette State Park, above the Mississippi River, to receive a book award from the Illinois State Historical Society. The society gives three types of book prizes, and what prize an individual has won is not announced until the day they are awarded. On April 28, 2007, when the awards were given before an audience of historians in the hundreds, I was very gratified to receive the society's highest award, its Award of Superior Achievement. This award is granted in "recognition of superior achievement that serves as a model for the profession and reaches a greater public." The chairman of the selection committee, in introducing me, stressed the wide variety of sources I had used and the virtually overlooked and unusual subject matter of the Portuguese in Central Illinois.

In 2007 Frances separated from me. Although she remained in my house, she fitted up a separate bedroom for herself in the parlor. She divorced me in 2008. I did my best to change her mind, and asked her to choose a counselor. That did no good. At our first session the counselor asked our motivation for coming. I said marriage counseling, but Frances announced she was there for divorce counseling. Frances thought me too compulsive and controlling. I probably am a bit compulsive, as anyone who has written a number of scholarly books has to be highly focused. Others have told me that I have a strong personality, so Frances might have thought that controlling, although I never intended to control her. I think the real problem was that our 23-year age difference had finally surfaced. She became interested in more youthful activities, such as political blogging, and had developed a number of blog buddies in Chicago with whom she wanted to be closer.

The divorce itself was amiable enough. Our pre-nuptial agreement took care of most of the details. She moved to Springfield, Illinois in May 2008. I had extensive visitation with the kids. I had custody of them during the summers, when they lived with me in Port Townsend, Washington. They visited me in Birmingham for Christmas and spring breaks, although we sometimes travelled together during the spring breaks. In addition I often visited Springfield in connection with my papers at the Abraham Lincoln Presidential Library, and I would at a minimum have dinner with the children if a very short trip. I also had four month-long visits when I rented an apartment and the children would visit, each one separately for an entire week. That daily routine, especially when I picked them up after school, was the most conducive for them to open up and tell me what was going on in their lives.

I had dated Grace Eskridge before my marriage with Frances. After the divorce Grace and I re-connected, began dating, and late in 2008 she moved into my house in Birmingham. Although this seems like a thirteen year U-turn sandwiching my marriage with Frances, I must emphasize that Grace was not in any way whatsoever the cause of the divorce. Indeed, I did not want a divorce and did all I could do to prevent it. On December 27, 2014 Grace and I married. We're still together, and I tell her that she will make an admirable widow. Before marriage we negotiated my absence from Birmingham during the hot and humid season that I cannot abide, late May through early October, when I live in my Puget Sound home, Greystones. Grace comes out for at least two ten day visits. She owns a picture framing shop in Birmingham, and this is all the time she can take away.

From 2000 to 2020 I made many trips to Europe, many not as a tourist but to visit friends or my daughter Virginia, who has lived in Europe since 1999. I visited with Virginia when she lived in Ireland, England, and Sweden. I rendezvoused with her at other European destinations, Norway, The Netherlands, and Scotland, for brief vacations or cruises. I also traveled to Europe as an unabashed tourist, usually with a small group. I visited the Czech Republic and Hungary in October 2003; Northern Italy in March 2006, an opera tour; Madeira and Portugal in November 2009 with Grace who accompanied me on all the following trips; Rome, in March 2011; Sweden and Britain, in September 2012; Barcelona with return by cruise in November 2014; cruise down the Danube River in April 2016; Dutch and Belgian waterways in April 2017; and Venice, the Balkans, Malta, Sicily, and Naples, in November 1919.

From 2011 onward Grace accompanied me on all these touristic trips to Europe. Frances joined me on trips to Tuscany and Britain in 1997, but thereafter refused to accompany me. She said her gift was not to have to go. She did join me on a trip down the Ottawa and St.

Lawrence Rivers, by the 1,000 Islands, in summer 2006, and we took a short cruise as a family from Mobile to Cozumel, Mexico in March 2007. I took David, Jr. all over England in conjunction with seeing Virginia receive her Ph.D. from Cambridge. in 2011. Later, in August 2017, I took all three of my younger children from New York to England on the Queen Mary, and thence spent a month visiting London, Amsterdam, Copenhagen, Oslo, and Stockholm, where Virginia came down from Umeå to visit us. One of the highlights of that trip was to visit our ancestral family farm, Langum, in Drammen, Norway, a farm dating from the middle ages and still owned by the Langum family. From 2000 through 2010 I traveled to Europe nine times, and from 2011 through 2020, six times. An altogether different experience, but in June 2004, and by myself, I drove the long journey straight across Canada, from Montreal in the east to Victoria in the far west. I spent several days in Manitoba looking at churches where Frederic Sandeman de Mattos had served and checking local historical museums for photographs.

The trip to Madeira and Portugal, October 27-November 9, 2009, was memorable for more than the tourist sights we enjoyed in Madeira, Lisbon, Coimbra, and the Douro River. It was a working trip, of a sort, and most of my expenses were paid by others. The local Presbyterian Church in Funchal, where António de Mattos had preached for a time after he returned from Illinois to Portugal, organized a commemorative celebration and invited me to travel over, at their expense, to give a talk about António de Mattos and the Protestant Portuguese in Illinois. This effort was spearheaded by an academic at the University of Madeira, Zina de Abreu. Zina had been a reader of the de Mattos Papers in Springfield, and we had already met and knew each other. In addition to my talk at the church, with an audience of about fifty, and done with the aid of a translator, Zina arranged for me to speak to a group of about forty undergraduates at the University of Madeira on the history of American federalism.

A very friendly fellow involved with the church, Claudio Gouveia, took us on a splendid ride through much of the island, and on roads running along cliffs higher and more dramatic than those of Big Sur,

California, with which I am very familiar. He and a friend, Eddie Kassab, gave us a thorough tour of Funchal, the many parks and churches, and showed us where the de Mattos family lived and the church where they were married. The pastor of the Presbyterian church, also an António, gave us a tour of the beautiful Funchal botanical garden, high on a hill, and he proved to be incredibly knowledgeable about birds, various plants, flowers, and trees.

They put Grace and me up in a wonderful hotel, and had several dinners with us. Everyone was exceptionally friendly, especially Zina and Claudio, and expressed hope that we would return. We did return to Madeira, but with only enough time to visit the Monte Church and have lunch with Zina and Claudio. In November 2014, our ship headed for Tampa from Barcelona was scheduled to call at the Azores. Because of bad weather we were diverted to Madeira, and by use of email we were able to arrange for a short visit.

On the 2009 trip, after our visit to Madeira we flew to Lisbon where we were hosted by the national Presbyterian church, the Evangelical Presbyterian Church of Portugal. This group published a Portuguese language edition of the de Mattos book, being primarily interested in his role in organizing the national church in Portugal. However, they published the entire book, with a slight change of title more directed toward its Portuguese readers (in English), *António de Mattos: A Pioneer Protestant.*

I was the main speaker at the formal launch of the book, and the church paid for our accommodations and took us to most meals. Our immediate hosts were David Valente, the Secretary-General of the national Presbyterian church and his wife. She spoke nearly perfect English and served as translator for my remarks. We received tours of Lisbon and the south of Portugal just beyond Lisbon. Just preceding the launch event, the church had arranged for a television reporter's interview. There were several speakers at the launch besides me. Deb Kleber, whom I had not seen since 2001, spoke briefly, as did also the local church pastor. David Valente, the Secretary-General, stressed the importance of my book as the first detailed view of de Mattos, who was upon his return from Illinois, the first openly practicing Protestant minister in Portugal, and it was also the first book with so many details on the founding of the Portuguese Presbyterian Church. A young graduate student in history praised my book for its criticism of various aspects of both Kalley and de Mattos, making them appear as real humans. He also liked the technique I used in the book in murky areas of clearly separating out what facts were known and also what were unknown, and only then going on to give my own clearly labeled speculations and tentative conclusions.

We spent another four days in Portugal. We enjoyed a lunch with Deb Kleber and her husband. Grace and I then visited the Castle of St. George followed by Belem Tower. The next day we took a train up to Coimbra and visited the old medieval university with its many interesting features. The following day we went by train to Oporto, and then took another smaller train out along the beautiful Duoro River.

It was really a marvelous trip. Most of my expenses were paid either by the local or national Presbyterian church. I saw the launch of the Portuguese edition of the de Mattos book, my first and only entire book to be translated and published abroad. And I had the pleasure of being hosted by such welcoming, gregarious, and warm people.

From 2000 to 2020 I also became involved in several book projects that I abandoned. The most significant in terms of the amount of research I had done before dropping the project was the study of the legal history of American prostitution. I had visited several manuscript collections and archives, and had written the first quarter of the book. I have explained earlier why I dropped this project. Another project was a proposed history of the Sedgwick family, a New England family of multi-generational accomplishments. Here I was pre-empted by a family member who wrote and published it first. A third major unfulfilled work of this period was a projected trade book on the many European composers who visited the United States during the nineteenth-century. I did succeed in attracting the attention of an agent on this project, but she wanted an emphasis on how these visits changed either American or European music. I thought just the facts about these visits, what the composers did here, what tourist attractions they visited, their reactions to America – for example, the Waltz King Johann Strauss, Jr. hated American beer, while his wife loved the shopping – would be of interest to a general reader. The agent insisted that the book had to show the effect on music, but with the notable exception of Dvořák, I did not see any musical impact, just interesting stories. This would never have made a university press book, so with my agent's disinterest in the project I dropped it, keeping the collected materials for my own reading since I am a classical music fan.

I had another project that was moribund, almost totally abandoned, before I brought it back to life. This resulted in my latest book, at least before this memoir, *Quite Contrary: The Litigious Life of Mary Bennett Love*, published in 2014. Mary Bennett Love was a rambunctious American woman of the mid-nineteenth century, who crossed over the plains to Oregon by wagon train, and then came down to California while it was still Mexican. She separated from her husband, moved from Yerba Buena (San Francisco) to Santa Clara, and obtained a Mexican land grant by forging her oldest son's name to the petition. At various times she had disputes with her oldest daughter and separately her two husbands. She litigated over her land grant, trespassers, creditors, and property claims in Santa Cruz County and San Francisco. She was a large, sometimes cantankerous woman, six feet tall and over 300 pounds, and at times mean-spirited and at other times open-handed with her generosity. Mainly she was always interested in land acquisition, and stirring up or getting into one trouble or another.

I had been researching this fascinating woman while I was still in law practice in the 1970s. Bernadette, my first wife, was also interested in Mary Bennett Love's story and accompanied me on many of my early research expeditions. My earliest efforts to publish her life story were all rebuffed by publishers, and that was probably a good thing, since I was in no way ready to write her account. I had all my research notes and a few draft chapters in a metal box I kept in my basement. When I began law teaching, I thought Mary's story, while it had plenty of litigation, was not of a sort I could put into an analytical legal framework. In the 1980s I came close to just pitching out the materials. She came to mind again at the time I was donating all of my

California books. I thought that the Mary Bennett Love story was a piece of California business that remained unfinished, and I would feel better about my loss, albeit through donation, of hundreds of books on early California history, if I wrote up the Mary Bennett Love material into a book.

In some ways it became more of a legal story than I thought it would. The larger point was not simply that Mary engaged in so much litigation, but that, even though uneducated and illiterate, she knew so much law. For example, as soon as American troops invaded California in June 1846 Mary squatted on land she thought was public land to take advantage of the pre-emption laws giving actual occupants preference to public lands. No lawyer told her to do this, because there were no American lawyers around. She did it because she knew the law, and her example helps to support the thesis common among at least some legal historians that nineteenth-century Americans were more conscious and knowledgeable of the law than in other historical periods.

Looking through the papers in my metal box in the basement about 2010, I was surprised at the amount of good, primary source material I had gathered in the 1970s, and somewhat shocked by my abysmal 1970s draft chapters. I did have to return to the Bancroft Library at the University of California for about three days to read the land claim litigation records. They contained a number of affidavits about Mary that I had overlooked in the 1970s. However, the purely research phase of this book, at least at the time I wrote it, was the lightest of all my books, simply because I had done so much of it 35 years earlier.

I had a hard time placing the manuscript with a publisher, and about ten presses turned me down. Bradley Williams, executive director of the Ninth Judicial Circuit Historical Society, wanted to publish the manuscript as a book, and we had gotten as far as to draft a contract, but his board forced him to decline. Ultimately I sent it to Gordon Bakken, a fellow legal historian and friend, to whom the Texas Tech University Press had recently given editorial charge of its new series, "American Liberty & Justice." Gordon liked the manuscript and sent it out to a second reader. They then recommended it to the university press, whose bureaucratic wheels turned very slowly, but ultimately agreed to publish. Production details sometimes snagged, but that is usual. Gordon Bakken contributed a foreword, which may have been among his last academic writings since he unfortunately died on December 4, 2014.

The book came out in June 2014. The public library of Santa Clara, California, Mary Bennett Love's hometown, hosted the launch, with a few of her descendants in the audience. I signed books, my daughter Anna assisting by opening the books for signing, then gave a talk, with a slide presentation, and answered questions. I was disappointed in the number of reviews, and even more disappointed by the size of the sales, the lowest of any of my books.

True West thought that Mary was "thoroughly examined in this well-researched volume," whereas the *Midwest Book Review* gushed that the book was "an impressive work of meticulous biographical research and definitive scholarship ... written as smoothly as any historical novel. As entertaining a read as it is informed and informative." Only two academic reviews appeared, a generally favorable review in the *Western Legal History* and a mixed review in the *Western Historical Quarterly*. The most satisfying review came from a reader who wrote a letter to the publisher, passed on later to me, where she wrote, in part, that my "writing was scholarly and obviously scrupulously researched, yet easy to read and fast paced. In parts, believe it or not, I actually laughed out loud." I felt so gratified to see these wonderful words from an ordinary reader whom my words had touched.

The Mary Bennett Love work won two book prizes. The more lucrative was Cumberland's Lightfoot, Franklin & White Faculty Scholarship Award, funded by a local law firm and awarded annually. The prize was approximately $2,500.00. The more prestigious was the Willa Literary Award, granted by an organization called Women Writing the West. This is a group of female writers, all writing with settings in the American west, which grants annual awards in different categories for writing focused on women in the west. I won the prize for the scholarly non-fiction category. I am not certain that I am the first man to ever be so recognized, but I looked at the past winners in this category for about 7-8 years back, and they were all women. I took my daughter Audrey with me to a resort near Redmond, Oregon where the awards were given in 2015 for the preceding year. Hundreds of women were milling about, with an occasional husband here and there. I believe I was the only male winner in any of their categories that year. Of course, I am genuinely pleased that they liked the book, which, I whimsically surmise, may also have helped strike a small blow for diversity. These two awards brought my total number of book prizes to six.

I wish now to attempt to reach some conclusions as to my life and career, hopefully within just a few pages.

I regret that I have lost so many wives to divorce. These things are seldom entirely the fault of a single party, but I acknowledge that I carry more than half of the blame. Undoubtedly I left undone those things which I ought to have done, and did those things which I ought not to have done. However, I do have the benefit from my first marriage of many fine stepchildren: Gene, Patricia, Roberta, Dina Marie, Dean, and Willie, all of whom I love and with most of whom I still visit. From my second and third marriage I have four wonderful children, Virginia, David, Jr. , Audrey, Anna, and also fond memories of John. Although I chiefly remember the angst of raising a quadriplegic, non-verbal son, I always loved John and still do, and also have fond memories of the many times he could be fun-loving and sometimes even funny. Grace is a wonderful wife. I'm never abusive or unfaithful, but I know that I sometimes fail to treat her with the full degree of love and respect she deserves, and I only hope that she will aid me in my attempts to improve.

An academic life has been a great career. I earned more income that I ever did in practice, and with the IRA and 403(b) plans I have been able to accumulate more. My economic goals have never been for wealth, only a level of comfort. I believe I have achieved that, although I admit things were much more comfortable prior to the Great Recession of 2008-2009 when, along with millions of others, I suffered considerable un-recouped losses. Book royalties have never amounted to much. I once remarked to a fellow legal historian,

Gordon Bakken, that the sales on my Mann Act book and Kunstler biography were each about 3,000 copies. He said those were bestsellers for legal history, and that none of his own books had done as well.

I have genuinely enjoyed research and writing, probably the research a bit more than the writing, but that is true for most academics. I have never sold large volumes of books, and therefore never attained much of a name recognition. Scholarly books seldom gain their authors much fame, but I had hopes I could do better with biographies. However, an inherent problem lies with my approach to biography. I would rather not write a biography of someone who has already been adequately written up. I do not feel any urge to do "another" biography of someone, and would rather be a pioneer or at least the first biographer for a good many years.

The problem is that the public does not want to buy biographies of someone without name recognition, and that has kept my work on obscure personalities, however interesting, from selling more. Nevertheless, I find being a pioneer much more personally satisfying, although I know full well that I probably could have garnered more recognition as a writer and scholar by staying within the boundaries of well-known topics or personalities. I hoped I might have a winner with the Bill Kunstler book – a well-known figure for whom I was the first real biographer. I thought that was a winning combination and was very disappointed that there was not more interest.

I should close these reflections by remarking on the support given me by the administration of Samford University. I am not a Baptist, I am not even a southerner, and in fact in the midst of some of my email campaigns I was even a bit of a troublemaker. Yet I have never felt under any pressure from either the central administration or the law school administration. No one has ever said: quit the criticism. No one has ever attempted to influence the topics or contents of my writing. Moreover, the financial support of my work, mostly travel expenses to conferences or talks, and to distant archives or manuscript collections for research, has been very generous.

In sum, I have been given the financial means and the freedom to do what I want, and I have used those means and that freedom, especially the time that academe affords to faculty, to produce a solid body of scholarship in which I take some modest satisfaction. It has been a gratifying career.

INDEX

Birmingham-Southern College, 196

Black Panthers, 217

Bolla, Alex, 154, 155

Books-a-Million, 185

Borchert, Norman, 82

Boston Athenaeum, 257

Boston College, 90

Boston University, 215

Brandeis University, 202

Bray, Gerald, 195

Bread and Roses Shelter, 222

Breen's, 31, 32

Brooks Brothers, 38

Brown, H. Rap, 217

Brown, Ira, 56, 57

Brown, Jim, 194

Brown, Martha, 23

Bryant & Sturgis Papers, 76

Bryant, Bill, 16

Buena Vista, 34

Bulow Award, 228

Bulow, Jack, 229

Burnette, Rand, 272

Burns, G. Frank, 203, 204, 205, 206

Burns, Steve, 192

Caldwell, Jack, 188

California Alcoholic Beverage Commission, 33

California Collection Room, 28

California District Court of Appeal, 21, 22, 23, 24

California Rodeo, 82

California State Bar, 117

California State University at Long Beach, 133

California Supreme Court, 17, 21, 22, 23

Cambridge University (England), 95, 276

Cambridge University Press, 179

Campbell, Don, 77, 79

Carroll, John, 252, 253

Caruthers, Robert L., 203, 204

Castle of St. George, 278

Chama Station Lodge, 60

Chinatown, 3, 26

Christenson, Bruce, 27, 41, 42, 43, 45, 164

Chronicle for Higher Education, 221

City Lights Books, 33

Clapp, Becky, 169, 194, 195, 217

Coif, Order of the, 10

Collins, Harold, 26

Colorado College, 38

Colorado College Special Collections, 241

Columbia University, 76, 95

Columbia University Press, 219

Comstock, Anthony, 224

Connelly, Mark Thomas, 168

Connie's, 36

Conrad, Joseph, 221

Conservation Committee of California Oil Producers, 15

Corregidor, 41

Corts, Thomas E., 150, 156, 157, 158, 191, 225, 238, 252

Cosmos Club, 146

Craig, Edward, 203

Creative Montessori Directorship, 230

Cumberland Colloquium on American Legal History, 196

Cumberland Colloquium on Law, Religion, and Culture, 196

Cumberland Law Review Advisor, 153, 154, 251

Cumberland LL.M./S.J.D. Program, 196, 197, 198

Cumberland School of Law, see generally chapters six through ten, ii, 7, 136, 201
Cumberland Student Bar Association, 186
Cumberland University (Tennessee), 203, 204, 205, 206, 207
Cumberland Yacht Club, 153
Cumbres & Toltec Scenic Railways, Inc., 58, 60
Currier, Barry, 192, 197
Custer, George, 163
Dalkey, Alexander, 59
Dalkey, Franklin, iv, 47
Dartmouth College, 1, 2, 8, 18, 19, 29, 134, 135
Davis, Richard, 154, 155, 156
Davis, Rod, 192
de Abreu, Zina, 276
De Giulio, Alan, 122
de Mattos Family Papers, 244, 245, 249
de Mattos, António, 244, 259, 260, 261, 262, 263, 264, 265, 266, 267, 268, 269, 270, 271, 272, 273, 276
de Mattos, Dunbar W., 260, 261, 266
de Mattos, Frederic, 244, 261, 269, 270, 271, 272, 273, 276
de Mattos, Isabella, 262, 265
de Mattos, James, 244, 261, 263, 264, 265, 270, 271, 272, 273
de Mattos, Phyllis (grandmother), 18, 27
de Mattos, Richard, 271
De Voto, Bernard, 28, 48
DeBaussaert, Kenneth J., 76
Deconstructionism, 167
Defense Law Review, 126

Delaney Southwest Research Library, 241
Denver Public Library, 166, 241
Department Store Employees Union, 34
Detroit Athletic Club, 67, 73
Detroit College of Law Review Advisor, 94, 95
Detroit College of Law, see generally chapters three and four, 66, 67, 135, 159
Detroit Institute of Arts, 99
Diggers, 37
Donaldson, Frank, 188
Donaldson, Sharon, 188
Donnelly, Thomas C. Library, 241
Dougherty, Michael H., 100
Draper, Murray, 17, 22, 24, 25
Drayton, John, 131, 163, 164, 180, 181
Drinking Gourd, 34
Dunne, Phelps & Mills, 24, 25, 26, 32
Durrell, Lawrence, 76
Dvořák, Antonin, 279
Earthquake McGoon's, 3, 33
Eichhorn, Irma, 49
Elu's, 31
Episcopal Church, 267
Equal Employment Opportunities Workshop, 198
Evangelical Presbyterian Church of Portugal, 260, 277
Fannie Mae, 3
Faust, Ashley Simmons, 230, 231
Federal Reserve Bank of Chicago, 242
Federal Rules of Evidence, 101, 144, 145
Ferguson, Colin, 217
Ficzere, Martha, 19, 57
Finkelman, Paul, 211

University of Oklahoma Press, 130, 131, 136, 139, 140, 141, 163, 164, 179, 180, 181, 223
University of Umeå (Sweden), 95, 257
University of Washington, 133
Use and citation of David J. Langum, Sr.'s scholarly works, 225
Valcourt, Richard, 219
Valente, David, 277
Vanderbilt University, 206
Vandever, Donna K., 212
Vesuvio's, 34
Veterans Memorial Building, 23
Vietnam War, 4, 21, 41, 190, 191
Virginia Lake, 121
Volunteer of the Year Award, 228
W Affair, 154, 155, 156
Walthall, Howard, 170, 205, 206, 211, 213
Wang, Jane, 148
War on Drugs, 179, 222
Wardner, William R., 16
Warner Brothers, 43
Washington Post, 192, 220, 221
Washoe County Bar Association, 120
Wayne State University, 78
Weber, David, 76, 141, 225
Weeks, Arthur, 170
Weisberger, Bernard A., 184
Wells Fargo Building, 18, 38
West Publishing Company, 7
West Side & Cherry Valley Railway, 59
Westen, Peter, 84, 85, 126
Western History Association, 98, 99, 160, 165, 214
Western Michigan University, 90
Westerners Corral, 98
White Slave Traffic Act, 168

White, James, 114
White, James Boyd, 216
William S. Boyd School of Law, 123
Williams, Bradley, 270, 271, 280
Williams, Parham, 142, 147, 148, 150, 156, 169, 170, 191, 194, 195, 196, 204
Wilson, Woodrow, 146
Wolf, Morris, 121
Wright, Peter, 231
Wunder, John R., 99, 107, 132, 142
Yale Law School, 190, 216
Yerba Buena Bar, 34
Zandy's Bride, 43
Zunil, 104

LITERARY PRIZES AND AWARDS RECEIVED BY DAVID J. LANGUM, SR.

PUBLICATIONS OF DAVID J. LANGUM, SR.
(excluding book reviews and most encyclopedia entries)

Antonio de Mattos: A Pioneer Protestant (Portuguese edition), 276, 277, 278

Antonio de Mattos and the Protestant Portuguese Community in Antebellum

   Illinois, 259–273

"A Personal Voyage of Exploration through the Literature of Abortion

   History," 224

"A Short History of American Prostitution and Prostitution Policy," 215, 224

"Autonomy and the *Cumberland Law Review*," 143, 153–156

"Californios and the Image of Indolence," 49, 62, 63, 64, 76

"Californio Women and the Image of Virtue," 49, 62

Crossing over the Line: Legislating Morality and the Mann Act, 168–171,

   175–186, 203, 225

"Expatriate Domestic Relations Law in Mexican California," 75, 83

"Frederic Sandeman de Mattos: Gentle Rogue and Talented Priest," Part One,

   "Ritualistic Controversy," Part Two, "Parish Work in Neepawa and

   Beyond," 271, 272

"From Condemnation to Praise: Shifting Perspectives on Hispanic

   California," 49

From Maverick to Mainstream: Cumberland School of Law, 1847-1997, 169,

   170, 171, 203–214

Lightning Source UK Ltd.
Milton Keynes UK
UKHW022127050820
367766UK00006B/168/J